B
044529

DEC 08

ED

DIGGING FOR DIRT

DIGGING FOR DIRT

THE LIFE AND DEATH OF ODB

JAIME LOWE

FABER AND FABER, INC.

An affiliate of Farrar, Straus and Giroux / New York

Faber and Faber, Inc.
An affiliate of Farrar, Straus and Giroux
18 West 18th Street, New York 10011

Library of Congress Cataloging-in-Publication Data
Lowe, Jaime, 1976–
    Digging for dirt : the life and death of ODB / Jaime Lowe.
        p.   cm.
    ISBN-13: 978-0-86547-969-2 (hardcover : alk. paper)
    ISBN-10: 0-86547-969-0 (hardcover : alk. paper)
    1. Ol' Dirty Bastard, 1968–2004.   2. Rap musicians—United States—Biography.
I. Title.

ML420.O536L69 2008
782.421649092—dc22
[B]

                                                                2008029144

Designed by Abby Kagan

www.fsgbooks.com

            1   3   5   7   9   10   8   6   4   2

To my brothers—Matt for making me mix tapes

and David for listening to mine

And tonight, you're going to see somethin' that you never seen before. Somethin' that, that nobody in the history of rap ever set theyself to do. This fuckin' guy, that I speak to you about, is somethin' crazy. He's somethin' insane; he's the greatest performer ever . . . From the moons of Pluto, back down to earth, ladies and gentlemen, one more time, give it up for the Old Dirty Doggy, I mean the Ol' Dirty Bastard. I love that guy!

— RUSSELL JONES

CONTENTS

CONTENTS

DIGGING FOR DIRT

PROLOGUE: VITAMIN SUPPLEMENTS, AMAZONIAN APOCALYPSE, AND A SEVERE ACID-ALKALINE IMBALANCE

Last summer I was in a bar in North Hollywood—a vegan, alcohol-free bar with hand-carved bamboo stools and a mud-caked floor. I can't remember what it was called—maybe Moonbeam Unicorn Happy Energy. Instead of alcohol they served tea that tasted like dirt. The tea was named Universal Tonic or Earth Energy and carried a paragraph-long property description promising not just wellness but also enlightenment and gastrointestinal peace. The backyard was freckled with Christmas lights and Guatemalan tapestries tangled in trees. There were peasant blouses pleasantly lifted by spinning barefoot ladies getting dizzy to the communal drum circle. I had a bite of a vegan biscuit that tasted about as good as it sounds and made my way, dirt tea in hand, to the outdoor supplement bar, where I was allowed to choose two potent, energy-inducing liquid additions to my already brown tea, which I drank out of a coconut shell.

This was the last place on earth (or to be fair to the alien conspiracies to come, in this galaxy) where I would have expected to find a devout Ol' Dirty Bastard worshipper. But there he was behind the bar, hawking Amazonian teas and supplements, looking almost too punk-rock for the setting. Troy was in all black and Birkenstocks. He talked fast and expansively, doling out squirts of Calmazon—an anxiety-and-stress-reducing supplement that costs roughly the same as one therapy session. He started talking about his childhood in Connecticut and how his parents' longtime marijuana farm there had been busted by the FBI, despite years of being ignored during the cocaine era of drug enforcement, which had turned a blind eye to pot farming and dealing. When Troy was fourteen, his folks went into exile in Europe, where he also moved until he realized he wanted to finish out his childhood in his home state. He went back to Connecticut and, like every other white boy on the East Coast and some on the West, got gripped by the Wu-Tang. The nine MCs built a haven for thugs and suburban teens alike, who could slip into their fantasy as if they were living virtually through Wu-Tang's literate, precise, and hungry rhymes. Their beats and the worlds they spoke of were street but fantastic and escapist at the same time. For Troy, an adolescent orphan, it was Ol' Dirty Bastard who really drew him in—the way he lived, the way he talked, the way he took a crowd, internalized its energy, and spat it back out in comic obscenity and poetic prowess. It was ODB's unhinged approach, his lack of that natural psychological armor that adults hide behind. ODB was open, honest, and unglued at every turn. If he had a problem, he told whoever would listen what it was. Who among his fans doesn't know that he was burned not once but twice by gonorrhea? ODB talked and talked and talked; he loved his voice, and though there was only a fifty-fifty chance that what he was saying made sense, people listened. They lined up to listen.

Troy was alarming to me because I believed everything he was saying—we talked for hours about alien abductions and the necessity of eating "four-legged creatures." We spoke about apocalypse, government mind control, and the power of undiscovered plant life. This random, sandaled So Cal man seemed to be channeling ODB's mania and some of his quaint, almost endearing paranoia. He had a frenetic energy and a dedication to his liquid wellness products that made me suspect their true potency but believe that even if they had only a placebo effect, they were potentially magic. It was like he had joined a pyramid scheme of holistic energy and was so entrenched that he had me convinced for at least an evening, and curious beyond that.

He talked about Amazonian ritual ceremonies, Ayahuascera, that he'd participated in: "They'll make you nauseous from your toenails to your intestines and make all your cells shit." He talked about his decade or so in recovery from drug addiction and why he thought the Wu-Tang had fallen off creatively: "They're tapped into a certain amount of consciousness and they think the pot makes them further tapped in, but it really shuts them down emotionally." He asked me to ask RZA to join him on an Amazonian trek. He seemed to think RZA would be down with the shamans, and knowing RZA's journeys (he traveled with a Shaolin monk to China in 1999), it didn't seem entirely improbable. So I nodded. We talked about the growing biblical Rapture movement online, something that I am unhealthily obsessed with. Of course, we touched on the Illuminati conspiracy—the theory that half a dozen white men make all the important political and social decisions regarding world affairs and naturally control the majority of wealth and power.

RZA had been talking Illuminati backstage at Rock the Bells days earlier with an online camera crew. (RZA nodded in agreement when the interviewer asked whether or not he believed "the Government" placed microchips in the palms of U.S. citizens. And when the producer of the segment asked RZA to sign a personal release, he was such a believer in the New World Order that he refused, saying he had to consult his lawyer before signing anything. Anything.)

But then Troy unveiled his grandest conspiracy theory—that intergalactic aliens were interfering with human capabilities of telepathy and teletransportation and that his Amazonian herbs could open humans to the most powerful machine on earth: themselves. (I didn't want to tell him that his belief in intergalactic aliens might prevent some sales.) While we were talking I couldn't tell if he wanted to sell me herbal supplements, sleep with me, or serenade me for hours into the night about shamanistic prophecies of the end of the world (that's in 2012 if you're making plans). He kept returning to a library of pamphlets that featured shamans and religious followers in full native garb, eyes rolled back, sweating through their hallucinatory visions. The pictures reminded me of how ODB looked onstage and how people describe him performing, possessed with almost religious awakening, like he was sweating epiphanies.

Troy had clearly lived something of an ODB life and come out the other end a self-help guru, armed with Amazon juice and herbal deities. He was convinced of the possibility that ODB was off mentally and in the end unstable because of an infection. "All that gold on his teeth fucked up the acid-alkaline balance in his mouth, and he got a bacterial infection and it killed him." Fair theory; it could have been the decade of crack or the bag of coke he swallowed hours before death, but yeah, maybe the gold teeth did it. Bacterial infection aside, I was struck that almost two years after his death, ODB was living in the most unexpected places—not in posthumous albums or *VH1 Honors*, but in his fans' fervor.

For me, liking the Wu-Tang Clan started as posture. I didn't grow up a B-girl, break dancing and tagging. I barely liked the Beastie Boys until I picked one to have a crush on (first Mike D, then MCA when he got me into a concert at a skate park in Sacramento). Initially, I'd drop the Wu-Tang slang with the boys I liked, knowing it would be a surprise to hear a girl rattle off some hip-hop catchphrases. I loved Wu-Tang for the same reason white boys are obsessed with black MCs: it was a way of understanding and embodying something you could never be. For me it was a gender clue—Wu-Tang is what boys I liked listened to, and so I thought it might explain something about those boys. For those boys (and for me) it was a race clue—Wu-Tang is a way to understand black culture, to emulate it. But it was a surprise and secret that I—a girl with a round face, pale-ass skin, and red hair that grows fluffy with anxiety—could love hip-hop so much that it sent me into a fervored state. What was posture became a code, a test that defined whom I wanted to hang out with. I'm not saying it was a good test, but it was how I spoke to people in college—you list a series of things you like and see if it matches the person you're talking to. ODB was always part of the test. Like testing a new boyfriend on whether or not he would help a blind person cross the street. Loving ODB had to be unconditional—just being aware of ODB was the first step. It seemed like a weird requirement from a middle-class Jew who grew up on Madonna and musical theater in West L.A., but ODB has always been more than a rapper, more than the fool splayed out before his public during his short, tumultuous, but somehow inspired life.

My interest in ODB started as a curiosity and as social currency but watching his slow, public demise made me wonder who was really behind the cracked-out headlines; who was he in real life, in hip-hop, in his day-to-day? I followed this thread and it lead to questions, subcultures, social issues, characters larger than life, and some so behind the scenes you'd never know they were there. Mostly it led to a vortex, a kind of rabbit hole that I could deliriously jump into and get lost in. And that's what's always been so appealing about ODB as a character. On both his solo albums, *Return to the 36 Chambers* and *Nigga Please*, he came across as a loose-tongued lounge singer from a warped bygone era. He was intimate and off the wall, he was willing to strip naked for the mic, but he still seemed to have a costume on in his own skin. He created this character, this guy who was wild and honest and lived in a world where rules were a concept and boundaries were optional.

In addition to the usual Wu-Tang elements, some of the odd clues he left behind in lyrics were references to the song "Over the Rainbow," the movie *The Warriors*, and his idol Blowfly. There's a theme embedded—it's escapism and fantasy. Dorothy had a world she could disappear into and find her ruby-slippered self, the Warriors could self-identify with suede vests and feather headdresses and live by the chase, and Blowfly, well, he's permanently stuck in a bedazzled pornographic cape. ODB believed in life just past the rainbow and I think lived in constant pursuit of it. But I don't think he ever woke up from his fantasy, which is weird considering he'll always be remembered as a raw MC, a man who rapped about reality in detail. In some ways he embodied a stunning duality—he coaxed the make-believe from life because reality wasn't for him. At some point ODB got stuck in that rabbit hole, in Oz, in hot pursuit on the subway, in cartoons, in a cartoon version of himself. When fans caught a glimpse of him, they could vacation in his delirium, but we all had the ability to climb out. ODB never did. In the wake of estate lawsuits and eulogies, I tried to find the man behind the myth. I want to unmask the enigmatic MC because he deserves to be more than a teary footnote in hip-hop history, more than a couple of clucks and a head shake—he deserves to be remembered as full-fledged artist and man.

ODB was a force. He was a genius. He was a fool. He was happy, sad, high, sober, loving, and selfish—everything at once. He'd deliver a sermon about how the black man is God, how whites were born from blacks, and recite texts from the Nation of Islam, all while wearing gray sweats lowered to the pelvic bone and track pants over the sweats, cupping his thighs at an odd angle just below his ass. It took two pairs of pants sometimes to contain him. And onstage it didn't matter what he wore; when ODB hopped on the mic, it was a show. He dominated the stage. He took the time to talk about whatever came to him. Sometimes it was cocaine stored in his shoe; other times he'd just address one person in the front row. To sum up ODB from his headlines, he was a tragic, comic mess. He was a cautionary tale and an adventure. He was the guy whom everyone talked about but no one really knew. He was the heart and soul of Wu-Tang—a childlike presence who brought mischief and menace to grave matters. It seemed like everyone in Wu-Tang used rap as an escape, everyone except ODB. He used rap to describe exactly where he was in each moment and exactly who he'd been in moments before and exactly what he wanted in moments after.

The Wu-Tang Clan itself was born as a reaction. Consider it hip-hop's early stages of adolescence. The urban beat-popping, turntable-massaging, street-humping, hair-fading genre had only begun a decade and a half earlier in the Boogie Down Bronx, one long train ride (and a ferry) away from the Clan's home of

Staten Island. Hip-hop in the early nineties was nothing but an identity crisis—on one hand you had Will Smith, clean enough for prime time, and on the other you had Dr. Dre's West Coast gangsta rap low-riding its way up the charts. Up to this point hip-hop had been a social conscience (N.W.A., Public Enemy), a banned obscenity (2 Live Crew), a fashion statement (MC Hammer), a few cartoonish white boys (Beastie Boys), a cover of *Rolling Stone* (Run-D.M.C.), appropriated (Vanilla Ice), a mainstream hit (Sugarhill Gang), and, originally, a brand-fucking-new genre (Zulu Nation).

By the time the Wu-Tang Clan had gathered themselves together in whatever remote Wu-Cave they used to convene (as RZA explained in his book *The Wu-Tang Manual*, it was somewhere in the Stapleton projects, Park Hill, and the Shaolin temple of their minds . . .), the genre had damn near been accepted as nothing short of revolutionary. The problem was that by the early nineties the revolution was not simply televised, it was bought and sold. When hip-hop first broke in the late seventies, it was a pure art form born from the gut of necessity; it was a voice aching to be heard. It was all the frustrations of poverty, inequality, and injustice funneled into break beats and spontaneous rhyming and limbs tangled and spinning and defying gravity on any corner that could house a strip of beat-down cardboard. It sounds ludicrously romantic now—the idea that art can be pure and a vessel for information, emotion, and political discourse, the idea that art can erupt and materialize without material aim. Hip-hop in the eighties was an unformed being, a childlike presence that rock purists didn't take seriously and the mainstream shunned because it was ethnic and fractured. It sounded *funny* to audiences expecting traditional melody. The Furious Five wrote the first hip-hop lyrics to describe the desperation and pain of living in the ghetto: "The man repossessed my car . . . scare my wife when I'm not home . . . It's like a jungle sometimes, it makes me wonder, / how I keep from going under." The lyrics were reprinted in *The Paris Review* and the song was the first single with a political message to crack the R&B top ten. Sometime in the late eighties, there was a shift. After a decade of Reagan-era greed, when our government fought drug wars while funding the contras feeding the inner city, hip-hop was recognized by the mainstream. Madison Avenue noticed that hip-hop was speaking to the youth market coveted by corporations. The genre itself was a moneymaker, but so were the products embraced by MCs. What once was an expression of the streets, raw breath from heaving asphalt, became packaged. It became the Hammer dance. Hip-hop came out from the underground and now, by the early nineties, hip-hop had matured into an all-American dream, a thriving business plan. It wasn't just a ghetto fantasy anymore—to grow up, spit rhymes, and get paid. Now, the suburbs were paying attention.

Enter the Wu-Tang, whose work was different because it was street infused with fantasy. It was admittedly nerdy. They even rap about chess and now have a website devoted to it. GZA's a fanatic—he studies moves every day, and RZA won the first annual Hip-Hop Chess Federation tournament. In fact, they treated the rap game like chess, calculating moves, establishing roles, and countering the industry standard with surprise attacks and highly evolved strategies. They almost operated like a crew of chess pieces—ODB was the kid who lifted the board and turned the whole thing upside down. Each MC was like a Wu superhero, complete with elaborate backstories, street identities, alternative identities, and alternatives to their alternative identities. It couldn't be said better than how they introduced themselves on their first album: "Wu-Tang Clan ain't nothin' to fuck with."

Their urban origin myth was based on kung fu, chess, numerology, and the Five Percent Nation (an offshoot of Islam). The Wu-Tang brought a culture of bricolage to hip-hop and in the process they geeked out an art form that had increasingly become terrifying. Ripping and reassembling has always been part of the music. Hip-hop started with DJs talking over beats; it evolved into a Public Enemy–esque fury of samples. But in the early nineties, when artists who were being sampled sued over copyright infringement, the landscape changed. Instead of paying a dozen artists for the rights to thirty-second interludes, producers started creating their own beats. All of a sudden the sound shifted from thickly layered to bare-bones, and producers like RZA would lay homemade beats under Wu-Tang freestyles. He had the best of the best MCs: Method Man, Inspectah Deck, Raekwon, GZA, Ghostface Killa, Masta Killa, U-God, and the one and only Ol' Dirty Bastard.

By the time the Wu-Tang Clan came along, they entered the fray with RZA's business plan in hand. They were all about the "dolla dolla bills, yo." Their first b-side, "C.R.E.A.M.," was an acronym for Cash Rules Everything Around Me. They saw their rhyming skills (and RZA's raw, almost militaristic production) as a way out of the ghetto a decade after the founding fathers of rap had done the same. Only this time they wanted to get paid and they wanted control of their product. Beginning like a franchise operation, RZA, GZA, and ODB gathered their resources and built a business out of mix tapes and word of mouth, centered around their first group, All In Together Now, and a loose collection of six other Staten Island MCs. They MC'd block parties, took over talent shows, and hustled at every turn to get the word of mouth flapping.

The Wu-Tang Clan East Coast rap revival was in stark contrast to what was happening on the West Coast with Dr. Dre—while he was all about street survival and muscle (not to mention slapping Dee Barnes), Wu-Tang was more like a health food co-op. They were dark: RZA's beats are nothing if not ominous, strong, and stripped to the bare essentials, and most of their lyrics are about fighting and survival and the projects. But Wu-Tang was different. Rather than sling a red or blue bandanna in their back pocket (left side, right, Snoop?), they rejected gang affiliation and created their own psuedo-gang sans murder. Wu-Tang was proud of Shaolin (their name for Staten Island), but they were prouder of having the cash to get the fuck out if they wanted. They rejected corporate record labels and created their own. It didn't make a difference if it was the Crips, Bloods, Sony, or Capitol Records; the Wu-Tang Clan was all about control and fair profit. Why sign up with anyone when they could use co-op resources to flourish? Wu-Tang was rough and tumble, no doubt—some members have done time, others boast about dealing; they have rap sheets, and their rhymes are aggressive—but the group managed to infuse character and creativity into their work. It was no longer just rap; Wu-Tang became a legacy of mythic proportions that speaks to multiple generations—which in hip-hop, is damn near impossible.

On *Enter the Wu-Tang (36 Chambers)*, RZA chants "bring the motherfucking ruckus" over a beat that's so simple, it almost feels like an afterthought. Wu-Tang layers come in the multitude of voices—the MCs battle-rapping, overlapping and challenging one another through verse. The Wu-Tang sound is as raw as a cipher on a street corner, nine dudes circled around asphalt spitting words. And with the simplicity of nine voices intertwined, Wu-Tang slowly built in pockets of depth and humor. It seemed so simple, like a return to the beginning of hip-hop. In addition to hooks, RZA sampled kung fu phrases, comically violent musings from ominous Asian narrators like, "If what you say is true, the Shaolin and the Wu-Tang could be dangerous. Do you think your Wu-Tang sword can defeat me?" Then he'd counter the absurd fantasy of sword fighting as a metaphor for freestyle battles, the sword representing the tongue, with faint nostalgia for the projects. Wu-Tang's third single, "Can It Be All So Simple," released in 1994, is an intimate back and forth between Raekwon and Ghostface about growing up in Staten Island and the fantasy of success and the pressure to get away from drug-riddled families and bullet-laced walls. There's a sense on the track that Rae and Ghost are both realizing that success won't fully erase or change where they're from—their roots are always with them. Wu-Tang brought to hip-hop a saga. They seemed authentic and open, splaying their pasts, their anxieties, and their fantasies into albums. They were hungry and they were human. They were sensitive and mortal but wouldn't run from a fight.

And this was the first time a hip-hop collective dreamed entrepreneurial dreams. Wu-Tang, in addition to being raw and authentic, had the good sense to capitalize on their moment. At the height of Wu-mania everything from clothes to shoes to comics were for sale. Shit, even RZA's sister had a Wu–nail salon next door to the original Wu-Wear store in Staten Island, and everything was branded under one yellow-and-black flag sporting the fat ax blade W that fans would throw up during concerts. For the first time in rap history a band of brothers branded themselves. (Dave Chappelle's "Wu-Financial" skit took it one step further, with RZA and GZA advising a lily-white couple on investments across a cherry conference table. "You got to diversify your bonds, bitches," GZA said.) All of a sudden a lifestyle was for sale—a way of thinking and looking and walking and breathing. It straddled the comic stores and corners. Little white boys in suburbs even imitated RZA's marbled speech impediment, walking the mean streets of Greenwich or Pleasantville under the guise of a hoodie pulled tight. Wu-Tang's appeal made sense. When sheltered middle-class kids played gangsta, rhyming lyrics of South Central war, it seemed ridiculous. But Wu-Tang was selling something different.

If you understood, if you followed the origin myth, the characters, the affiliates, and the slang, you were in, not to mention that trying to decode the Wu-Tang way was fucking fun. It was like Mad Libs, Dungeons & Dragons, karate, and chess rolled into a Gat-laced maze. Comic-Con dorks, original gangstas, and future Pitchfork Media editors could adopt the Wu-Tang way with vigor, intensity, and authority. Wu-Tang spoke to anyone who would listen. They're the only hip-hop collective that's managed to remain credible across ethnic lines and span multiple generations. (It's baffling, but sixteen years after their first concert, the average age of their audience is nineteen. And they've spawned affiliate groups from Wu-Tang Killa Bees to Wu-Latino.) It's no accident that Quentin Tarantino employed RZA to score *Kill Bill* vols. 1 and 2, or that Jim Jarmusch paired RZA and GZA with Bill Murray in a segment of *Cigarettes and Coffee* that famously had the two MCs addressing Murray formally by his full name every time. He sat drinking coffee straight from the pot as GZA and RZA advised him on holistic ways. Jarmusch recalled a time when RZA was scoring *Ghost Dog* and brought ODB by the editing facility while they were both tripping on 'shrooms. Jarmusch mentioned it during an indie awards ceremony like a point of authenticity—he *knew* from Wu. In the same vein, when Wu-Tang was a guest on *The Larry Sanders Show*, it represented the new guard, the kind of band that Jon Stewart would have on if he had taken over Sanders's job. Naturally the network was terrified of so many black men gathered together onstage and Hank, trying to impress Stewart, who was guest-hosting for Sanders, kept asking after the "Old Dirty Bitch." The Wu-Tang Clan had cross-culture capital to spare.

But while most of the Wu-Tang flourished in cameos and collaborations, ODB acted the part of king clown, owning the role like no one before or since. (He was part of the best punch line in Chappelle's "Racial Draft" skit, when RZA and GZA accepted Chinese racial identity and RZA announced before leaving the podium, "Ol' Dirty has now changed his name from Dirt McGirt to the Ol' Dirty Chinese Restaurant.") Everything separated ODB from the rest of the Clan—he rapped out of breath, warbled nonsensical interludes, and crooned out of tune, sometimes holding an off-key note till he was blue and out of breath. Every time he opened his mouth, you knew who you were listening to. He would rap about sneezing, then act out a sneeze and incorporate "achoo" into a rhyme scheme. Onomatopoetics were never limited to actual words, and ODB took the Cab Calloway "Hi-dee, hi-dee, hi-dee-ho . . ." improv approach to music making. If he forgot the words to a song, he'd mumble something to fill the stanza. ODB wailed verses whether he knew the words or not. At first he played up his most dysfunctional qualities, letting MTV film him while he cashed a welfare check years after dropping gold records, but slowly and sadly the dysfunction took over from hyped-up persona to too-true reality.

But before he was a social spectacle, ODB was a voice. He was a dog in heat howling, always on the brink of pleasure and pain, and you could hear it in his elasticized notes, each long-winded breath telling of something. Great musicians transcend genre, and he was as punk rock as the Sex Pistols, as soulful as James Brown, as moody and brandy-laced as Nina Simone, and as combustible as Courtney Love. Starting in 1997, his public disintegration overshadowed his enigmatic voice. First he was arrested for failing to pay child support. Then he was shot in the back by a burglar. A few weeks later he walked out of a store without paying for a pair of Nikes. He got into a fight with a security guard at the House of Blues in L.A. and was charged with making "terrorist threats." He was accused of firing a gun at a cop. A couple of months later traffic police found twenty vials of crack in his Mercedes-Benz. Instead of going to jail, he went to rehab in Pasadena and walked out two months before his court-ordered year there was up. He toured the country on the lam, popping up at various Wu-Tang shows until he was caught with a mob of admirers at a McDonald's in Philly. ODB went to jail when he should have gone to a psych ward. He came out broken and barely able to control his tear ducts. And in November 2004, he died with a public legacy that eclipsed his true character, one that was so free and so raw that it was hard to know who he really was.

He lived a life that most people can't even imagine. He was so seemingly willful and spontaneous and gifted, it was as if he was possessed with godly determination. Or was it that he was high, drunk, manic, and intoxicating in his inebriated states? People watched as Ol' Dirty Bastard *lived*, they watched him tear through a day impulsively, in awe. Middle America, urban America, rural America—we're all losing our ability to physically live. We sit behind gray cubicle walls, refreshing our computer screens hoping for manufactured excitement, someone else's life digitized: a DUI caught on tape, a crude animated political statement, social networks that require e-comment friendships. We live in an urban environment with walls and limits and boredom and we've become voyeurs, content to watch as other people do (even if all those other people do is get a tall latte while wearing gigantic sunglasses). We live in a consumer ghetto, where art is commerce and idols are bought and sold. Well, you could never buy the ODB dream, because it was also a nightmare. But you could watch idly, as if he were a character in a virtual reality game as he destroyed his world, his self, and ultimately his life. He was willing to put it all on the block to succeed, for an audience, to live a life without worry or consequence, because he *had* to. For Russell Jones, life was not a series of choices and obligations and decisions, it just *was*. It was what was in front of him, that day, that moment. But that wild abandon led to a monumental and ultimately deadly downfall, one that rivaled most Shakespearean characters'. And in a way ODB was hip-hop's Shakespearean fool. He spoke in seemingly nonsensical terms but managed concise clarity and wisdom between bouts of madness. There was truth in what ODB said because it came to the world unfiltered—ODB, live and uncut. The court jester is meant to distract with humor but also to speak the truth. The fool knows more, sees more, and speaks more than most main characters because he is commenting outside the situation. ODB made audiences laugh. He made them pay attention because it was never clear exactly what he would do or say. His face—high cheekbones, wide eyes—was like a template. His expression reflected his mood; his eyes raged from excitable darting to glassy wonder. He was a tempest.

ODB died on the floor of the studio he helped build, curled in the fetal position. He was surrounded by family and friends up until the final hours, but really, he was alone, dancing in his thoughts, haunted by his fear, paralyzed by life. He was scared of everything and nothing. And in his final days, he was barely functioning. He had no one and nothing but a small vision of life on a beach, sitting in the sun watching the glitter rise from the green blue tide, in Hawaii, somewhere far away from everything he'd known—a fantasy. My fantasy is that he staged his death. That someone else swallowed a bag of blow on or before November 13, 2004, and that he broke away to roam the streets as just who he was born to be: Rusty Jones. No more monikers, no more trouble, just him and his birthright: his voice and his very first name.

ODB was omnipresent—the guy you'd run into on the corner or sticking his head out of an SUV window. Everyone I've talked to has an ODB story or a friend with an ODB story. I chatted online with someone who specialized in offshore gambling and said he placed all of ODB's sports bets because his ex-girlfriend worked for Elektra and handled ODB. Another friend's ex-boyfriend was in rehab with Dirt and would put ODB on the phone begging her to take him back, as if ODB could somehow convince her. (He doesn't seem like a great spokesperson for fidelity.) My brother was a tour guide at Universal Studios and watched ODB refuse to put shoes on before getting on one of the rides. Security had a twenty-minute conversation with him and guess who prevailed?

But I know he didn't stage his death. I know he died painfully, emotionally dead and physically dependent, bored with life, unwilling to engage in anything. I first saw him onstage, a shell of his former glory. His teeth sparkled, but so did the drool making its way down his chin. When people ask me why I'm searching for ODB, I can say only that I'm deeply affectionate toward this man for reasons beyond me. I love his lounge act, the way he interrupts and ignites a phrase. I love his style and complete lack of grace. I love his contorted face wincing with each elongated syllable. I think I'm searching for more because his life was complicated: it was laced with bad luck and bad decisions and talent that couldn't quite outshine the chaos of his reality. Sasha Frere-Jones, the music critic for *The New Yorker*, repeatedly references the force of ODB as a performer, but when ODB died, the magazine's coverage was a jokey "Talk of the Town" item about a middle-aged white man with the same name who kept getting calls for Russell Jones, ODB's given name. It just seems like he could have been remembered for who he was and what he contributed to the cultural lexicon. You didn't see the same treatment for Hunter S. Thompson.

In the wake of his death were a slew of clues and contradictions, babies and baby mamas, arrest records and freakish moments of honesty and dysfunction, and clubs full of devoted fans. As one, I guess I just want him to be more than a tragedy, more than an addict, more than the sum of his parts. And I can't explain my affection for him without digging a little deeper, knowing a little more.

PART ONE

DRUNK DAYS AND KUNG FU NIGHTS

I.

THE BEST SPEECH SHAWN COLVIN NEVER GAVE, 1998

Witty Unpredictable Talent And Natural Game
—acronym for Wu-Tang

When ODB was asked what his plans for 1998 were, he said he was "lookin' for new girls to put babies in." If only . . . For a month, there was a stillness surrounding ODB, the mellow before the storm. No headlines, no bullets, just ODB, at home watching cartoons and CNN—President Bill Clinton was on TV denying allegations of an affair with a White House intern, Monica Lewinsky, while balancing the budget for the first time in thirty years. Against all odds, the year began with a sense of righteousness and virtue. ODB spent February 24 wrenching four-year-old Maati Lovell from underneath a 1996 Mustang whose engine was pressing into her chest. The car was on fire and combustible. He was recording with the Brooklyn Zu at his cousin Popa Wu's studio in Bedford-Stuyvesant off Fulton. ODB saw smoke from an open window and ran out with affiliates to pull the girl out from under the engine. Afterward, he went to the hospital to visit the girl and her family, declining to sign in. He just wanted to see that she was all right.

The following night, he left Brooklyn in a limo. It was a black-tie evening. Guests politely walked the red carpet, smiles frozen on already frozen faces. Aretha sang when Pavarotti called in sick. That was supposed to be the only hiccup of the show. Producers with headsets cued predictable orchestral interludes. It was the fortieth annual Grammy Awards, held in Rockefeller Plaza, a midtown castle glittery from flecks of nearly forgotten snow. Awards shows have a way of triggering my tear ducts. I can't watch without a sense of cheesy awe and enlightenment; my investment in who wins amazes me sometimes, as does the feeling of being slighted when my favorites inevitably lose. But awards shows are really worth watching for the off-script moments, when you can tell who someone is by their reluctance or their embrace of the fanfare, when you can detect a human behind the voices and faces that otherwise serve as entertainment. With ODB in the audience there was never a doubt that *something* would happen. He was the one performer that wore his blemishes as badges.

And so the oh-shit moment of the 1998 Grammys was born. It was the period of televised time that halted ceremonial procedure and disregarded polite customs of clapping and sitting and waiting your turn and not showing emotion. The audience was aghast; the producers were scrambling. It was a glorious oh-shit moment. More than twenty-five million people watched it. Some understood why, how, and what the fuck? Others couldn't even fathom his name. Ol' Dirty Bastard took the stage that otherwise belonged to Shawn Colvin, who had just won Song of the Year for "Sunny Came Home," an unremarkable girl-with-guitar tune. Sweet but boring, the song lilts in a conventional folk style; that it's about a housewife burning down her home (and metaphorically her boring life) barely registers. While it held on to the number one spot on the Adult Contemporary chart for four weeks running, the song is mostly known for its quiet ability to disappear into the background of *The L Word* and *Veronica Mars*. So you could see why ODB had something urgent to say.

He was dressed in a deep red suit—a velvet Versace. His hair was braided tight and woven neatly to his scalp. No flyaways, no pipe-cleaner antennae; he looked sharp. He wore glasses, his gaze focused and serious, real serious, his right arm punctuating as many words as he could unfurl. Erykah Badu and Wyclef Jean, who had presented the award to Colvin, stood mute, likely stunned into silence. ODB took Badu's microphone upon ascending the Grammy stage stairs. He gave Badu a kiss on the cheek and whispered something in her ear. At the same time the camera was focused on Colvin waltzing out to the stage. She opened her mouth but it was ODB's unmistakable, undeniable voice that carried. It was the best speech she never gave. "Please calm down, calm that music down." The camera was, originally, zoomed in on Colvin, but when it was clear Colvin was not actually attached to the voice commanding the audience's attention, the lens realigned with ODB. He owned the moment. "I went and bought me an outfit today that cost me a lot of money, because I figured that Wu-Tang was gonna win. I don't know how you all see it, but when it comes to the children, Wu-Tang is for the children. We teach the children. Puffy is good, but Wu-Tang is the best. I want you all to know that this is ODB, and I love you all, peace."

A statuesque model stood in the background, unsure of her role, her blank face not even acknowledging that something out of the ordinary was happening. She kept looking to her right at a production assistant who eventually rushed out to escort ODB backstage. Colvin, stunned but still a Grammy winner, said "I'm a little confused." Naturally. It was confusing for everyone except for those who knew ODB. They knew exactly what he was talking about.

As ODB explained later, he was pissed that the rap awards weren't presented during the main ceremony. They were given out earlier at a ceremony held somewhere else in front of a different, smaller audience. In 1998, the only way the Grammys recognized rap was if you were Will Smith. And this was *two decades* after the birth of hip-hop. Smith won Best Rap Solo Performance that year for "Gettin' Jiggy wit It" and explained in a post-awards press conference, "Gettin' jiggy with it is, like, the next level of cool. It's cool to the eighth power. Some people are fly, some people are kind of hot. But when you are the jiggiest, when you exude jiggy-essence, it's the acme of cool." To anyone who knows the Wu-Tang and their nine-volume definition of cool or whatever, jiggy is just nauseating. The foundation of Wu-Tang is in its lore, its urban mythology, its appropriation of kung fu, chess, Buddhism, Islam, Bible studies, cartoons, comics, Staten Island; anything they came across was woven into an intricate web of culture and identification and a constructed community that bordered on cult. They made themselves a world when the projects didn't provide. And they sold that world to this other world (a primarily suburban one) in rhymes. And here were the Grammys saying fuck you to hip-hop, to ghetto black boys who were aggressively creative. Wu-Tang wasn't just rhymes, not ever. It was a collage of culture—recontextualized and reimagined—into a wholly new and fantastic universe. Wu-Tang was into fantasy but they were not so into jiggy; Wu-Tang would never employ a word so seriously deaf to street semantics. And so, yeah, ODB was mad, but not at Will Smith or anyone in particular; it's not like he cared that Will Smith was a little bit more marketable. On that stage, with the audience and his mama sitting in the seventh row watching, they saw how deeply ODB believed in himself and in the Wu. When he felt compelled, when he had something to say, he said it. It was impulsive and childlike, but honest. And really, what do the Grammys amount to, anyway? A pat on the back, a celebration of mainstream music—like they needed a boost in record sales. ODB had been nominated before and the presenter Patty Loveless snickered at the cue cards next to the cameras: "I've been waiting all day to say this, Ol' Dirty Bastard," when she announced the nominees for Best Rap Album of 1995. Consider the other selections: *E 1999 Eternal* by Bone Thugs-n-Harmony, *Poverty's Paradise* by Naughty by Nature, *I Wish* by Skee-Lo, and *Me Against the World* by 2Pac. It's surprising the academy recognized his debut album at all, not because it wasn't critically fit and musically inspired, but because the Grammys don't often acknowledge musicians who live outside the Billboard top ten. That's why when he was up there, he had to mention Puffy, the most criminally corporate character in hip-hop. That man was a hustler, not an MC.

ODB brought up Puffy because no one else would. Puffy could package a song with guest vocals and recognizable samples, but his rapping was more posture than actual performance. *The Onion* ran the headline "New Rap Song Samples 'Billie Jean' in Its Entirety, Adds Nothing" and credited Puffy as the producer. He'd been riding the giant coattails of Biggie Smalls for most of his career. His album *No Way Out* was no exception. The entirely unremarkable single that served as a tribute to Biggie was really more of a vanity project for Puff. Even after Biggie's death, Puffy continued to attach himself to his star performer and was tenderly remorseful via a hit single that had already been a hit single in 1983 on the Police's *Synchronicity*. "I'll Be Missing You" is nearly identical to "Every Breath You Take." Isn't it disturbing that he changed one word in the chorus and won two Grammies (one for the single and one for *No Way Out*, the album it appeared on)? Isn't it also disturbing that in this ode to Biggie, the only screentime Big gets is in a still photo at the end of the video, almost an afterthought. He's not pictured once; he's not even sampled or quoted. It's all Puffy doing his odd spastic-knee *Fiddler on the Roof* dance, clad in a spotless white suit shifting side-to-side in an alley with his elbows up and his sunglasses faded just right. Puffy plays to the camera, looking up, looking down, looking off in the distance, like maybe he might see a vision of Biggie on the horizon. The song is just the start of Biggie, Inc. By itself, it's tired, the chorus is soulless, the flow truncated by sheer ineptitude. *Wu-Tang Forever*, however, was an innovation, a double disc that sold more than four million copies and was critically heralded as nothing short of the second coming in the form of a second album. In contrast, Puffy's equally commercially successful *No Way Out* (the Grammy winner) was heavy on sampling and light on substance and intellect and real rhyming and personality. Puffy was a nostalgic favorite because of the tribute to Biggie, and it was an easy, safe, Grammy-tastic choice. Replacing that one word and wearing white was apparently enough to earn the golden gramophone. Ol' Dirty Bastard was speaking the truth in his protest—he was claiming rightful recognition. And incidentally, Biggie was also nominated for Best Rap Album that year and also lost to Puffy.

ODB knew all along that he was going to the awards and

that he was going to lose. He stopped by his producer Steve Rifkind's house a few blocks away from Rock Center just before the ceremony. ODB was going to the Grammys with his mom in a rented white limo stocked with champagne and water and Perrier. He didn't drink any of it. ODB asked why Rifkind wasn't going to attend. "We lost. I already saw it in the pre-ceremony. I mean, we lost to Puff Daddy. I don't want to watch that." Now hip-hop dominates the Grammys, but in 1998 the rap awards were distributed in a pre-ceremony like the tech portion of the Oscars. ODB collected his mom, Cherry Jones, and asked Rifkind, Why did I get all dressed up then?

ODB got on that stage for a reason, with conviction and confidence and purpose. He wanted the world to know that you can speak your mind; that some things shrouded in false grandeur need to be taken to task. After all, this is the same awards ceremony that welcomed to the stage the Olympic gold medalist Tara Lipinski—better known for her triple toe half loop than for any contribution to the music industry. The Grammys needed to acknowledge hip-hop and black culture beyond Will Smith and Puffy. ODB opened his mouth, unscripted and spontaneous; this wasn't a calculated breast exposure à la Janet, this was ODB raw and uncut, impulsive and real. And, of course, he was sensitive; let's not forget the children.

Backstage after the speech, he was handed another mic, and another forum, by Chris Connelly of MTV News, asking for an explanation. (As if he needed one.)

ODB: I dunno, something just jumped into my blood and I was up there. Puffy and all the artists are good artists, but I think Wu-Tang, hey we number one, and that's basically it.

CONNELLY: Do you think that was the appropriate venue to say that?

ODB: Yes.

On the ride home in the limo, ODB's mom stroked his head, which was resting on her lap. She said, "You really wanted to win that Grammy, didn't you?" And he said, "I didn't really care." They stopped at Rifkind's apartment again and ODB asked him, "How did I do?"

Rifkind smiled. It was obvious ODB did care.

Maybe by the time ODB got in that limo to ride home, he really didn't want that statue anymore, but he certainly believed Wu-Tang deserved it. And maybe he didn't want it because it never meant what it should. Maybe he didn't want it because he knew it didn't matter. It is undeniable that announcing "Wu-Tang is for the children" had more of an impact than winning. It was a lifestyle proclamation, a lifestyle for generations to come. It was a political slogan. It was free advertising. It was a secret code for followers . . .

" 'Member when?"

"Ya, man."

"Wu-Tang is for the children."

And in ODB's mind, it *was* for the children; it was for the four-year-old burn victim Maati Lovell, it was for the twelve inner-city children receiving full academic scholarships to college from the Wu-Tang Clan, it was for his own kids, for his nieces and nephews and cousins, it was for Steve Rifkind's kids; any kids he encountered, ODB loved. "Wu-Tang is for the children" simply meant that the collections of MCs were more than Grammys and albums and dolla dolla bills; Wu-Tang was in it as a movement. Maybe it was self-referential. Maybe the reason ODB believed in children had more to do with justifying his own behavior. A child would run up onstage and speak his mind, but an adult knows better; an adult exists in social parameters and inhibited instincts. ODB never sat and thought, "What am I going to do?"; he just did. And there on that Grammy stage in 1998, he lived in that fine small space between lucidity and delusions of grandeur. Somewhere between unacceptable and admirable, between brazen and buffoon, ODB flaunted freedom. Johnny Cash walked the line; ODB saw no line to walk.

2.

NICE LIKE THAT: THE KNIT, 2003

You never thought hip-hop would take it this far.
—Notorious B.I.G.

The first time I saw ODB play live, I cried. It was his first post-jail performance, at the Knitting Factory in New York, and though we were just fifty blocks away from that Grammy podium, ODB was nowhere near what he was. He took the stage around four in the morning. I'm a girl who prefers to see dawn after a sound seven hours of sleep. I like it when the sky is gray with slow high pockets of light, and a rosy blush tickles an otherwise dark and forgotten night. I like my sunrise with coffee and knowing that the day is ahead, not behind. I take early plane flights, when everything looks flat—subtle shades of a milky blue secreting definition as the morning blooms. That night, in fall 2003, I stayed up till dawn. I stayed up to see ODB. I had a CMJ pass from a Slovakian day trader who played bass in my friend Max's band. I bought him a hot dog wrapped in bacon and vowed to stay up every night, all night, to see the shows that I normally never would have, because I'm a lazy music lover. (It doesn't help to be five feet four on a good day and consequently jaded by having to hop up and down just to barely see who's onstage.) Well, the only night I actually saw dawn was when Ol' Dirty Bastard was on the bill. I wanted to finally witness the man I'd been reading about since college. I wanted to see him move, react, turn his voice inside and out the way he did on his albums. I wanted the impossible. First, I wanted him to show up. Second, I wanted him to live up to my expectations, to exceed them. I wanted to see him own the stage the way he did at the Grammys, with no real sense of boundaries, just raw impulse and need. He needed to be up there.

The show, organized for the last night of CMJ, was an odd bill. CMJ is supposed to be an arena for new small bands with tight smelly jeans and an aesthetic awareness of who they want to be—white boys with tattoos and slow suffering drawls. Which is why ODB's fresh from prison, fresh from a Mariah Carey/Roc-A-Fella press conference, fresh from the psych ward comeback show was odd. ODB has a lot of fans; some are overly educated white boys who take their cues from Pitchfork and love him like a patron saint. That night, for some reason, straight-edge emo prog rockers the Dillinger Escape Plan opened. They scream real loud and play real fast and perspire angry drops of sweat with each hoarse word. I got there early and planted myself inches from the lead mic, thinking if I can make it through DEP, I'll be well positioned for ODB. And this is the kind of thinking that a short girl has to employ at every show. It takes only one giant head blocking my view to make concert-going a yogic exercise. So, there I was with a gutter-punk kid I met behind the velvet rope outside. We talked about skateboard-ing, tagging, and how he used to sometimes live under the cube sculpture in Cooper Square in the East Village. He also told me about how when he was short on funds, he would go to the gay bars in Chelsea and enter amateur stripping contests. He'd win, then run out of the bar with his earnings. He was like an extra from *Kids*. He carried a journal. He checked his skateboard. He talked about forties and nights wandered away. He was young but not in college, not in school at all. He carried a sense of abandonment—he was a kind of psychic orphan. There's that time before a show when hunger and anticipation and annoyance and excitement converge—all just by standing there. My new skater friend and I stood together ready to pass time until ODB arrived. We both wondered if he would. But before ODB, we had to get through the Dillinger Escape Plan with our posts in front of the lead mic intact.

I didn't realize DEP would be such a violent experience. The music was loud, hard, fast, and tribal riotous. I held the stage, felt my hip bones pressed into the splintered wood in front of me, then panicked because the overwhelming force of so many bodies against mine had me worried that I'd eventually collapse into a pile of fractured bones, only to be further trampled under the footsteps of a vengeful mob (vengeful for what, I'm not sure, because they all looked like middle-class white boys sweating through Calvin Klein shirts). But there was no way I was going to relinquish my spot inches away from where ODB would be, and so I held on. I lost track of my skater buddy in the violent eddy of the crowd and played possum, letting the beating continue, while occasionally hitting back or swatting away a stray limb. I just let my eyes roll back and waited. And waited. And finally they finished in one burst of angry emo. The bulked-out lead singer drenched in salty sweat greeted his fans: all male, all eager, all delirious in admiration. Then the true crowd pushed forward, the CMJ white boys who wanted their token fucked-up

black man to dance. There were drunken shouts, doubtful murmurings. The floor was carpeted with a layer of crushed plastic
cups.

Brooklyn Zu and members from Sunz of God took the stage
first, peppering the audience with taunts and braggadocio. The
MCs floated cross-stage hunched over and hyping the hell out of
the tightly packed room. They kept asking if we were down with
Brooklyn Zu? If we were ready to make some noise? If we were
wanting to welcome Dirty hooooooome? Each line hung half
finished, unpunctuated, meaningless without ODB. The stage
was crowded but empty, limbs crawling all over the place, mask-
ing what was missing. It was still unclear: was he there, was he
willing, was he alive? Then those slow, methodical, deep-ass
beats from "Got Your Money" rolled out. From offstage a voice,
cool and calm and seemingly dirty, overcame everything. The
crowd cried. Buddha Monk, ODB's right-hand man, emerged,
mic in hand, sounding exactly like ODB, feinting left with a false
start. It was like he was the fucking Wizard of Oz, doling out
elaborate antics to distract from the fact that Dirt was maybe or
maybe not gonna grace the stage. He should have done the
whole thing from behind the curtain because when Buddha
revealed himself and he wasn't ODB, the crowd hissed like a
deflating balloon.

They continued, dodging full cups of beer, and to no fanfare,
to no announcement, in the middle of a song, ODB emerged.
He was in a fog, slow, like someone pushed him from the rafters.
He shuffled, staring at the floor, looking fat and stunned and
unprepared, hovering, frozen with fear.

I was worried for him. I wanted him to lie down and get
some rest. There was something wrong in the air, like we might
as well have been at the Bronx Zoo a hundred years ago mar-
veling at the pygmies on display, in cages. When Dave Chappelle

was on *The Oprah Winfrey Show* he talked about the reason he infamously walked off his own set and away from $50 million: that one of the production assistants laughed in a way that seemed menacing, judgmental, racist, ignorant. In these later days, when ODB performed it was to an audience populated by people cheering him, celebrating his dysfunction, excited by the prospect of having a tall tale to tell on the L train. Like they'd seen Bigfoot in a cage at the freak show. There seemed to be no awareness that he was dead onstage; that he was slack-jawed and crying, unaware of the tears streaming down his own face. He was drooling and looked desperate. Mumbling, he delivered each line with only a couple of words dropped in, Buddha Monk picking up the slack as this evening's resident ventriloquist completing each verse. ODB was a mess. Buddha Monk, playing cover, turned to Dirt and said, "I don't want you to do NOTHIN'. I want them to feel the VIIIIIBE." And turning to the audience, "In order to be like we be, you got to be . . . HIIIIIGH." But there is no amount of high that hides terror or that induces talent or that convinces an audience that the one-man army, Ason (as ODB is self-described on "Brooklyn Zoo"), is fine *even though he can't close his fucking mouth by himself.*

And when it came time to mumble-rap "Shimmy Shimmy Ya," he did; he got in at least ten lines straight of "Brooklyn Zoo," stringing the words together like he was saying the pledge of allegiance. When reciting his lines, he stood still like a tranquilized animal, his gaze directed toward his feet because he could not open his eyes. If you've ever been to a mental ward, one that prescribes Thorazine or Klonopin, you'd have recognized that this person onstage had narrowly escaped some facility and probably should have still been in treatment. The only thing missing was the ass-open gown, which he wouldn't have known he was wearing anyway.

The dancer grinding next to ODB worked her hips back and forth. He didn't notice; at that moment the Loch Ness monster licking his cheek wouldn't have given him pause. Dirt was checked out. The dancer took off her shirt, wiggling around like he might react to naked flesh—nipples, areola, anything. But he was still crying like a helpless baby, eyes closed, mouth open, limbs limp. After thirty minutes of performing, two men held his arms and escorted him offstage. The concert continued, the CMJers booing, fists pumping with righteous indignation like they didn't get their fifty dollars' worth. I decided to walk home because it was late or early enough that it was light. I made my way from Tribeca to the Brooklyn Bridge, my throat parched, my body bruised, and my mind reeling. It was the dawn of the next day and though the gray light slowly exposed the cityscape around me, I felt consumed by darkness.

3.

BIRTH OF A BASTARD, 1968

Hip-hop is a culture given birth by inner city youth in the mid-70's, consisting of four basic elements (graffiti, break-dancing, DJing and MCing) and a creative ideology.
—*Grandmaster Caz*

At four in the morning on November 15, 1968, Cherry Jones gave birth to a quiet baby boy named Russell Tyrone Jones. She was asleep, still knocked out from the epidural when he emerged in the maternity ward at Lutheran Hospital off Pelham in East New York. "I had all my children natural birth up until him. They gave me something for the birth, something intravenous. It knocked me out. He was a good baby, though, didn't cry."

It's ironic or some ill coincidence that of all Cherry's seven babies, ODB was the one who required drugs to be coaxed into the real world—that somehow the only way he'd swim out of that fetal paradise was if the passageway of life was baited with some IV of numbness.

I sat in Cherry Jones's living room on a crowded sofa populated with pillows, looking at pictures of this sweet, serene, fat-faced baby. She had stacks of pictures, but these are the ones, when Rusty was immobile and quiet, that she paws gently, her lips stretched to a sad smile. ODB was born special: "He *was* a show, just came out with a certain kind of charisma. People were drawn to him. And he was nice about it."

Jones's home is littered with stacks of CDs and books and pens and Post-its and other normal clutter. There's a phone that rings periodically, which she answers with concentrated nods and quick goodbyes. Her living room may as well be mine except for the dozens of gold records, framed limited-edition CDs, newspaper clippings, and promo posters strategically placed. It's like a shrine with no fire—every piece of memorabilia is a reminder of whom Cherry Jones gave birth to.

A life-size cardboard cutout of ODB is tucked away in an alcove next to the washing machine. It's the photo of him from *Nigga Please*—his head tilted toward the sky, shoulders dropped back, lips slightly parted. He's wearing a wig that belongs on Cher, and a jumpsuit that seems fitting for a soul train Evel Kneivel. The zipper is open to mid-chest and he seems to be looking up at a bedazzled mother ship that will any minute now drop a passageway from the heavens, where he'll be sucked in through a pneumatic tube. There's no menace in his eyes, just silent recognition that he is ODB, and if he wants to wear an Elvis jumpsuit with gold-capped sleeves to meet intergalactic ambassadors, he will. And he will do it in a way that is not ridiculous. He will do it in a way that is majestic. He will do it in a way that is not only his own but an homage to Rick James, a loving portrait of himself in a poly-blend onesie and some rainbow platform shoes, with glitter in his eyes.

Cherry's brownstone was one block away from an apartment I had once shared with a militant Malaysian lesbian obsessed with BET (she named her pit bull Missy Elliot) and with about a million aggressive yet sluggish roaches. The block is in the heart of Park Slope, Brooklyn, just down the way from Prospect Park and half a block from sidewalks clogged with Bugaboos and Labradoodles. I couldn't stand to live there because it reminded me of the life I'm supposed to lead, one of urban sophistication sheltered by suburban isolation. A life based on years and babies and monetary achievement and plans and commitment. For me Park Slope was a step backward from my illegal Chelsea loft. (I've always wished I lived in a *Tootsie*-era New York, for the cheap lofts and the casual muggings that in my mind's eye seemed more endearing than threatening.)

In 2003, when ODB got out of prison, he moved back in with his mom. Instead of Bed-Stuy, where he grew up, ODB lived in Park Slope, which must have felt like a bizarro world where the black-white ratio was proportionally inversed. Regardless, ODB's method of fitting in was to stick out. But now he was older, subdued. ODB had a favorite sushi restaurant around the corner, much to his mom's confusion: "He loves sushi. I don't know why. Raw fish?!" (Remarkably, she didn't think he was all that crazy, except for the raw fish.) Cherry's house was across from a junior-high playground that one day stopped, silent and awestruck, when ODB emerged on the stoop. First it was silent, then riotous. The kids wanted autographs or just to touch the man. He obliged them with his scrawl and his drawl, passing time while the principal of the school tried desperately to redirect the preteens' attention to something else, like class. Even on this block, not really his own, ODB was king.

When I asked Cherry Jones how Rusty, the younger, sweeter ODB from her pictures, got involved in music, she clasped her hands across her chest—"From me!" (On the song "Drunk Game" ODB said, "My Momma taught me this shit and my Daddy learned from my Momma, which is good. Which is goarrr-ood!" As the song progresses he gives echo-chamber shout-outs to Cherry Jones, Patti Labelle, and Gladys Knight in between murdering the notes of "Sweet Sugar Pie.") ODB and Buddha Monk (his lifelong sidekick) used to hear their folks' records spinning from open windows. "We'd sit outside and while they would be playing the music, we would be hearing it. And we'd listen to the soul music and try to sing it exactly the same, and you know, growing up his voice wasn't all that good," Buddha Monk said. Cherry Jones was a soul singer with pride in her LP collection, and though she happily takes credit for ODB's music appreciation, she doesn't quite feel the same way about technical aspects of his voice. "I raised my kids on good music. I told Rusty, 'You have the nerve to get out there and sing when you know you can't sing. I'll tell you something, sounding that way, I'd shoot you." And at the time she was a parole officer. But there was something moving about the way she spoke of him as a mother who loved her son with devotion and ferocity but who was also a little relieved when he died, a little happier to remember him than live with him. At least live with him in the end, when there was so little left of who he was.

Cherry and Rusty used to sing along to her Marvin Gaye and Al Green and Millie Jackson records in the living room. "He was always the entertainer. Rusty taught all of them, he taught RZA . . . They knew nothing," Cherry said. In those days RZA's mom, Linda, who was Cherry's niece, would stay for days with Cherry's family on Linden Street in the Bedford-Stuyvesant section of Brooklyn. "Linda was more like a sister to me." RZA and ODB spent most of their youth trekking back and forth from Fort Greene and Bed-Stuy to the Stapleton and Park Hill projects in Staten Island, where Linda and RZA ended up living.

At age ten, Popa Wu (ODB's cousin and mentor) introduced Five Percent Nation teachings to ODB, RZA, and GZA. The

Five Percenters, a sect of the Nation of Islam, have been historically tied to hip-hop's founding fathers. Their beliefs are based on the tenet that the black man is God. "Next thing you know, [Ason] Unique had his knowledge from Popa Wu," Buddha Monk said. "Popa Wu would come around and talk about what we are—the purpose and the truth in life, and it just was something that I knew was right and I had to have it in my life too." Most of hip-hop slang is rooted in Five Percent lingo. A cipher, or a group of MCs rapping in a circle, is directly evolved from Five Percent gatherings, which began in Harlem and involved groups of young men standing on street corners reciting memorized teachings from Clarence 13X. The expressions "word," "dropping science," "what up, G," and "peace" all stem from Five Percent lessons that were memorized and recited. "That religion, I don't know anything about it," Cherry said. "To me they're crazy. Their god comes from atoms or something. He would try to tell me that and I would say if you don't believe in God, you better stop that mess in my house, so he took it in the streets." And every week, sometimes twice a week, the three cousins would file out to civilization classes (part of the Five Percent lessons) and attend meetings and rallies. Lessons involved reciting the Supreme Mathematics, a system of understanding numbers alongside life teachings and philosophical concepts. Knowledge was represented by the number one, wisdom by two, and the addition of one and two equaled understanding, or three.

ODB found himself in the Five Percent Nation and, more specifically, in the teachings of Clarence 13X, a former Nation of Islam believer who studied under Malcolm X. In 1963, as a student minister in the Nation of Islam, Clarence 13X formed Nation of Gods and Earth (NGE) based on the theory that all black men were Gods and all black women were Earths (as opposed to the Nation of Islam belief that God *was* W. D. Farad Muhammad). Clarence 13X formed this social movement in Harlem in the sixties from the structure of Islam, but it included a specific emphasis on youth leadership and oral history. This included a rhyme scheme with abstract references to NGE teachings. The word spread from Harlem to the Bronx, where MCs like Eric B. and Rakim Allah, Big Daddy Kane, and Brand Nubian laced lyrics with references to Nation of Gods and Earth. One of the fundamentals of Clarence 13X's teachings is that people are divided into three groups: 85 percent of the population is blind, deaf, and dumb to knowledge and self improvement; 10 percent exploits these ignorant souls; and the remaining 5 percent are truly enlightened and selfless individuals who are trying to help the 85 percent. The 5 percent are meant to navigate their own moral code and to save the unenlightened from self-destruction. There is a sense of trickle-down intellectual righteousness in that 5 percent of the population has the power to bestow 85 percent with a moral code and psychological redemption. The percentages and which side you're on delegate civilization versus savagery, thinking versus acting on impulse.

GZA, RZA, and ODB would go to weekly meetings and monthly demonstrations and would study NGE literature known as the Mathematics and the Science. "Some neighborhoods had civilization class and meetings but we also had the parliament and the rally at the end of every month. We had gatherings of the young Gods and Earths, mostly Gods, and some of the older Gods would speak," GZA said. In terms of being a Five Percenter, you have to wonder how much ODB really subscribed to their theories and practices. "They'd go through it for hours and then there were speeches and these powerful men would speak and if anyone had anything else to say they would get up and say it," Icelene, ODB's widow, explained. "It was hard for

Unique [ODB] *not* to talk." It was like his first stage. He went to meetings. He read the lessons and privately believed. GZA when asked said, "One hundred percent, he believed it one *hun*dred percent." But he had to recognize the split: that when he was onstage, when he was chasing the camera lens and courting the casual observer, he was acting antithetically to the NGE code. Of course one could see things as Lord Jamar of Brand Nubian does: "In the Five Percent Nation, each man is the sole con-troller of his own universe. If you're the god of your universe, you set up your own laws." ODB certainly followed his own code; he didn't eat pork, he went to meetings, he knew his les-sons by heart, but at the same time he lived a life of so-called depravity. And it's possible that ODB was drawn to NGE teach-ings because he struggled with the sense that he was actually one of the 85 percent of souls destined for self-destruction. There's nothing particularly enlightened about accepting the name Ol' Dirty Bastard, let alone living up to it on occasion. And it's hard to imagine a religion with such strict rules embracing ODB—a public figure who rapped about drug abuse and sexual promis-cuity, and proclaimed the virtues thereof. But even ODB's form of devotion is surprising—who among his fans would guess that amid all his outlandish behavior he restricted his diet or believed in anything outside himself?

Originally, Russell Jones rapped under the moniker Ason Unique (a name given to him through NGE), meaning quite lit-erally that he was a unique son. "As a teenager, Rusty was an entertainer, he had to be the star of the show, he always had to do something to stand out, and he's always the one that got the beating," Cherry said. ODB, RZA, and GZA would skip school and haunt the Forty-second Street cinemas that would play dou-ble, sometimes triple, features for a buck-fifty. Sometimes after chasing open mics, the three cousins would round the evening out in midtown watching staggeringly nonsensical kung fu fighting. They'd plant themselves in the theater seats once occupied by vaudeville audiences. The Broadway theaters in the early eighties were reduced to screening pornography and kung fu imports. These were the days when Forty-second Street whispered to passersby, offering girls or joints or bags of coke. Back then tourists ran away from hustlers and whores only to dine out on the stories of poverty, lawlessness, and the struggles of brown-skinned folk in shows such as *Dreamgirls* and *A Chorus Line*, musicals that compared to today's Disney adaptations seem positively cutting-edge. Broadway in the early eighties was pockmarked with cavernous subterranean culture. You could lose yourself in rerun cinema or half-priced hookers.

It was in this world that the three cousins formed All In Together Now, a precursor to the Wu. "He and RZA and GZA would do all these sideshows and it was so crowded that you couldn't even breathe," Icelene said. Their playground was grainy prints of Martial Arts Maniacs; they'd skip school and hide in front of the flickering light of a projector, miming whiplash-fast kicks and chops, holing up till bright lights moved in on some inner-city peace. After one marathon kung fu session, RZA or GZA or ODB himself (no one remembers, everyone's willing to take credit) knighted Rusty the Ol' Dirty Bastard after one of the flicks they'd just seen: a Meng-Hwa Ho joint named, depending on interpretation, *An Old Kung Fu Master* or *Mad Mad Kung Fu* or *Ol' Dirty & the Bastard*. The movie featured Yuen Siu Tien, a martial arts actor who often played an elderly lush who had mastered the art of drunken boxing; he was a kung fu disciple known as Drunken Master. And if ODB could empathize with a special skill, it'd be drunken anything. Even as a teenager, ODB was known for shoplifting forties as fast as he could drink them. One of his early managers said that when ODB drank, he drank it all and whatever was around—that was before he replaced the bottle with a crack pipe. In some ways ODB's life was thirty-five years of drunken boxing. He was a man numb to pain and punches because he was drenched in a substance that makes feeling an accessory. And if he lived a life defined by substance abuse, he started slow, with a simple malt liquor, a forty of Olde English. Like he said, "I drink Ol' En-glish, so I speak Ol' English."

He was kicked out of enough Brooklyn high schools that Cherry couldn't keep track of which one he actually attended. Eventually he was enrolled in Mable Dean Bacon Vocational High School on Fifteenth Street and Second Avenue in Manhattan. At the ages of twelve and seventeen Russell Jones was offered recording contracts. His mom put the kibosh on both, hoping he'd focus on academics, but Jones showed little interest in actually attending class. He didn't graduate from high school. Instead, he'd mount every stage, embrace every mic stand as if it were a lusty lady, and hop on any bill that would have him, primarily beat boxing and occasionally rapping in talent shows. Sometimes he'd take the decks and spin songs of the day, but it was Dirt at the table, so naturally he'd unleash a song with his right hand and waltz around the table dancing in front and around till he arrived back at the spot where the DJs are supposed to stay put—a whirling dervish, circling the tables as if he *were* a record. It was at Berkshim High that ODB met Malik Taylor (Phife) and Q-Tip, who went on to form two-thirds of A Tribe Called Quest. "Tip went to school at Berkshim and we'd go up for all the talent shows," Phife recalled. "Back then ODB still went by Ason Unique. He had a little rough style with him but if you didn't take him seriously that's when he'd get with you." Phife and Tip lived in Queens, ODB in Brooklyn, but they'd meet up in Manhattan for shows. "Occasionally it would break out into a battle, but for the most part it was really about wit against wit and respect. All the good-looking women went to high school in Manhattan, so there was that too. He'd be out there to impress women." It sounds so innocent when Phife is talking—like they were just average teenagers chasing skirt. Buddha Monk described equally typical teenage activities: "Dirt was incredible. We used to knock on people's doors, run across the street, and stand there like we never did it." And why should ODB's childhood be different? Antics and playfulness are what made ODB the MC that people loved; it's what he never grew out of. Phife paused, hiding beneath a small hand towel. "He just had a certain style that nobody else thought of." It sounded natural, like his breath just happened to exhale with words cupping the air. It sounded like he didn't have to work to get to the point when it felt right. It just did because ODB simply was.

In an appearance on Carson Daly's *Last Call*, RZA described an incident when they were teenagers in Brooklyn. "It was like, 'Yo, some guys from Bensonhurst beat us up!' So we went to go help. We ran out there and ODB thought it was going to be a couple guys. It ended up being fifteen guys lined up with broken beer bottles all over the place . . . and we had . . . a brown paper bag and he puts his hand in the bag and says, 'Back up! Everybody back up!' So everybody starts backing up. They was scared. But this one guy was so drunk that he just kept coming . . . So OD was like, 'Back up! Back up! Back up!' and the guy was like, 'Shoot me! Shoot me!' So OD took his hand out of the bag and was like moving his hand around, 'No man, you know I won't shoot you.' There was no gun," RZA recalled. "It was a bag of Dipsy Doodles."

Even backed up against a wall, ODB managed to improvise his way out of a dead-end alley with posture and confidence and really, in the end, honesty and self-preservation. He knew he had to reveal his hand, but at that point the fire was out—it was a joke with a Dipsy Doodle punch line. The best entertainers are those who are willing to promote themselves, to use themselves as bait for audiences. R. Kelly followed his child pornography charges with a single called "Sex Planets," which makes the not so subtle Uranus pun that seems an obvious thing to avoid for a man in his situation. But R. Kelly is R. Kelly; he will always sing sweetly about doing it and he was found innocent of the charges anyway. That's his deal and he's not hiding it, packaging it, or trying to sing about something he cares less about. ODB's grace and charm was that he was riotously embracing every moment, wreaking havoc as he walked down the street.

There's a Cee-Lo song that's drenched in horns and circuitous hand clapping. It's a song that moves. The chorus goes: "Think about it are you sure you're really living?" ODB never had to think about it. He knew he was really living; he knew he was really singing even though it sometimes sounded like he was choking on a mouthful of marbles and dandelions. ODB didn't care what he sounded like; he cared that he did it, did something, and he liked the sound of his own voice. He wanted it bad, wanted to be the one that people watched. If he didn't spend half his life running from the law and the other half breaking it, he'd have been on the cover of *Time* as Man of the Year. Right, I know, that's absurd, but I like the idea of the layout, those red borders and ODB with his head cocked to the sky, calm, his mind occupied by living inside a rhyme, and his face, handsome, childlike, and impulsive, beautiful in its stillness, and his mouth parted, ready to explain whatever. He could talk in and out and around everything—hugging strangers, demanding the impossible, declaring greatness, and then delivering the promise.

4.

CASCADING YELLOW CHIFFON AND A CANOPY BED, 2004

I have no feelings towards the future because feelings
are emotions and I don't have those.
—ODB

I was lost and in a rush. I'm always in a rush when I'm lost. I took the subway from midtown to the Kensington section of Brooklyn to meet ODB at his apartment. Even though I lived maybe a mile and a half from Kensington, when I got out of the subway I had no idea where I was. I waved down a car to ask for directions to 38 Kermit, and the driver told me to get in and wouldn't take any money when he dropped me off. I was forty-five minutes late and when I approached the street, it was cold enough that the manholes were exhaling steam.

A large man standing in the middle of the street (I assume ODB's bodyguard Jerrome, though we weren't formally introduced) asked me if I was looking for Dirt. I said yes and he pointed to a red door on an average-looking building. Jarred Weisfeld, ODB's new and already infamous manager, answered the door. (Damon Dash called him a "fucking clown" on a VH1 special and "not of the culture" during an argument between Weisfeld and Dash over which jersey ODB should wear on air. The two grown men were arguing as if ODB, who was standing right there, had no say regarding his wardrobe.) He was young, twenty-three or twenty-four, and was wearing a baseball cap, the brim curled the way frat boys used to do it before the flat bill was reintroduced. He whispered at me, "Dirt's asleep. I'll get him up. Hang on." The hallway leading to the living room was dark.

A single beam of light cut across his living room. Dust motes danced in the fluorescent air, drifting from the cracked window to the carpeted floor. I sank into a black leather couch that must have been a Staples special. I noticed a pair of eyes across the room watching from the doorway. He hovered, walked to the bathroom, turned the light on, took a closer look at me, turned the light off, turned it on again, looked again like he hadn't just seen me sitting there a minute earlier, turned off the light for a second time, and shuffled in. He was wearing a terry cloth bathrobe with the tags still attached at the back of the collar. The room was musty, and smelled like an assisted-care facility. Weisfeld sat across the room in a chair, out of eyesight. Dirt didn't talk and neither did I. We had originally scheduled the interview for a few weeks earlier. We were supposed to go to Junior's together. I liked the idea of sipping matzo ball broth at the counter with him, little braided girls and their mommies running up for autographs and pointing. We would have taken a walk after dinner through the Fulton Street Mall; he would have been mobbed by bootleggers and churchgoers and gold slingers. It's funny to reimagine that night—it sounds more like a date than an interview. Jarred called me to cancel the Junior's night. I waited a month for the next call, to be invited to his apartment.

And so we sat in silence. For a minute, he looked at me and waited. I asked him how he was doing. He nodded, shrugged, tilted his head, and said,

"Fine, I guess."

What do you mean you guess?
"I just been a bad boy, that's all, ain't nothing to it."

You were in jail.
"Yeah."

What was that like?
"Not good."

Why?
Impatient and sort of dumbfounded, he replied,
"It was *jail.*"

Right. In retrospect, my interview with ODB was one of the worst I've ever done, mostly because he didn't give a shit, bridling at whatever lame leading questions I had written down in my notebook and answering most of the others curtly. He didn't want to talk. He wasn't gonna talk. He didn't have to.

What was jail like?
"It just wasn't my scene. I didn't like it in there. I don't like jails. Thousands of threats were made against me because I was famous, because of my walk, whatever, whoever, just because."

What kind of threats?
"People were trying to kill me. All kinds of shit."

Can you expand on that?
"It just wasn't my shit in there."

Does being on parole affect the way you make music?
"No, not at all."

You think your music will be the same?
"Yeah, wait say that again what? Naw, ain't no changes."

Are you in touch with Wu-Tang?
"I'm not in close contact with anyone, just RZA."

What happened?
"Nothing, they just doing their thing. We're doing our thing."

Are you gonna go on tour?
"Yeah."

Where do you want to go on tour?
"America."

The limited answers and yes/no responses continued to the point where we were laughing. At least I was laughing. Dirt was unfazed.

Is it hard being on parole?
"It's not hard being good. I just had to stop drinking."

Was that hard?
"Yeah."

How about with drugs?
"Yeah."

Do you feel like you wish you could keep doing drugs?
"Sometimes, once in a blue moon. Nothing brings it on, it's just when I want to have fun, that's all."

How many kids do you have?
"Three."

Do you see them a lot?
"No. They live in Long Island. I'm close with the kids but not with the mother."

What do you do every day?
"I be at home writing rhymes."

What are the rhymes about?
"Just rhymes. That's all."

Can you describe them?
"No."

What are your favorite things to do?
"Women."

That's it?
"Yeah."

Anything else?
"Nothing after women. I write my music, do my music, and enjoy myself. That's what I do."

Why do women make you feel better?
"I don't know. It's just how it is. Life is boring. There ain't nothing to do. I have money but there's nothing to do. This is boring to me."

This interview?
"Na. I do my music and I put it out and go on tour. Tour is not boring. That's the only time I have fun."

Why?
"I don't know. I don't have to think too much."

What does it feel like?
"I don't know what it feels like. It feels good. It's like women, I guess."

Do you have groupies?
"Na. Well, sometimes. In Paris and Japan. It's good out there."

Why did you change your name from Ol' Dirty Bastard to Dirt McGirt?
"Just having fun, that's all."

Are you a different person when you change your name?
"Na, same boring person, same boring life."

When you wake up, what do you wake up to do?
"Just live."

What were you thinking today?
"Just get up and take care of business. Whatever business there is to take care of."

Like what? I don't know.
"I don't know neither. I write lyrics, I go outside, and I run around and chase girls."

Where?
"Everywhere. Then I come back in and sit down and listen to music. I can't party at night no more."

Are you close to your mom?
"I guess so."

Why "I guess"?
"Because that's what I said."

Do you think she's supportive of you?
"I feel supportive of myself now. If I get off parole I'm gonna sit down, relax, and make music."

Where?
"Hawaii."

Do you know how to surf?
"No, I don't do none of that."

Why if you get off parole?
"You never know what could happen. Anything can happen."

But it's in your control . . .
"I guess so."

Do you feel like your life isn't based on your decisions?
"Nobody's life is based on something they decide."

Really?
"Yeah, and that's what makes it boring. If I decided what to do [yawns], it would be exciting."

So what would you do?
"I don't know. I would know better than I know now."

But you have this second chance, right?
"Sure, whatever you say."

What do you rhyme about?
"The streets. It's about everyday life on the streets. I don't want to be pinpointing what it's about. It's just about life. It's music, that's all."

And in some bizarre cinematic moment, he scrunched his face as tight as he could and glared at me with venom and hate and antipathy. He looked like a different person, gnarled and old and angry, not the nearly asleep and docile Dirt that had previously been dodging my questions.

Is there a problem? I asked.

His face muscles relaxed. No longer hostile, he shook it off. "Na, I was just thinking about something else."

What were you thinking?
"Get money. It's all about money."

Is there any part of your life that has nothing to do with money?
"Na, it's all about money. Where you live at?"

Downtown Brooklyn. Kind of between the water and Junior's.
"Oh yeah?"

Isn't that your favorite restaurant?
"It used to be."

Do you get recognized a lot?
"Yeah."

What do people say when they see you?
"Hey, Dirty."

Do you have any friends?
"Na."

Jarred interrupted, asking "Dirt, you all right?"
"It's nothin, I'm just tired."
"Yeah, I'm tired too," Jarred whispered.

Dirt rolled his eyes and squinted like this line of questioning was silly and consequently over. I came into this interview after the show at the Knitting Factory convinced that he was mentally ill and heavily medicated, a reasonable conclusion considering his unpredictable past. It was reported that ODB went from Clinton Correctional Facility upstate to Manhattan Psychiatric Center, where he was diagnosed as schizophrenic. When I asked about the detour to MPC, ODB said he went "not even for a minute, just for a second." And Weisfeld was quick to silence that part of the conversation. "He doesn't want to talk about that." An easier answer, and one that was given later by his lawyer Peter Frankel, was that every prisoner goes through a psychiatric evaluation. It's standard procedure. So why was Jarred defensive? He was always defensive and fairly transparent. If I were a better journalist, I would have snuck into the bathroom and checked the medicine cabinet. But decorum stopped me. Privacy and respect stopped me. Plus, it didn't occur to me until later in the day. Not that it really mattered. Jarred and Dirt and his lawyer could tell me that he was doing fine, that the rumors of mental illness were ridiculous and unfounded. That Dirt was A-OK, he was just being Dirt, which was a popular refrain among his closest people. I got the sense that wasn't true.

When we talked about the Knitting Factory show, ODB said the tears and the stillness were because of drugs, which is an odd thing to admit for someone who was newly paroled.

"At the Neon Factory? That's when I was nice like that? I don't know, man, I don't know. I was in another world. I wasn't myself that night because I had some Ecstasy."

Weisfeld, who'd been busy texting someone, stopped quickly and responded: "Naw, he's just playing. When Dirt went onstage at the Knitting Factory that night, it was a pre-rehearsed thing. Dirt got up there and just decided to say he was on Ecstacy." Why? "'Cause I was on Ecstacy. That's why," Dirt said, standing up, now as lively as I'd seen him all day. "You weren't on Ecstacy," Weisfeld said. "Dirt, what's wrong with you?" "I just do what I gots to do. Period," ODB said. How come it doesn't show up on urine tests? I asked. "It just doesn't."

"Dirt, why don't you tell her the truth. You don't do Ecstasy," Weisfeld pleaded. "Yeah. OK. I don't do Ecstacy. We don't do Ecstacy and all that stuff," ODB said reluctantly, pausing between each word for emphasis, like the school principal had him by the ear. He sat back down. The truth is, if you had to choose between mental illness and drug addiction to explain erratic behavior, addiction is a little easier to explain. But the two are almost always intricately tangled.

When it was clear that every answer Dirt gave more than a word to was a gift, I came back to the subject of his mother. His eyes rolled back, his face screwed up tight again, and he started talking in another voice, answering a question I never asked, in a really aggressive way. A second or two passed and he was back to Dirt, unaware that he had said anything. There was a second flash of another person, just for a second, and I thought about Jarred's nondenial denial about MPC.

A man claiming to be a childhood friend of Dirt's (we'll call him John) showed up with his girlfriend that afternoon as I was getting ready to go. I was scheduled to fly home for my grandfather's funeral that day and John offered to give me a ride back to the subway. He was a white boy with a puffy fur-trimmed jacket on. He slipped a mix in that was his voice, featuring ODB. Then he looked at me and said, "If you don't name me, I'll tell everything you need to know about Dirt." No one before or since has ever claimed to know everything about ODB, not even his mama, so I was skeptical but listening.

"It's all about Dirty. He might be polite, but he doesn't like talking about things other than him. I'm tryin' to live the life as if I'm Dirty. People want a nice big friendly handshake and Dirty's not that person. My job is to coldcock the guy in the mall who's bugging Dirt. We went to buy some leather hats and it turned into mayhem at Kings Plaza. He just wants to be a person. He wants to go to IHOP early in the morning without having to sign autographs out of syrup." I asked John if he was at the Knitting Factory show and what he thought.

He said that he had heard it was a rough night, but that he wasn't there in person. And without prompting he started talking about the pills Dirt was on for schizophrenia or multiple personality syndrome, he wasn't sure which, but that he was definitely on something. "There's a gay ghost that fucks with him named Christoph. It's all in his head, but Dirty'll just start laughing. When you hang out with him, he'll go through different changes. He can be alive and up and wild, and he can be depressed. It just depends," John said. But even in these days of isolation and darkness, Dirt still had a humanitarian heart. John went on to describe the time his brother, a firefighter, was hospitalized in the burn unit at Cornell University Hospital. Dirt dropped by after a show to see John's brother and wish him well. "He was shaking little kids' hands and telling them about a burn he got on his collarbone once. He was just delivering words of kindness and confidence. He just does that, he takes that kind of time, even though his problems are worse than everybody's out there." John ended up driving me a few stops farther than the closest F and I got out at Ninth Street halfway between Dirt's house and his mom's house in Park Slope. I thanked him for the ride and got a call later from Weisfeld, who said, unprompted, that he didn't know who John was and that he just showed up one day, attached to Dirty's entourage, and that he's a liar and I shouldn't believe anything he says. Jarred was spinning, but I wasn't sure what to make of John either. Does it matter that he confirmed my suspicions of ODB's mental illness? Does it help now to have a diagnosis for someone who's dead? The way ODB talked, the way he walked, his truncated swagger now more of a stagger, he shuffled like a mental patient—full of twitches, pauses, and paranoia, often seeming sedated, as if his former personality was hovering somewhere nearby.

Back at the apartment, Dirt fantasized about the life he'd

rather lead, basking in the sun, surrounded by sand. "It's all about myself now," he said. "It ain't about mothers and fathers and sisters and brothers." He was out for survival, but there's a difference beween survival and living. As I left his apartment, full of functional furniture and bare walls, I caught a glimpse of his bedroom and his fairy-tale canopy bed shrouded in cascading yellow chiffon.

5.

DOLLA DOLLA BILLS Y'ALL: WU-TANG SIGNS TO LOUD, 1993

*I sell ice in winter / I sell fire in hell / I am a hustler baby /
I'll sell water to a well.*
—*Jay-Z*

In 1991, Russell returned to Brooklyn from Florida with his girl-friend Shaquita, who would eventually change her name to Icelene. They met at a sweet sixteen in Linden Plaza. "He had so much energy, the kind of energy you would never see in a normal sixteen-year-old," Icelene told me. "He just wanted to take over the whole world. When I first met him I just wanted to soak up that energy. He kept saying he was a better dancer than me. He'd dip all the way down to the ground and a lot of people couldn't do that because their knees would give out." He'd worked odd jobs at Universal Studios, cleaning the shark on the *Jaws* ride to support their newborn baby and the one on the way.

He came back to Brooklyn broke and in the system and without a place to stay. "It wasn't nothing to be proud of but he was such a dedicated father that he would steal to provide for us,"

Icelene said. "We didn't have no money, we'd have to go to a family member's house to eat. Sometimes they wouldn't want us to come to their house." Once their second child, Barson, was born, the family signed up for welfare assistance. "We needed help. He'd get five dollars and buy something to eat and we would all share it. One meal for all of us and I was pregnant at the time. And he would steal food so we wouldn't go hungry."

Icelene found a homeless shelter in Bed-Stuy, which, in order to place the family together, recommended strongly that Russell and Icelene get married. So they arranged a quickie wedding, to be held at Brooklyn City Hall, where vendors wait outside with Polaroid cameras and bouquets of plastic red roses, dew drops glued on. The marriage was small and perfunctory. ODB said, "I do." Cherry encouraged the union with the hope that he'd stay with his legally bound family, but watched her son walk away immediately after the ceremony. His mom now says Dirt never wanted to get married and that she pressured him into it. Icelene and Russell lived in the shelter for six months while ODB worked as a mechanic in a garage in Bed-Stuy. He kept up rapping, MCing talent shows around the city, trying to get some time in a studio to record, but mostly he was about performance. "A lot of times he would just perform for himself. He wouldn't run into a room and say, 'Come on everybody, gather round.' He just loved music and he would just be singing in the streets," GZA said. "I always had good lyrics but I didn't want to get up there, and that's when Dirt would step in." Dirt would push GZA into performing. "He'd say, 'Let me get that, get me that mic.' He used to get on me about it, he'd say, 'Man, all that nervous shit.' It wasn't like Dirt was a therapist, he'd just tell me straight up, 'That shit's bullshit.' That was his way." Dirt was a natural performer. He craved the stage. He couldn't understand someone, even his cousin, too shy to steal a moment.

A year later, RZA was charged with attempted murder for a melee that left one woman dead. He faced a jury trial and up to eight years. "It was self-defense, that's the truth," said RZA, in retrospect, to *Entertainment Weekly*. "But I also was not a mother-fucker to fuck with, nah mean? Listen, I could have been on the public enemy No. 1 list. But I'll never forget the smile on my face [when] I got eight years of my life back in my own hands. Ever since that day I been focused. 'Oh, it's me? I'm the man? I'm the one who can fix my life?'" Four months after the trial, RZA formed Wu-Tang Productions—a collective of nine MCs who at the time would have been in the first round of any Fantasy MC draft. They were all amateurs looking for the elusive music contract that offered a way up and out. They were power players in their own right and in their own neighborhoods. RZA told each MC to come to the studio armed with a verse and a hundred bucks.

That first day Wu-Tang recorded "Protect Ya Neck" at Firehouse Studios in Manhattan. The single is a study in unified one-upmanship: nine MCs competing for space and spitting verses laced with battle-rap rhymes and underscored by dirty-ass beats due to some seriously low-fi production elements. Their words introduce and complement one another—Raekwon would complete Inspectah Deck's thoughts and Meth would chime in for the chorus after ODB's verse. But underscoring the Clan's togetherness is a sense of talent-show bravado: who's the best, who's gonna win, who's gonna slay? The raw samples and gritty sound only add to the creation myth: these guys just showed up with words and drive and ambition like someone had restricted them with a giant rubber band and finally let go. Each MC got a verse to prove his worth, to flash his style; most stepped up with haughty boasts and tossed out some pop knowledge. ODB spit some aggressive nonsense; he boasted too, but his *shit was funny*. His last line leading into Ghostface Killah was "Niggaz be rollin with a stash / ain't sayin' cash, bite my style I'll bite your motherfuckin' ass." And right there, in his first verse on his first single, ODB embraced his status as a serious clown, but not for nothing. He laid it out in full: the one thing most important to him beyond cash and drugs was his style, his delivery, his teasing intensity. Not that anyone before or since could replicate what came out of his mouth.

ODB was just starting, but already people knew who he was. At first, when Wu-Tang started getting airplay, "we didn't know what to do with ourselves," Icelene said. "The album was all over the radio stations and media and we were just running through the apartment screaming. He was so happy, my husband would give me some money, like sixty dollars, and I could finally go to the store and buy things. I mean sixty dollars isn't much but it's a lot more than nothing."

RZA sold the single from his car, getting local airplay and attention when a hundred, then thousands, then hundreds of thousands of CDs passed through his trunk. He'd already been burned by Tommy Boy, where he had been dropped in favor of House of Pain, a bunch of Irish-American hip-hop hooligans. And GZA was equally frustrated by his experience in 1990 with Cold Chillin' Records, the inspiration for his revenge single "Labels." This time RZA was in control and the plan was local—generate attention in your backyard, infiltrate the DJ booth at parties, get the word out. Buddha Monk would throw on the single at block parties across the boroughs. "I was a known DJ, and people would come to the house parties or the block parties and I'd play the first single, 'Protect Ya Neck,' and they'd wait for ODB's part and go crazy. It was like people were waiting for a change in hip-hop and when they heard him, it was like they found it," Buddha Monk said. A&R reps were frothing at the mouth, but RZA had a plan. He wanted Wu-Tang to be a brand, each MC a personal rep in its expansion. The goal was to take over the record industry one label at a time, and where there's a Wu, there's a way. Most labels wouldn't agree to RZA's concept, thinking that by signing the Wu-Tang the label was entitled to release solo projects from each MC. The longer they waited, the more traction "Protect Ya Neck" got on the streets and in air time. Their first record pressing of "Protect Ya Neck" sold five hundred copies within a week. So they pressed ten thousand more. Those sold through within a couple of months. Finally, they sold enough to warrant the attention of the label execs who had rejected RZA's demands earlier that year.

It took a mailroom kid at RCA to walk into a listening session with CEO Steve Rifkind to confirm Rifkind's already strong inclination to sign Wu-Tang. He doesn't even remember the kid's name; he just remembers the single playing, "Protect Ya Neck," looping dark circles in a fog. "This kid just ran into the room and said, 'That's that *shit*,' and he ran out. I never saw him again." ODB and RZA came up to the RCA office in midtown with a list of demands, the same demands they made of all the other labels. They wanted their contract set up in a previously unheard-of way to protect the royalties of future contracts. It was a hip-hop conglomerate vision, and one that was conceived more like a militia operation than a conventional creative deal. Recording artists were constantly getting worked over by the labels, and RZA had a vision for how to stop that by essentially forming a small union to protect the rights of those involved with Wu-Tang recordings. He understood from his failed experience at Tommy Boy that hip-hop was equal parts business and creation and that control was imperative. Rifkind said, "ODB came in like a businessman. He was quieter than RZA and mostly let him talk, but he knew what was going on. And at the end of our meeting I asked if they had any questions. And he said, 'How come you keep saying yes to all these demands?' And I said, 'Because they make sense.' " Rifkind also said yes because he wanted to sign Wu-Tang, but he wasn't the only businessman in the room. RZA and ODB would show up at the office every day at six or seven with a notebook in hand, flip to a certain page, and start hashing out marketing ideas. "The public never saw the businessman side of Dirty," Rifkind said. "They saw the clown."

Within the group, Wu-Tang established roles and characters. Each MC had a personal hook: GZA the genius, RZA the professor, Meth the popular pothead, Ghostface the menace, and so on. Dirt was naturally assigned court jester in the Wu world because he brought chaos and smiles. Before the Wu-Tang signed, they were vying for label recognition by performing at corporate events for executives. Rifkind remembered one event in Connecticut at a retirement home where "ODB came out with a stocking mask pulled over his face and singing 'Over the Rainbow.' Singing! As loud as he could." He later recorded a howling dog version of the same song on *Return to the 36 Chambers*. The single "Goin' Down" began with a joke, an extended deep gravelly note, a sound from the bottom of his throat held as long as his breath could hold, and when it broke he laughed and the RZA beats looped in like a death march. On the track, Dirt thanks some people, announces who's in the house, sneezing and breathing and panting. It sounds aerobic, as going down should, and between growls he's fronting like a murderous hood, shouting "What?," challenging the listener. But from the trills of his voice and the longing that underscores each breath, it sounds real, like he's looking for something beyond, something that happens when you're out of breath and following an imaginary golden path. ODB had extraterrestrial gifts—*extrovert* was an understatement; *normal* was simply a word that never applied to him. In the beginning he knew when he was onstage and when he was there to perform. But after a while, his life was the performance that people watched. And like he said at the end of "Goin' Down," "You KNOW not to touch my HO / I like livin' my own fuckin' show."

A few months after Wu-Tang was signed by RCA, Dirt pled guilty to petty larceny and served a hundred days in jail. His career, on full blast, never interfered with his side project—getting busted. While Wu-Tang wasn't exactly gangsta, its MCs weren't squeaky clean either. The Clan's reputation and record rotations were based on street whisperings and block parties and blunts—more than a few Clan members served time and they most definitely endorsed pot smoking, except for ODB, who was more interested in the bottle. Buddha Monk told me, "In the beginning, when each one of them would only make fifty bucks a show, I'd provide all the weed. We used to have twenty bottles of Olde English in the back of my Plymouth Sundance and six to eight pounds of weed at every show. I never smoked and Dirty was definitely not a weed smoker, at all. Dirty was straight alcohol. Dirty was an Olde English mothafucker. I'm personally surprised they didn't endorse his ass."

When ODB performed, it was impossible to look away. When he sang or rapped, it was impossible not to hear his voice—louder, grainier, grittier than the rest. He courted the audience. In a Swedish TV interview, he sat next to Meth, who was actually answering questions while Dirt periodically burst into a wide gilded grin and waved at the camera like a kid on too much corn syrup. He'd already built a healthy reputation in Brooklyn from parties and mix tapes. Though he and Biggie never collaborated, there's a shaky home video of Biggie and Dirt performing for Biggie's birthday on May 21, 1993. To watch Biggie swaying side to side and lilting up and down next to Dirt, who's rapping "Shimmy Shimmy Ya," and "Baby C'mon" a full two years before either song was pressed to vinyl—it's like they're just regular people messing around onstage, Dirt rapping in Big's shadow, Big bowing to the spastic rapper. It was before Biggie's *Ready to Die* and before Wu-Tang released *Enter the Wu-Tang (36 Chambers)*. They form a perfect contrast, Biggie's mellow heartfelt delivery complementing ODB's clowning and indeterminate sounds. The sound system's in and out, the audience seems only half in it, but had they known that these two MCs would shape hip-hop, they might have recognized the love onstage. Biggie died even younger than Dirt—a full eleven years, at age twenty-four. He missed having to live through the celebrity backlash; he missed having to grow up in the spotlight. He was taken down in his prime and the album released fifteen days after his death went on to sell more than ten million copies. That night, Dirt just took the stage, shoved Biggie aside, rapped until the muddy music stopped, and bear-hugged Big. Watching him perform in these circumstances—in a small club, before fame, among friends—made me wonder whether celebrity was just as much to blame in his death as addiction and illness. Biggie never had to disintegrate publicly. It's a gift to watch ODB on this small stage (Biggie Smalls's stage) where he looks happy and aware, like he's at home stealing a spotlight, and close enough to the crowd to lock limbs. A few years later, after both Biggie and Tupac Shakur were murdered, Dirt told the European station ZTV, "Notorious ain't dead. Tupac ain't dead. They exist within me . . . I went to the next dimension and I saw a poet in the land of nobody. Tupac and Biggie they just on my shoulders, right here. You just can't see them." The off-camera interviewer asked ODB if he thought those kinds of killings would go on. "Well, if it does, then it does. That's life and life and death is the same."

6.

BACKSTAGE AT B. B. KING'S: PASS THE MIC, 2004

You ain't imitating me on this fuckin' tape.
—ODB

The next time I saw Dirt, after talking at his apartment, was February 9, 2004, at B. B. King's in Times Square, his last New York show. I got there early and sat backstage with his mom and his stepfather, Frank, while Jarred waited for Dirt's limo to arrive. It was painfully quiet and sterile in Dirt's dressing room, like a high school cafeteria just before the lunch bell. Cherry was fidgety. She kept saying, "Rusty doesn't like it when I'm backstage. I fuss over him. He hates to have his mama around before he performs." (At a show a month later in New Haven, ODB told his mom she couldn't be there.) The first thing she said, though, when I asked about Rusty's homecoming was that it "was wonderful because he's been away for so long. I just wanted him to come home and get his career back, get it back on track like it was." Cherry kept looking over her shoulder as if he'd arrive and throw her the stink eye for showing up. There were bottles of water and fruit baskets and a leather sofa that looked just like the one ODB had in his living room. Frank was silent, nodding his head to say hello, but there for Cherry and little else. At one point he piped in to talk about the commotion Dirt caused when he went outside their apartment across from the asphalt yard at John Jay Middle School. Cherry said, "The kids kept telling the cops, 'Do you know who this is? This is Ol' Dirty Bastard.' And the cops said, 'Well, Mr. Bastard, can you tell these kids to go back to school?' And he did, he said, 'Yo yo, you kids go back in school.' And they all went back in school. All of John Jay was out there and the man in the barbershop got mad because there was practically a riot just because Rusty left the house."

Jarred's girlfriend was backstage rolling her eyes. She told me that Jarred's welcome-home present to ODB was a deluxe basket full of condoms. She rolled her eyes again and said, "Not that he'd use them anyway." I asked Cherry about his babies and baby mamas and the women in between, and Cherry dealt some excellent mama spin: "He's a sweetheart. There's not a woman that he's been around that don't love him. That's the whole problem. He's caring. If they need something, he gives it to them. He's sweet-hearted. He just has a nice personality about him. He's a pussycat." From the brief time talking with him in his living room, I could see some remnants of the ODB charm in spite of everything—he sat there and he tried. And he wasn't picky. "Let's just say he put a lot of feelers out. I was with him once, just in the lobby of an office building in midtown, and he asked out every girl he saw, like seven in a row," his former Elektra A&R rep Dante Ross said. "Now that he's out of jail, when it comes to the women, he's the same. In every other way he's quieter," Cherry said, nodding her head out of nerves, not wanting Dirt to catch her backstage.

Cherry and I talked about ODB's transition from jail to home and she answered, sad and reserved, "He's always lived with me. He's handling it. He's kind of lonely. He doesn't call anybody except for Jarred. I call him four or five times a day, especially when he doesn't answer. He never answers the phone. I don't think he likes to be bothered. He doesn't like talking to people too much. He gets in that mode when he likes to be by himself. He's quieter now. Maybe he's growing up." Cherry talks fast and enthusiastically, like any minute she'll get the boot from Dirt. Looking left, then right, she whispers, "He just doesn't want his mama around. I don't know, it's silly, most of the time I want to punch him because all these other singers are fine with their mama around. Just look at Beyonce with her mother. Now that's nice. And Brandy. But if that's what he wants, it don't make no difference." It's hard to tell how aware she is of her son and who he is and that he might make some irrational demands. "He had some emotional problems . . . anybody coming out of jail would have that. He was in there all by himself." And then, while she was talking, the hallway started to pulsate, a dozen or so men arrived walking tightly together like a flock of migratory birds—V formation.

Jarred tells Cherry, "He's here."

"He's here? Oh, OK." She looks uneasy and puts her hands on the arms of her chair, but doesn't move, because Rusty's already landed. He grabs some water, leans in to kiss his mama's cheek, and she says, "Don't kiss me, you don't want me here anyway. I'm doing an interview. And I'm leaving." She gets up playfully.

"Look how good-looking he is," Jarred says. ODB's thinner than the last time I saw him; he's shed the bathrobe in favor of a letterman's jacket with a cursive D on his left breast. He's swooped into the room, fellas in tow, and there's an energy, an excitement about him that was missing when I saw him last. He's awake. He's punchy. He's more like the Dirt I've read about but, still, he eyes me suspiciously.

"I don't feel like doing an interview right now, but I'll say a few words," he says.

Dirt recognizes me, narrows his eyes, and shoots darts in my direction.

"Yo, I did an interview with you already."

Yeah, I just wanted to follow up and see how you were doing. Um, how have you been doing?
"I'm walking destiny, that's all."

Did you record that last track for the album, the one with Pharrell?
"Na, I'm gonna do it though."

You have the lyrics set?
"Yeah."

What's it like living on your own now?
"It's regular, man. It's cool, it's cool. I don't know, man."

He suddenly takes the tape recorder from my hands.

He holds it like a mic, cocked at a forty-five-degree angle to his lips. He finds exactly where the machine is perforated and exactly where he needs to speak to make his voice heard and lasting. "This is Dirt McGirt, you know what I'm saying, I don't like answering no fucking questions, you know what I'm saying? You know how we get down, we been doing this for years and we'll continue doing this." He presses stop and hands me back the tape recorder. I can only imagine how I looked: shocked, pale, delighted, at a loss for words. *What the fuck?* He seemed manic but alive, elevated even. And twenty seconds later, he caught the edge of the leather sofa next to me and sat real close, so our shoulders were touching and I could smell his breath and feel the heat of his words.

"You okay?" he asked, at once soft, serene, sweet, and concerned. I nodded yes. And he touched my shoulder, got up, and left the room. I sat for a minute, knowing that rather than a follow-up interview, he had given me a brief glimpse of who he was. The old ODB was back.

He performed with more ferocity than at the Knitting Factory, meaning he was at the very least conscious, which was a welcome change, even if it was artificially induced. He ran from the fire-exit doors to center stage breathless, but with enough air to resuscitate a medley of his singles. He was fueled by either a lack of prescribed meds or a prescription of street meds.

"Throw those W's up! Throw those W's up!" he said.

The crowd countered with "Wu-Tang, Wu-Tang!" Then he said "Throw your R's up, throw your R's up!" for his new label Roc-A-Fella and much to the confusion of the mostly Wu-centered crowd. They obliged, sort of, as much as you can form an R out of attached digits. Flanked by Buddha Monk and 60 Second Assassin, Dirt worked though "Shimmy Shimmy Ya" and "Got Your Money" and maybe two other songs before booking it backstage. As soon as he left, Buddha Monk stepped forward and said, "I never really wanted to leave anyway." He rapped for the rest of the hour, and judging by Jarred's wide smile, those four songs that Dirt rolled through were enough to warrant a comeback. The crowd was left wanting and chanting "O-D-B," but they got a taste, which was more than most who saw him perform post-jail.

7.

THE MIDAS TOUCH: SINGLES, RECORDS, TEETH, 1994

Only in the rat race of the arena, does the heart learn to beat.
—Rainer Maria Rilke

Before jail, before addiction, before ODB had to redeem himself onstage, he was a star. He was the person to watch. And though he was faithful to Wu-Tang, ODB could get only so much attention when he had to share the stage with eight other MCs. According to RZA's plan, ODB was set to soar as a solo act. The year he launched his solo career was also the year his life became noticeably unhinged. ODB started 1994 in Queens heading to the store at two a.m. to get ice cream. He noticed a car following him. He ran from the car, assuming it *was* following him, jumped a fence, and landed in a yard with three ravenous rottweilers. The owner came outside and ODB crawled into the house through the doggy door. Inside, the owner called the police at ODB's request but he couldn't shake the feeling that he was being followed. The dogs, still snarling and snapping but secure in the backyard, freaked ODB out enough that he jumped through a glass window on the second floor. Several broken bones later, the police arrived on the scene and came to the conclusion that ODB was under the influence of drugs. He was charged with burglary. The woman whose home ODB leaped from tried to drop all charges but legally couldn't because of ODB's prior record. Dirt checked into a Brooklyn hospital, which he walked out of the next day, only to be shot in the back around the corner from the facility. The bullet, from the gun of a rival rapper, entered his lower back and came out through his stomach. The shooting only served to increase his paranoia and he would again (against his doctor's advice) check out of the hospital where he was being treated. Was his fear rational or the beginning of mental illness? Running from a gun pointed at your back seems like a perfectly normal instinct but jumping through a stranger's second-story glass window because of barking dogs certainly was not. Mere months into 1994, ODB's behavior, what once was just his persona, was starting to be a little too real. Within a year, ODB's manager quit over his drug use. But this was just the beginning, a time when it was hard to distinguish justified paranoia from drug-induced paranoia from mental-illness paranoia from I'm-a-celebrity-now paranoia.

Professionally, he was one of, if not *the*, standout MC of the Wu-Tang debut. He stood apart because he was nuts. He'd stay at the back of the stage wearing overalls with one strap hooked, pumping his fists at the Wu-Tang flag, angrily and repeatedly beating the wall. In recordings he'd scream, "And ever and ever and ever . . ." on loop until it sounded like an angry diatribe. In 1994, Elektra signed Ol' Dirty Bastard for his first solo album, *Return to the 36 Chambers*, which dropped on March 27, 1995. According to Dante Ross, the parceling out of Wu was all RZA. "RZA asked me who I wanted and I started listing with Meth and ODB, and before I could finish, he was like, 'Meth's going to Def Jam, but you can have Dirt.' He already had it all laid out. When I first met Dirt, he was already a star, you know, he was the Ol' Dirty Bastard and he not only sounded like the Ol' Dirty Bastard, he sounded punk rock." When Dante Ross says the name Ol' Dirty Bastard, it's like the most important phrase that's ever passed his lips, like each syllable conjures a memory, some laughter, some tingling in his limbs. Most people who knew Dirt pronounce his name with a reverence that insists on punctuating each word, rolling the L, dropping the D, pausing in between words to pay proper respect and then with that last word *Bastard*, it's like a small explosion. ODB was signed to Elektra with most of the album already recorded. He'd done the majority of the studio work with RZA and Buddha Monk at Firehouse on Twenty-eighth Street in Manhattan. DJ Mike Nice, a hip-hop historian, told me that Dirt recorded *Return to the 36 Chambers* in one sitting and just single takes. That's the kind of story that's whispered in the back rooms of record stores; it's what cements a legend. ODB had confidence to spare—he could wail on a chorus, breathe through a backbeat, or wild out on one syllable, but no one knew if he could carry an album. "Once the record was done he came in the office and told us what the cover would be, what the back art would be, and what the teaser ad would be on television," said Brian Cohen, Elektra's head of marketing. "This man knew what he wanted and we were happy to give him what he wanted. Most artists don't have a fucking clue who they are and this guy knew. So we were happy to give him everything he asked for."

And what he wanted, exactly, was a reproduction of his ID for public assistance, his food stamp card, commissioned by "The City of Brooklyn Zoo." Rick Posada, the engineer on most of *36 Chambers*, came up with the idea and executed the actual

Photoshopping. The card, real with some type adjustment, had a small parental advisory sticker on the lower right corner. The sticker was the only indication that this was an album cover and not actually a giant welfare card. His picture on the ID is a classic ODB pose: eyes staring directly into the lens, confrontational and quizzical, with his tangential dreads crawling up the wall, his mouth slightly parted, his lips puckered like he was just about to say something. "He wanted the art exactly as he had imagined. His welfare card on the front, and on the back, he said, 'I want it to be my room, shit all over the place, no shirt on, and I'm just gonna be standing looking at the camera,' " Cohen said. "Marketing, my department, is usually called in to mediate, and my normal job was to talk the artist out of spending a lot of money. But he basically didn't want to spend any money. My impression was that he was not crazy, *at all*. This is the music industry. He was the most rational guy who walked in here. He understood his craft, he knew his genre, he was all business."

As promotion for the album, ODB went with his family and an MTV crew to get food stamps, to see if his welfare card cum cover art still worked. He walked into the government facility in Brooklyn after having been driven via limo and collected a week's worth of stamps and a fistful of cash. ODB stood in line to get welfare cheese while his debut album was a top-ten seller. Media outlets went bananas . . . *how classless and bizarre and illogical and ghetto to take a TV crew and a limo to your local check-cashing storefront and demand poor-people money*. How self-centered and ignorant and grandiose. Kurt Loder probably blushed at the thought. This welfare incident was mentioned nine times out of ten in his obituaries and eventually made #22 on *Spin* magazine's list of music's hundred sleaziest moments. ODB was just testing the system, as was his way. He was just cashing in because he wanted to see if he could. Every time he got onstage it was because he wanted to see what he could get away with. And now, as long as the cameras followed him, his stage expanded.

He was notorious because he did what no one else would— *taboo* wasn't a word he recognized. What people don't mention, though, is what he said afterward: "I had no idea the card was still gonna work. I can't believe we're still in the system but I'm not giving back the money, you [the government] owe me 40 acres and a mule anyway." So ODB accepted government money for an audience. Everything about ODB's public image was like a running montage of blaxploitation characters. He had a ghetto glam swagger that made everything he did cartoonish. His pants were baggy, his head was always shifted one way or the other, and if his teased-out 'fro was only half-braided, it didn't stop him from stepping out. In the video of "Shimmy Shimmy Ya," he struts haphazardly through a line of clapping dancers clad in metallic hot pants and tall Afro wigs. He gets down, he gets up, and then he chops a wooden board in half with his bare hands. He was a nut, but he embodied a sense of new free-dom—the *I don't give a fuck* kind of freedom. ODB went to collect his food stamps in a limo because that's what Dolemite would do, that's what Redd Foxx would do. It was outrageous. It was even more outrageous that they actually gave him food stamps and money. Sure, it could be sleazy, but isn't it worse that our government doesn't update its records? He hadn't been collect-ing from the system for at least three years.

You're just encouraging him, I imagine his mother saying, pursing her lips, her eyes squinting toward a frown. *He's acting a fool.* His father probably thought, *He knows where he came from, he knows he had two working parents and a place to rest his head.* ODB's father gave a lengthy interview to the *Daily Press* of Newport News, Virginia, about his son's upbringing, and claimed that they were not wel-fare recipients and that he used to take ODB fishing on Long

Island on weekends during the summer. I had lunch recently with a black author who, as we sat down to eat, said, "You know, black folks have a word for people like ODB and it starts with N and it rhymes with digger." I was surprised. It was the first time I talked with someone who took ODB simply at face value, who saw only his baker's dozen brood, his gilded teeth, his ode to Olde English, his cracked-out cornrows—his ghetto celebrity. I wondered if the black community, the upright black community represented by Bill Cosby, was embarrassed by ODB and everything he represented.

He went to get food stamps as a publicity stunt, as an experiment, because MTV encouraged him with its cameras, those same cameras that broadcast his spontaneity to lily-white living rooms. Yeah, he kept the money and yeah, he was equally shocked that the card worked, but why do it in the first place? Was it to sell records? Was it to make an elaborate point about a ghetto boy who never grows out of the ghetto, especially when the government still has his file? Was it just to point out some banal inefficiencies of the system? Was it to start a conversation about poor communities? Plainly put, I believe he collected his stamps because he could. He was a showman and I don't think he would have set foot in that line without an audience and without the right timing. Boom, boom, his album was coming out and it featured his welfare card. Let Snoop and Dre handle the Gats and bandannas. ODB dealt with a different, more universal reality, getting food on the table. It's telling that his dad went to great lengths to give an interview that disavowed ODB's ghetto upbringing. Most people, normal people, are ashamed to be poor, dependent, or desperate. But ODB shouted about it on the corners. He had no shame about poverty. He wanted out but he was never sheepish about embracing what he knew and where he came from. At the same time, it was also part of his act—he was a rapper who identified with being poor. "He really just wanted to stay in the ghetto," Icelene told me. I took my children and I ran. He stayed because he didn't want anyone to think that he thought he was different from them but really, he wasn't, he just had fun, and he loved living in the ghetto. People robbed him and put guns up to his head and he still wanted to stay there." While MCs like Snoop were theoretically rolling blunts and firing AKs and lining up their hos, ODB was visiting the welfare center. Much like his erratic behavior, fact and fantasy were meshed together in ways tough to distinguish, and there was something real in what ODB was doing—something fans identified with whether they were from the ghetto or not.

It was a career-defining moment, and inevitably what's remembered is the absurdity. The incident was followed by shock, outrage, and not very well stifled laughter. It was his first real *oh shit* moment. Dirt got attention and his album got a second-week sales bump. Dante Ross said the day it happened, "Dirty called and said, 'What did I do? Can we fix this? I wasn't even thinking,' but that shit probably got him the duet with Mariah [Carey] in the end. If he wasn't already well known, *everyone* knew about him after that." What does it mean that he felt sad and manipulated and full of regret and panic? Well, ODB was willing to trade some face for notoriety. And still, at this point in his life there seemed to be a distinction between Russell Jones and Ol' Dirty Bastard. Ol' Dirty was the character that notoriously "came outta my mother's pussy, I'm on welfare, I'm twenty-six years old, I'm still on welfare," as he sang on "Raw Ride," one of the tracks on *Return to the 36 Chambers*. Just before he announces this, he raps, "Who the fuck want to be an MC? You can't get paid to be an MC." And here, it's clear that ODB is well aware that he has to be more than a rapper to make it . . . he had to be a show.

And his showmanship paid off. In September 1995, Mariah Carey enlisted ODB in a remix of her single "Fantasy," from her fifth album, *Daydream*. Before her duet with ODB, Carey came off as an adult contemporary ice queen, stuck in a Rollerblading contest with an R&B soundtrack. She lacked substance and seemed desperate to sell herself, like those hour-long loud infomercials about very sharp knives. She was talented and pretty with a saccharine earnestness, but bland; her vocal range was acrobatic, but soulless. Then she met ODB. What Carey had in natural talent, Dirt matched with intensity and reality and sheer willingness. I mean this is a girl with a flawless voice and three octaves of range working with ol' Dirt Dog, who would occasionally hit the right note and just wail but more often than not would sing into transcendental moments that you could not concoct by being merely on key or even through training. He just got that moment and rapped himself into a marbled frenzy of rough and throaty verses that augmented Carey's sweet reverence and polite skill. And of the two voices, one classically trained and the other an outsider's, Dirt's prevails. It is brilliant because it has character. His voice has lived. He makes that song move; he brings a sharp reality to the fantasy, like lemon to an open wound. He makes you feel the pain and the joy of Rollerblading with Mariah Carey—the ecstasy of appreciation and the sting of defeat. He's allowed in because he's a curiosity, but Dirt could never really have Carey, could never take her on the kitchen table. "Fantasy" was recorded before her divorce from Tommy Mottola, before her meltdown, before Mariah was ubiquitous with tiny jeans shorts and low-cut spandex tank tops. She was still squeaky clean and ODB was there to Dirty her up a bit. He was servicing her, but only in a professional manner.

On the track, as on many others, ODB introduces himself like a circus caller bringing in the elephants, referring to himself in the third person: "Introducing the Ol' Dirty Bas-taaaaaaaaaard." And then Dirt answers himself with a couplet: "Me and Mariah, go back like babies and pacifiahs." That line is so obscenely funny it eclipses everything before and after: it evokes Freudian mommy lust with its suggestion of ODB suck-ing on Mariah's breasts, and establishes the absurd claim that they've been friends since birth. It is a tremendous ghetto fan-tasy, a warped *West Side Story* redux that these two stars would kick it to a Tom Tom Club beat. But they complement each other in every way, her sweetness, his roughness, wrapped neatly together. John Norris said this song was Mariah Carey's single greatest contribution to pop culture. I'd argue that the song belongs to Dirt. ODB's voice is the anchor—his growl, his yelp, his raw enthusiasm for every moment. He's infectious, hilarious, and imperfect. At one point he's just exhaling and laughing with the beat. He does more than lend street cred and grittiness with his presence; he lives the words he exhales. He's as wrapped up in the fantasy as anyone. This single formula, R&B princess plus Street MC, was the first of its kind. Now every rap album is loaded with at least one lugubrious duet, a grizzly rapper and a go-to girl.

The "Fantasy" remix with ODB was the number-one single on the R&B charts for six weeks. But the fantasy lasts only so long—even though Dirt had multiple platinum-selling albums, he was still ghetto. And even though Mariah or her producers capitalized on the image shift, she wasn't entirely down. If you watch the video, you'll notice Carey Rollerblading along the boardwalk with a troupe of hip-hop dancers. She looks at the camera lustily, indicating Dirt as her boyfriend. And for some reason, Dirt is shot separately at a completely different location on the boardwalk, next to a strung-up clown doll. They didn't shoot one scene together for the video nor did they actually record any part of the remix together. "Mariah Carey was never in any of the sessions to record it. For her, I think Dirty was too Dirty because she recorded all the other remixes with the artists in the studio. The character that Dirty was, I don't think she believed in him like he was on the level," Buddha Monk said. That is, until the single took off; then Mariah changed her tune. "One minute we were here in Brooklyn and the next we got a call to do Mariah's show at Madison Square Garden. At that point, she loved us so much, she gave us a twenty-four-hour limousine, and I called my mother and Dirt called his mother and they got dressed up in their furs and dresses and they had the time of their lives. The next day Tommy Mottola sent him a big-screen TV that was too big for the living room. They just started sending him whatever he wanted. She would call him and talk to him," Buddha Monk said. What made "Fantasy" such a good track was that Carey seemed distant and uncomfortable and Dirt just didn't care. He loved her and he knew a track with her meant tens of millions of new mainstream ears that had never gotten past the parental advisory stickers on his CD. And she knew that working with Dirt could help sully her clean-cut beauty pageant image. It changed her career and Carey never forgot it.

Mariah Carey wasn't the only one invested in ODB's ghetto grit. She and ODB were just characters in an MTV-generated entertainment culture. The network seemed to delight in the sexual undercurrents between the R&B diva and her urban prince. It was reminiscent of old Hollywood: starlets were paired with their leading men in order to generate more viewers and more controversy. MTV and VH1 are responsible for a lot of the public perception of ODB. Their cameras were rolling every time Dirt gave an interview high, they would lead off news segments with clips about his arrests, and they mourned his death like they had lost a commodity. ODB was great for punctuation—he'd speak enough lunacy that each segment on him ended with an exclamation, at least crazy enough for a sound bite on *MTV News*, something to counter the tired boy bands and the gangsta-rap wars. Naturally, the network tried to gloss over the complexities of ODB, but his unscripted life continued to reveal them. In some ways ODB knowingly took that white stretch limo to the food-stamp line to make a point. *Yo, MTV audience, want to go for a ride in ghetto reality? You want to see some real gangsta bullshit? Step in line, it starts with food stamps, it starts with poverty. You want to fetishize that, then let's go.*

A clown at a circus juggles and mugs to distract the audience from disaster. ODB used his life as a distraction. He used his reality to grab attention. He had STDs? He told you so in verse three. He wanted to fuck you? He didn't mince words. Unlike gangsta rap, his lyrics reflected who he was. He was honest— warts (or actually gonorrhea) and all. Unpredictable, he knew that people watched him, waiting for what was next. His songs are peppered with the words "What? What?," which he shouted in a hostile preemptive retort. He'd use these as punctuation, as invitations, as the simple question the words represent. "Everyone responded to him the same way, women or men. He was just a fascinating person to watch," GZA said. "A lot of times when we did shows, the crowd would look at him in awe, like what is he gonna say now." It was true in shows; it was true in life.

He ended 1996 with a Grammy nomination, a gold record, and a new name: Osirus [*sic*], after an Egyptian and Greek god of vegetation whose followers believed in immortality. ODB could easily have been a Greek god—he would've fit perfectly into the soap-operatic mythology of mortals and deities intermingling. Despite his larger-than-life stature, he was also famous for talking to anyone who approached him. Maybe he chose Osirus because it sounded like Cyrus from the 1977 movie *The Warriors*. Cyrus was the unifying gang leader who called the original peace meeting in the Bronx in the first scene. It's an iconic New York moment: thousands of people gather for collective bargaining and one hostile gesture tips the scales. Cyrus was assassinated by Luther, Luther framed the Warriors, and the Warriors spent the rest of the two-hour movie running an urban obstacle course from the Bronx to Coney Island. ODB loved that movie; it's mentioned in his lyrics more than once. I think he liked it because it's a furious chase ignited by one small menacing action—unplugging the speakers at a show. Luther upsets the balance and chaos ensues. Even though his new name subtly references Cyrus, I think ODB really related to the menace, the person who upset the balance and sparked a riot by winking sideways.

ODB was a predictably unpredictable factor. ODB interrupted a Roots show in November 1996—he was initially welcomed to the stage by ?uestlove and MC Black Thought who, knowing he was in the audience, beckoned Dirt up toward a mic to guest on a couple of songs. Naturally he overshadowed everyone onstage, which is no small accomplishment considering there are at least ten people up there at any given time. But then he wouldn't leave. So Black Thought started a scuffle with the newly anointed Osirus, trying simply to regain an already lost spotlight. Dante Ross said, "There were definitely instances of madness that a few people saw. He'd try to ruin people's shows. I saw him ruin the Roots show. He'd have a standoff with the bouncers in a club. I've seen him wildin' out. I wish I would have had access to him when he was out there but he was gonna do what he was gonna do." Ross described going to shows with Dirt as an exercise in restraint—he had to physically check ODB on more than one occasion. "He'd see people onstage and he just couldn't hold back. You could see it in his face; he just wanted to get onstage and perform. And sometimes he did. It was usually out of love, but then he'd always end up overshadowing whoever was up there. Nobody does a better show than ODB." Black Thought had been humbled by a performer who thrives in the heat of a spotlight and whose flow is recognizably his own. Just thinking about ODB fronting for the Roots makes me miss him and wish it were possible to see the egos jockeying for space on a stage big enough for a thousand but too small for these two. All devilish, all cunning, all smiles with his crooked teeth hissing and spraying, his chest heaving, and legs crouched low like a preying tiger, ready to pounce on any beat.

PART TWO

CRACK-FED CRAZY OR CRAZY-FED CRACK

8.

GHETTO SUPERSTAR, 1998

Don't try to psychology my shit, motherfucker. Cause you
never psychology it, motherfucker. Never. Never.
Never. Motherfucker. Never.
—ODB

After *Return to the 36 Chambers* was released, ODB's manager,
Sophia Chang (now RZA's manager and wife to Sifu, the monk
who heads the Shaolin Temple in Soho), stopped working with
him. It wasn't anything personal, it wasn't for lack of love, but
Dirt was heavily involved in drugs and she couldn't rely on him
to show up, to record, to fulfill contracts. It was a mystery as to
who had first introduced him to the pipe. His already erratic
behavior was only stoked by his steady embrace of what once
was his alter ego. Rusty Jones was becoming Ol' Dirty Bastard in
a literal sense, leaving behind the focus and piety of Ason
Unique. Dante Ross wasn't involved in the second Elektra album
(*Nigga Please*) or in its production. RZA barely touched a track;
he gets credit for two songs but according to Buddha Monk,
RZA lifted a couple of vocal controls and that was about it.

Most of the Wu-Tang splintered off in solo careers, reuniting for sporadic tours or festivals like Lollapalooza or the attempted tour with Rage Against the Machine that was hastily aborted (some say because of internal Wu-Tang spats, which most of the time involved Dirt pissing someone off or pissing on something). Dirt was left to his own devices, which was never a good thing. Cherry described him to me like this: "He was the kind of kid that would start all kinds of trouble, start a fight, throw a punch, whatever, and then run away as fast as he could." This adolescent menace seemed to underlay just about everything in his life.

He just didn't function the same as everyone else—he lived life impulsively and instinctually and without boundaries. In some ways ODB functioned on a higher level, not just in terms of drugs, but in action. He said and did whatever he wanted. *Like he was free.* On the few red carpets I've covered, I've always been amazed by how easy it is for TV shows to get artists and athletes to record an on-the-spot promo endorsing their show even though the celebrity in question has probably never watched it. Any camera crew that asks one question can get Nas or Jay-Z or Snoop to quickly say "What up" to the audience. The same writer who called ODB the n-word also said he refuses to listen to music made after 1993, especially hip-hop, and I can see his point. Hip-hop is such a commercial product these days, on a micro and macro level: you have crunk goblets for sale and Jay-Z choosing the hip-hop brand of bubbly to pour in them, but God forbid you drink bubbly at a hip-hop event since Hennessy sponsors just about all of them. You can't have a concert, promote a record, or make music without partnering on ring tones and PlayStation tie-ins, or dropping rhymes with product names laced throughout. I'm half waiting for GZA to write a protest lyric made up of all the usual hip-hop endorsement suspects, like he did on "Labels." Hip-hop sold out a long time ago, no surprise there. But indie hip-hop, with its high ideals and political semi-rage, should stand in opposition to mass consumerism and corporate culture . . . right? It's depressing that Common recorded an infectious flow for the Gap Christmas jingle, to hawk forty-dollar hoodies to suburban eleven-year-olds who think he's down, and that he signed up to be a spokesperson for the Lincoln Navigator.

ODB, in his prime, wasn't for sale. The only product he ever mentioned was Olde English, and he invested more in the malt liquor than the company did in him. Even announcing the TV station he was actually on was a fight. In 1996, John Norris tried about ten times to get Dirt to say he was doing an interview with MTV but Dirt wouldn't. He rolled his eyes or bugged them out and brushed off whatever attempt was made to pretend to have a conversation. Norris worked hard to act natural throughout the interview while Dirt lounged on the sofa, facing his crotch toward the camera. Finally Norris reached the point of exasperation and simply announced the next guest.

"Do you know Drew Barrymore?" he asked ODB.

"Na. Who?" ODB said.

"Drew Barrymore. She was in *E.T.*"

"Na, all I remember is that nigga that was riding the bike in the sky."

And that was the end. He never announced who he was or why he was there. Dirt just sat there in his royal blue tracksuit because his manager told him to. The producer, a voice in the background of the clip, and Norris struggled between takes with what to do. When they weren't rolling, Dirt was spaced out, off in the distance, and they talked like he wasn't even there. ODB later kicked off his second album with the lyric "All y'all niggas talkin bout commercial songs / This ain't no commercial song / Straight up, nigga, what?" He was aggressively independent, thrusting through that last "what" like an uppercut. MTV may have molded him, RZA may have managed him, but no one owned ODB. He sold himself. He marketed himself. He was his own product. And tragically, that meant his downfall was of his own making as well.

For someone who was so fiercely independent, someone who was perceived as such a loose cannon, it shouldn't come as much of a surprise that the one thing he found reliable, the one thing that was always there for him, was drugs. He would try just about anything but favored crack, and was pulled over at least half a dozen times in three years with vials stashed in the glove compartment or baggies of coke in his pockets or both. He had always been over the top and now, aided by drugs, he was bolder, overly self-assured, defiant, and riddled with otherworldly anxiety. "I'm pretty sure he has done just about every drug," GZA said. "All I ever done was smoke weed and drink alcohol with him. He didn't really smoke weed, though. It wasn't his thing."

At the same time that ODB was reaping the fruits of stardom, there was a shift of power between Dante Ross and Sylvia Rhone, now Universal Records' executive vice president. For some reason, Elektra (a subdivision of Atlantic Records, which is owned by Universal) let four years lapse between *Return to the 36 Chambers* and his sophomore effort, *Nigga Please*. That's a long time between projects—it's an eternity in the music industry.

If a rapper's lucky, his career will last four years. These days, an artist needs a mix CD two weeks before his real release just to whet the appetite of his fans and to remind the public of who he is and to buy his album. (And only sometimes will the FBI raid and arrest the mix CD artist in question, who is likely making the mix CDs for the record companies who are supposedly being protected. But ODB came up when albums actually existed, before digital piracy became integral to the hype machine.) In 2006 Ghostface dropped two mixes and two CDs for Def Jam just so he could ride the tail of *Fishscale*. Lil Wayne appeared on seventy-seven songs the year before his album *Tha Carter III* dropped. Lucky for everyone involved, ODB made a habit of being in the public eye, so it's not like his fans could forget him. There were more than enough moments when ODB was on-stage, in front of a camera, or hogging a mic, and most of those times he was likely intoxicated. He was drunk. He was high. He was crazy. Or all of the above. If he wasn't being pulled over for a suspended license, he was being arrested and charged with criminal possession, meaning he had enough crack on him that police assumed he was dealing. His music was almost superfluous. Dirt stayed relevant because he acted crazy. But more and more, it was less of an act. His fame stopped being about his lyrics—what and how he was saying shit—and started to be about the unpredictable, the absurd, and the dysfunctional.

In 1995, Elektra sent out a compilation of their artists that included a live recording of ODB at Clinton Studios in New York. It was sent to critics and industry people. The recording started out like any other—ODB gets into a verse, a freestyle, wraps his cheeks around some beat boxing, some rhythmic breathing—he was warming up, feeling his way through the stage and audience alike. Then, abruptly the music stops, and ODB monologues: "I got a goddamn announcement to make! Motherfuckas pulled me up outta my bed to come to this motherfucka's tonight! I'm serious! I didn't even wanna come to this motherfucka tonight. I'm in my bed, butt-nekkid! Fuck that shit!—I'm lettin' niggas know! You don't fuck with a nigga when he's butt-nekkid, especially when they didn't get no sleep yesterday from gettin' fucked up all night. Record companies be usin' niggas as fuckin' puppets, man," Dirty goes on. "I ain't no fuckin' puppet, man! Niggas are so used to getting used as a puppet, they be ready to get pupperized. You go to a fuckin' record company, and they want you to rhyme here and have a hook there, then a rhyme here, and a hook—fuck that! Let niggas do what they wanna do. Let a nigga be free! Only people that understand this music is niggas! And the white people gonna like it anyway, 'cause white people like anything a nigga do!"

Then Dirty goes on to flirt with a girl in the audience who's looking nice, he says. He serenades her, yodeling his way through Rick James and Teena Marie and Billy Paul a cappella for the lady and not surprisingly sounding soulful and from the heart. His raw R&B feelings pour out in elongated crooning, the kind of singing that flowed when he was dancing around his mama's living room. He turned his attention from the nice-ass woman in the crowd and plunged straight into "Brooklyn Zoo." Then suddenly, the music stops again and he and his Brooklyn Zu posse hit *that* a cappella. From the beginning and without music, Dirty steamrolls the lyrics that once were at the ready. He forgets the words. Mumbles. Doesn't do anything at all. The recording continues, he keeps fucking up, and in the background someone in the band is giggling and saying, "Damn, we always do this shit." After forgetting a few more lines, Dirty finally remembers the rest of his song but for insurance he asks the crowd to sing the chorus. They simply repeat his hometown borough over and over. "Brooklyn Zoo!" (heavy on the "oo") he exclaims with his people, shouting the same thing onstage and off. And click, his track is over.

It's not so shocking that this recording exists; it's that *this* was the song Elektra handpicked for their year-end review artist compilation, *this* is what represents Dirty and what they're selling. They knew what they had, and they knew how to market him. He was lazy (*don't pull a butt-necked negro out of bed!*), he was a street revolutionary (*the black man is not a puppet, I am my own man*), aware of his audience (*white girls love me; white boys wish they were me!*), he was a Lothario (*baby, that dress would look better on my floor, now let me sing you some Rick James!*), he was the life of the party (*I'm so fucked up, I can't remember the lyrics to my own goddamn gold-selling single!*), and in this, ODB was using his dysfunction to make performance art. His work was more about him and his stage time than his product; he had become the product. He'd show up and just be ODB, same onstage and off, with a near invisible line between the man and his creation.

And despite his protests about being dragged out of bed to perform, don't think for a second that when Dirt wanted to get onstage you could stop him—he got onstage. There are dozens of pictures and clips of someone in Wu-Tang or an affiliate or a manager with his whole arm wrapped around Dirt's waist, holding him back, pulling him out of the hot bright lights as if with the rounded handle of the Apollo hook. He wanted to perform, like mere mortals want to breathe. It just came to him out of need, desire, and impulse. "Gimme the mic so I can take it away," he sang in "Shimmy Shimmy Ya." It was no idle threat. He really would steal the mic. There were stories of how he pulled the plug on MCs in the middle of their sets whether he was booked to perform or not. He knocked over turntables at Prince's Glam Slam club in Miami. (No one could come up with a reason; ODB was sometimes a menace and liability.) In February 1996, Dirt showed up at the Palladium in Los Angeles, and after watching the Fugees open for Cypress Hill, he wangled his way backstage and then onstage to guest on "No Rest for the Wicked." Ross, who went to the show with Dirt, said it was like Dirt would get this look in his eyes, like a kid in a candy shop. "I'd go to shows with him and hold him back where he just needed to be up there. It looked like he was gonna cry if he didn't get onstage. Every show he watched, he looked like he was gonna cry. He was just crazy. I never knew what was going on with him." Now there's crazy (fun at a party crazy) and there's crazy (you need help crazy)—ODB was both and Ross could see which crazy was winning. Everyone around him would recite the mantra *Dirty being Dirty*, while he was slowly losing his grip on reality.

In the summer of 1997, ODB, entourage in tow, arrived at a recording studio in the San Fernando Valley, a half hour from Steve Rifkind's office on Melrose in Los Angeles. The sun was hot and the recording studio, called Enterprise at the time, was occupied by one of the founding Fugees, Pras. ODB was confused by this because he thought he had the studio booked. "He walks in and there was a commotion because he was in the wrong studio, the wrong state. He thought he was in New York. He thought we were in his studio space, and once we got through all of that he was like, 'All right, cool' and was about to leave," Pras said. "I can't explain why he thought he was in New York but I told him 'Actually, we in L.A., dawg,' so I clarified that right there. You have to remember this was the era when he changed his name from Ol' Dirty Bastard to Osirus and was about to change it to Big Baby Jesus. He was definitely in a zone. I think he was sober, though."

As ODB turned to walk out of the studio, no longer thinking he was in New York, Pras started to fiddle with the hook of "Ghetto Superstar." ODB turned around at the exit and said, "This thing is hot."

"And I was like, 'Ye-ah,' " Pras said. There was a hook already recorded but it was only a placeholder. Pras looked up. " 'Yo, you want to get on this?' I was just playing and he was like, 'Yeah, what's it about?' " Pras explained that it was for the soundtrack of *Bulworth*, the Warren Beatty vehicle about a corrupt senator who sees the light after a mental breakdown involving rapping his stump speeches and falling in love with Halle Berry, a South Central B-girl trying to save her brother.

"It was raw," said Pras. "Everybody's trying to conform to that mainstream shit and ODB was like, this is what I *do*. His process was unorthodox. I can't even explain it. He'd do two lines and come out of the booth and then listen to it. Then he'd do the ad-libs and go back and lay the verse around the ad-libs. It was a crazy method, but the verse always fit. And I never seen anybody do it that way before. Usually you add the ad-libs after the verse and you've got vibe for where they'll fit and how they should sound. But he'd be like, 'Hey . . . uh . . . ya . . . ri-ight' and then he'd do the verse and it'd fall right."

Although rappers record guest vocals on other artists' tracks all the time, it seemed like even this basic misunderstanding (apart of course from his complete geographical obliviousness) was glorious evidence that ODB lived and worked by chance. He happened to be there, so why not jump into the booth. "He walked in and boom, he was rapping and that was just crazy. He just came in and laid down his vocals. I don't even know who he was supposed to be working with that day. I only remember telling him this was not where he thought he was," Pras said. The incident was also remarkable because the song unites two of hip-hop's elite groups from the early nineties underground, the Wu-Tang and the Fugees. "Yeah, you got to remember, I had been a fan of Wu-Tang for forever, they came out a couple months before the Fugees but around the same time. We were having the same kind of impact, they were ahead of us by like nine months with 'Protect Ya Neck,' " Pras said. Mya, who sang the hook, wasn't there during the recording and ODB wrote his portion and recorded it in an afternoon. The song was mixed and released in 1998 to coincide with the premiere of the movie, and the following year it was certified platinum and nominated for a Grammy. "I mean, what was going through his mind for him to think that he was at Hit Factory or some New York studio? [But] when he walked in he felt like he was in the right place, and it was all good 'cause he got on the record and made it great. He added that ol' Wu-Tang vibe. I just thought, I love Ol' Dirty Bastard because he's out there. He was entertaining to everyone. He didn't care, he didn't give a fuck, he was like, whatever and something like that generates respect." It might generate respect, but clearly something was wrong. Over a remix of Kenny Rogers and Dolly Parton's "Islands in the Stream," he rapped "I'm paranoid at the things I said / Wonderin' what's the penalty from day to day," words that were meant to speak for Bulworth, but, really, ODB was just as paranoid as the fictional senator who hired a hit man to kill him.

The journalist Soren Baker from *Big Brother*, a skateboarding magazine, did a Q&A around the same time with ODB that's impossible to read without thinking the MC is mentally ill: he comes across as simultaneously paranoid, depressed, fatalistic, and elevated in his thinking. Baker interviewed ODB on May 28, 1997, just before the release of *Wu-Tang Forever*. Baker felt the quotes were unusable for the story he was trying to write on the Wu-Tang, so instead he delivered the raw transcript to the skateboarding magazine a few years later.

What's going on with your career at the moment?
"Well, what's going on with my career is that the CIA is watching me. They got a close eye on me like they had on Biggie and 2Pac. You know, I'll take it from there."

So what's up with the splits in your identity?
"It's just me. God, that's all. I'm God. That's my identity,

one of the low gods. One of the earth gods—one with a lot of wisdom."

Lyrically, what's the difference between Osirus and what you always hit us with?

"On this album, the Wu-Tang album, I'm just dogshit on that. On my album, you'll see a lot of positive, a lot of negative."

What type of positivity are you going to be touching on?

"I'm not trying to be really specific. I'm just rapping my ass off, that's all. I'm not trying to get all personal and shit. People will hear it, and if they like it, they like it; if they don't, they don't. This rap game, it's not me, man. That's all I'm saying. I'm just happy to be here, man. As far as the interviews and going into all the details and stuff, I'm not really good for that. I'm really into the Nation of Islam. I'm here to teach freedom, justice, and equality, man, as well as negative."

How long have you been affiliated with the Nation?

"All my life. I was one that was gonna be killed. I had a royalty order on me to be killed before I was born. I guess they failed. It's been three times already that I've been shot. And some other shit. That's a good thing. Now that I've got my powers, they're trying to figure out another way to kill me. They'll probably try to kill me through a disease, so I'm trying to find a cure to all diseases now."

You're doing that yourself?
"Yes."

That's pretty impressive.

"That's how far my mind stretches. I keep it down low, though. People think that I'm crazy—I am. I'm just equipped with crazy knowledge. Basically, the Wu-Tang album is going to be the bomb. There's nothing really to discuss. It's something just to see with your own eyes. You can talk about it for years and write books. The best book to me, for real, it's just to hear it yourself, because then you get the most positive and negative out of it. Then you can take the waste and throw it in the garbage."

I've read that you signed your mother to Ol' Dirty Bastard Records. What's up with that?

"The whole family. She owns it and she is it. The whole family is talented. We're like another Wu-Tang empire, but I call it Ol' Dirty Bastard empire. We're going to have Dirty Wear by Ol' Dirty Bastard. You'll see. There's going to be a lot of things. I don't really like talking too much because this phone is bugged. Plus, I'm not really a talker. The rest of the members, they talk their asses off. I can't really talk. I'm really all about money, about rap, about women, about babies. I'm about those things. I'm not really good at explaining things about a record or what I'm talking about on the record. I just do what's on nature. I don't like going back in history, because then I'm exploring the Devil. He likes to climb mountains and go all up into our bodies and learn what type of frequencies we got, and what type of frequencies he can make, to cancel out our frequencies. I leave that to them guys. Those are my children. I love 'em, and I hope they love me like I love them. Especially nowadays. It's fucked up when you got a helicopter over your head almost every day. People all on your back. Every time you turn around, somebody's winking at you, or there's a white man in a car or a black-suited guy in the car looking at me. Every day I see the same cars, and different days, there's different cars. It's kind of scary. That's all, man. I don't like it. I'll be staying in the house sometime. I'm tired of this shit. This is what happens to me every day. They came up to me personally and told me who they was—they work for the government—and that they tried to kill me three times already. Biggie and 2Pac, they did them in. I'm just tired of this shit. For real, I want peace. I don't want no war, and that's all they're about, it seems like. That's all they do: plot, scheme, and scam. Not only me, they're going to try to kill my kids. Everybody thinks it's a fucking joke and funny. It ain't happenin' to the rest of them niggas, the Wu-Tang members. It's only happening to me. They think it's a joke. This shit is real. That why I ain't happy to get on the phone just to be talkin'. If I die, the CIA killed me. That's real."

After reading that interview, it's impossible to believe that ODB's responses are an act, *Dirty being Dirty* as his management explained over and over. And this was in 1997, well before his post-jail diagnosis of schizophrenia. His mom excitedly told me in her living room, after he passed away, that her Rusty "was a working paranoid schizophrenic. I could never understand it." That he heard voices, that he thought his stepdad, Frank, was in the CIA and watching him, that he could never sleep, that he was a restless soul. And that even after he was an adult, when the doors were closed, she held him on her lap to soothe his ticks and calm the constant chatter in his head. When she and I spoke, she blamed it on jail; she said she lost her son behind bars. But the *Big Brother* interview was four years before ODB did time. His managers and cohorts would argue that it was the drugs, or that ODB gave Baker what he thought he wanted to hear, but that Q&A isn't a joke. It's not premeditated and it mimics a pattern of speech and paranoia found in bipolar and schizophrenic patients. He's euphoric, grandiose, anxious, and irritable. He's poisoned by the government, suspicious of doctors, and curing all diseases within one response to a question about the Nation of Islam. He's begging for help with something, with his addiction, with his mind, with his alienation, with his fear, with 'copter blades thumping just past his peripheral vision at all times. A psychiatry professor at Harvard, Dr. Alvin Poussaint, told me ODB's case is typical but hard to diagnose. It's difficult to diagnose mania when drugs are involved, and often they are. Were the drugs self-medication for mental illness? Was the illness a by-product of too many drugs? Why, when it was so clear that ODB was unstable, unpredictable, unstoppable, did no one seem to notice or at the very least suppress the giggle that accompanied each headline of blatant insanity? Maybe people did and he didn't listen. In the video for his collaboration with Busta Rhymes, "Woo-Hah!!," the two of them are connected in a full-body straitjacket with three legs made out of oven-mitt material. They undulate, pulling and pushing each other, trapped and connected and bouncing off padded walls. It's as if he were asking for restraints, not just hinting at insanity but scrawling madness on the padded walls around him.

But despite the seemingly obvious, nobody did anything. They were either profiting from the show or enjoying it. Creativity and celebrity and psychosis are sometimes intertwined, and this combination is nothing new. Billie Holiday's life made Ol' Dirty Bastard's look like an episode of *The Cosby Show*. In the abusive group home she grew up in, the mistress of the house locked her in a closet with the corpse of a child who'd been beaten the previous week; she went to jail for refusing a john while she was soliciting in Harlem during the Depression. And once she found her voice and her audience, Holiday also found heroin, and died from a drug overdose in her early forties. But as Charlie Parker explained: "Music is your own experience, your thoughts, your wisdom. If you don't live it, it won't come out of your horn." Holiday herself said, "You just feel it, and when you sing it other people can feel something too."

ODB was the kind of man blues women sing of—sweet, coo-
ing, and intoxicating in the moment of courtship and invisible
when the loving was done. And when Bessie Smith croons, "Just
like a rainbow I am faded away / My daddy leaves me most
every day / But he don't mean me no good, why? / Because I
only wish he would / I've almost gone insane / I'm forever trying to call his name," she very well could be singing of ODB's
proclivity to leave his lovers as quickly as he met them. And even
though he did indeed scatter broken hearts across continents,
he also seemed to be born to circumstances similar to those
of many blues women. Black women singers in the twenties
embodied a sexuality that couched their entire art form in low-
class culture. The blues came of age during the Harlem Renais-
sance, when black intellectuals stoked the efforts of sculptors,
writers, and painters, especially those upstanding efforts that
reflected a more refined sensibility. The movement never
embraced most of the blues women like Bessie Smith, Ma
Rainey, and Billie Holiday because they sang about working-
class women and they sang openly about sexuality and empowerment. ODB has never been treated seriously in part because
he's confusing—it's hard to strip the art from the madness. And
like the blues singers before him, ODB related to the working-
class struggle and was openly sexual. Sure, rappers who get academic nods like Talib Kweli or Mos Def or Tupac can rhyme
revolution and social awareness, but who would you rather sit on
a stoop and sip forties with? ODB every time, and it's because
his frankness reflected an emotional struggle that listeners could
relate to, with some silliness on the side. Holiday and ODB—
they trapped the authenticity of life and hardship and heartache
and love and pain in their voices. He certainly recognized the
similarities. He even covered Holiday's "Good Morning Heartache," not long before he died. It wasn't always good and it

wasn't always easy. Holiday and Dirt were so public, they both let their audiences watch as they broke down.

"He was the favorite among hipsters, you know; people latched on to him because they liked someone to laugh at. Some people think it's poetic to watch a black man self-destruct," Ross said. Isn't that what audiences crave—performers who are so publicly unstable, they live a soap opera? These days Courtney Love isn't known for her music—she's known for her plastic surgery, her iconic dead husband, her hissy fits, her drug addiction and recovery, her breaking and entering, and her poor daughter, Frances Bean. Will Hole even be mentioned in her obituary? Her music and talent have been so overshadowed by her public breakdowns that people love to debate whether she has any talent at all. But one thing that's undeniable is her skill at catching the eye and ear of the tabloids. Maybe that's the kind of talent a sedated society craves. While the masses satiate themselves with affordable designer goods at Target, it makes life more exciting to watch notorious celebrities live and self-destruct. A sick sense of schadenfreude makes noncelebrities root for disaster and dysfunction. Audiences live vicariously through personalities that know no barriers; they feel momentarily as free and as wild without any consequence. Do any of us actually care what happens to Britney Spears or Michael Jackson or Dave Chappelle? No, celebrities aren't our friends or relatives or even the guy at the bodega who knows how you take your coffee. Chappelle should be commended for getting out when he realized fame was laced with arsenic. ODB never had the sense to step away from the limelight because it was the only thing that kept him going.

A mentally ill person sometimes appears to be free, uninhibited, and intentionally uncaring (especially if hypomanic). But really this state is far from any kind of liberation. The so-called freedom becomes impulsive, destructive, and dangerous. "Part of our brain inhibits certain things," Dr. Poussaint said. "When you become mentally ill, that filter opens up and what is or is not obscene may change. You may think it's perfectly OK to express the emotions within you even though what's coming out is beyond social rules and boundaries. The mentally ill don't understand boundaries. It just all comes out in a very mixed up way with new associations and connections." So what if ODB's notoriety, his entire career, was based on his illness—this ability to be freer than free? "There's a human tendency to get vicarious pleasure out of what other people are doing, particularly if they represent repressed things in ourselves," Dr. Poussaint said. There is a human impulse to be depraved, but social boundaries prevent most people from acting on that impulse. There's a small explicit thrill, envy almost, in watching public figures self-destruct, particularly when it involves sex, drugs, and creativity, because it represents what we want, what we wish we could do.

In 1994 Kurt Cobain shot himself in the face after making a career of depression. His songs oozed from the pores of pharmaceutical-soaked skin. High school girls and boys, including me, mourned. Our sadness was contrived in a way, because if we actually listened to the lyrics, we'd have known his death was inevitable, that his death was what we were hoping would happen. We didn't know we were hoping for it to happen at the time but his death made him a martyr—when Jesus died on the cross, masses were looking for a savior. Cobain's death authenticated his character; it made the pain in his songs real, as tangible as the weave of his mohair cardigans. In every way Cobain's death was the opposite of ODB's. He was a messiah in the afterlife, and David LaChapelle even went so far as to directly evoke this in a photo, where Cobain (or at least a look-alike) is cradled by Courtney Love, his head heavy from the weight of thorns and bloody self-mutilation. Cobain made madness enviable. I don't think he went so far as to market his illness, but he didn't shy away from sharing it. He produced a platinum record with a single titled "Lithium," a drug to counteract bipolarity; Nirvana's lead video for *Nevermind* featured a pack of affectless teenagers bouncing limply to indecipherable lyrics. He embodied the disparity of anguish and ecstasy. To say that Cobain and his flannel following embraced depression is to understate the case—he made depression dazzle. He made grunge a runway statement. All of a sudden sad diary entries and cut wrists were adolescent accessories, as common as band patches sloppily sewed to backpacks—teen angst was embraced by the cool kids, the loners, and the popular alike. His smeared eyeliner, sallow cheekbones, and un-sunned skin were factors of his success. His dirty, near dreadded locks served as evidence of his humanity, his weakness, his depression, his self. Suburban offspring were envious of his pain, his feeling, his deep fucking poetry, because it meant that he had depth, or at least publicly perceived depth. Cobain was a rock star—one made whole by being broken.

ODB was likely as depressed, as clinically ill, and as dysfunctional, but was diagnosed too late. Both Cobain and ODB flaunted their disregard for social norms. But with ODB, it wasn't a sickness, it was just his cracked-out personality. "In the studio he was unpredictable, sometimes amazing, sometimes six hours late," Ross said. "I've worked with a lot of characters but Ol' Dirty Bastard was the wildest. It hurt him in the end because he always had to outdo himself, be wilder than he was before. Whatever it was, it was a little too much. Sometime after the first record came out he lost control of what he was doing." His instability was the show that people paid to see. It wasn't quite as acceptable for a black man of the projects in a hip-hop world to cop to a weakness, to be mentally ill, or to seek treatment. It certainly wasn't encouraged to rap about it. There's been only a handful of rappers like Eminem whose lyrics include doubt and self-analysis and insecurity to counter his alter ego's boasting, or like DMX, whose lyrics reflect his depression. He's the only mainstream rapper who's self-identified as mentally ill, and that was only after threatening an interviewer with a baseball bat and then having to admit that yes, he was bipolar.

Dr. Poussaint, who specializes in mental illness and suicide in black communities, linked a reluctance to talk about mental illness to slavery and to the church. A black man is supposed to stand on his own, he said. Having some kind of mental illness is a weakness—a stereotype that white slave owners projected onto their slaves. "Black Americans view the medical and mental health care communities as co-conspirators in a political and social system that was designed to obstruct black progress," Poussaint writes with Amy Alexander in their book *Lay My Burden Down*. Many early white doctors based their concept of black physiology and psychology on a core of racist stereotypes—that black men needed to be in shackles because they were wild, unpredictable, crazed, and unfit for "normal" life. And as an extreme reaction to centuries of oppression, real mental illness in the black community is often overlooked and undiagnosed. As recently as 2006 a special report on mental illness in the black community was published in the *Psychiatric Times* that instructed doctors to "learn not to automatically ask black patients for their 'Medicaid cards,' but should rather ask, 'How does the patient intend to pay for services?' " It's telling that an academic journal has to instruct medical professionals not to assume that black patients are poor. Even more recent studies about mental illness in ethnic populations found that while there is stigma attached to it within the black community, the study groups are small and limited. Another study published by Columbia University in 2006 found "African Americans' negative perception [of mental illness] did not necessarily result in endorsement of harsher treatment of mentally ill persons," which is a conclusion that doesn't deal with the root of why mental illness is stigmatized in the first place. In fact, that issue has only recently and sporadically been addressed in academic and medical communities. In 2001, U.S. Surgeon General David Satcher published two reports dealing with mental illness—both addressed the issue in relationship to black communities. The first report "noted that suicide rates for African-Americans 10 to 19 had more than doubled from 2.1 per 100,000 in 1980 to 4.5 per 100,000 in 1995." The second report concluded that roughly one in five Americans suffered from mental illness and that that statistic was as true for the black population as it was for the general population, but that a tremendous gap exists between the need for mental health services and their availability in minority communities, leaving a greater percentage of black individuals untreated. Attitudes toward mental health are complicated to begin with—symptoms often appear as exaggerated normal behavior, so it's hard to distinguish normal from elevated.

"Schizophrenia can take hold in many different ways," Poussaint explained. "It makes people behave outside the norm, like it may seem OK to shit in the studio or masturbate in public, and sometimes with mental illness among musicians, the music is what's guiding the illness. Sometimes patients believe the music is directing them." Mental illness is perceived as a weakness in almost every profession. Schizophrenic behavior is not functional behavior, and certainly not something accepted by polite society unless, of course, you are a musician. In that case adolescent behavior is encouraged, winked at, and planted in media columns. (Any publicity is good publicity, after all.) Bizarre potty incidents are embraced, and being deemed crazy is a badge of honor. ODB often urinated onstage or in public or somewhere other than a toilet. Pushing the limits is nothing new—there's beheading a bat with your teeth and eating it onstage, pissing on audience members, snorting the ashes of your father with a line of coke, shooting up onstage, performing in strategically placed tube socks, regularly trashing penthouse suites . . . Rock stars acting crazy is like a banker counting money; it's all part of the job. And sure, it's *all* an act. The fanfare of misbehaving onstage and even what's reported in tabloids are not real, for the most part. These are the performers who define their product by drawing outside the lines, but look at Ozzy Osbourne now—he's a declawed pussycat, housebound and needy. The job of the clown, after all, is to disguise tragedy with a real good juggling trick. That's what ODB was doing. He was distracting the world—his family and friends—from his own tragedy. He sat for an interview in 1997 and explained calmly that yes, in fact, the government had placed chips inside each of his gold teeth and one in his foot. And Meth sat next to him, egging him on. But Dirt really believed those chips were there.

According to the U.S. Department of Health and Human Services' Office of the Surgeon General, nearly 60 percent of older African American adults do not utilize services that they need for their mental health. In the same study the Department of Health found that "African American attitudes toward mental illness are another barrier to seeking mental health care. Mental illness retains considerable stigma, and seeking treatment is not always encouraged." One study found that the proportion of African Americans who feared mental health treatment was two and a half times greater than the proportion of whites. Another study of parents of children meeting criteria for ADHD discovered that African American parents were less likely than white parents to describe their child's difficulties using specific medical labels. Yet another study indicated that older African Americans were less knowledgeable about depression than elderly whites. Ultimately, the black community doesn't simply mistrust psychiatry; there's skepticism about the medical community in general. As recently as 1972, 399 illiterate black sharecroppers were still engaged in a forty-year clinical experiment called "Tuskegee Study of Untreated Syphilis in the Negro Male," in which the subjects were denied penicillin even after it was established as a cure for syphilis. It took five years of protests within government agencies to even publicly aknowledge the abuse and a newspaper leak to reveal the medical ethics violations and that human beings were being used as guinea pigs.

When ODB was checked into the emergency room, on more than one occasion he walked out, bullet holes still gaping. He didn't like doctors—he didn't trust them. He didn't like hospitals, but would occasionally make a rare exception, like that day the four-year-old girl was trapped under the car outside his recording studio in Bed-Stuy. He went to the hospital then, incognito. A psychiatrist works toward diagnosis to treat a patient, to understand actions, to prescribe, and to heal—what good does it do now to identify an illness in the deceased? Well, there's curiosity. I wonder what would have happened if just before he released his second album, Dirt had gotten help and accepted it. I wonder what his life would have been like if he had taken medication and that medication had actually helped. Who would he have been? Could he perform? Would he have wanted to? More important, would ODB have twelve misdemeanors, two charges of making terrorist threats, various theft charges, bullet wounds, palimony delinquency, a pair of shoplifted Nikes, and stray crack vials found in his glove compartment? Would he have lost eighteen months of his life to Clinton Correctional Facility? Would he have died so young? But then under the quiet blanket of medication, would he have lived his life his way? "Should we have salvaged him with high doses of something that might have made him into a zombie and prevented him from making music? I can't make that call. He wouldn't be able to either, but he'd probably choose creating the music. He'd probably think, 'Even though I'm suffering, I'm creating.' If he didn't have his music he might have committed suicide when he was twenty," Dr. Poussaint said.

There's a long history of creativity linked to mental illness. Would it matter if what he did was a result of a chemical imbalance and not raw bravery, not bravado bucking the system, not just a personality quirk? Some people who create art would be called mentally ill in the lexicon of psychiatry, but it's still part of what we call life, Dr. Poussaint said. And what is life without variety, surprise, and individuality? And what is life without fate? Perhaps ODB's life, tragic and inspired as it was, happened for a reason.

In 1999 Mike Gelfand published a book, *Dead Pool*, in which ODB was listed as the second likeliest celebrity to die, after Idi Amin Dada, the former Ugandan dictator who died fifteen months before Dirt. "ODB seems like a swell fellow and all, but hey: he's a rapper . . . and it's not like he hasn't already been shot," Gelfand said during an interview promoting his book. Included in the price of the book was the opportunity to enter the official annual *Dead Pool Guide* national contest. The winner of the contest won an all-expenses-paid vacation for two to Mexico for the festive Day of the Dead celebrations. I guess we should be grateful or surprised that ODB lasted as long as he did, a solid five years longer than Gelfand thought. ODB's fearlessness came naturally—he instinctively knew that in this society you can work your way out of the projects but you can't outlive societal projections. He was lucky to live to thirty-five; by twenty-nine, he was already living on borrowed time.

9.

CAN'T STOP, WON'T STOP, 1998

My rhymes come funkier than your grandfather's feet.
—ODB

If you took out two years of ODB's life and just placed the time and all that happened in those years on a shelf, separate from his other days, he'd be considered a model citizen. But Dirt managed to pack so many petty crimes and obscure felonies and run-ins with the law into 1998 and the first half of 1999 that it seemed as if he broke the law out of habit. He had a *Thelma and Louise*-style fervor, as if he was thriving on his arrest record. Sometimes it seemed as if he had a LoJack on his ankle and was being tracked by police, they would show up so often. Other times it seemed as if he was always scrambling away from or toward something. He led an erratic life, crossing a few different states, his days mostly concentrated in Los Angeles, New York, and Virginia. The only consistency of his life was that Dirt had a knack—a divine skill—for getting into trouble. It was all part of the joke, with continuous headlines announcing his latest fracas, but he had to live the joke, and at some point it stopped being funny. When I reviewed his New York State rap sheet with a district attorney, he said that it was pretty standard, and he was surprised ODB got any time at all. Perhaps it was his notoriety or his escalating drug addiction or his race or the fact that he *did* break the law (no matter how petty the offenses), but ODB spent two years of his life fucking up. His crimes were self-destructive; even his assault attempts read like thinly veiled schoolyard babble. But for two years he lived a crime-blotter life, instigating arrest and courting minor disasters by magically merging phenomenal bad luck with astoundingly bad decisions.

In April 1998, two short months after the Grammys, ODB was charged with second-degree harassment of his estranged wife, Icelene Jones, endangering the welfare of children (his own), and failure to pay child support. ODB was granted a conditional release and his wife was granted full custody of their three children, Barson, Taniqua, and Shaquita. Three weeks after that ODB declared to *Vibe* magazine, "There's no more ODB no more. No, there's no more Osirus, that's all lies. From now on, my name is Big Baby Jesus." He later told *MTV News*, "I always been Jesus. I don't know what the big secret's been all these years. Hanging pictures up on the wall and crosses and things of that nature, I mean, it's all good, but the truth's gonna be revealed one day, and one day the truth's been revealed."

The Big Baby Jesus phase is one of the most popular reinventions in American pop culture. Funny, outrageous, provocative, ODB as Big Baby Jesus is perfect. Is it explainable? Probably not. Five Percenters believe that the black man is God, so let's say ODB or a relative, like his mom, believed in Jesus and that Jesus is divine and godly. If you combined both religious systems, ODB would in fact be Jesus. Alternatively, maybe he was just trying to further the "*Wu-Tang is for the children*" rallying cry by becoming a child savior. Maybe it was a joke. Or maybe he was distancing himself from himself, a separation that would prove useful in the coming year.

A month after Big Baby Jesus was born, ODB responded to the third bench warrant issued regarding his back payment of child support. He agreed to give Icelene Jones $35,000, which was less than she asked for but enough (for the time being). The negotiation of and the continuing battle for child support was the one thing that kept his teenage sweetheart close to him, at least in litigious ways. "He fell off and he was lost. He forgot who he was. It got really bad at the end of the nineties. He just started disappearing and becoming this Ol' Dirty Bastard person for real. He had problems way before that but they really got bad around then," Icelene said. She described Dirt as loving and doting and affectionate, but more often than not he wasn't around. And when he did show up to play Dad, it was a problem. By the late nineties Icelene had moved her brood out to the suburbs. "He was just too rough, he'd come out to Long Island and act a fool. He would come out and really embarrass me and the children and I'd always be like, 'Oh my God, you need to go back to Brooklyn,' " Icelene said. "My kids were on the football team, the little league team, the track team, I had them in every sport, and he would show up and call people names. People would ask for an autograph and he would sit there and argue about it. My husband could be really difficult to get along with sometimes."

These were the rare family moments—ODB clearly loved his children, but he just wasn't around. I don't see how he could have been, between touring and jail and rehab. ODB, according to his mom, would give chunks of money to his baby mamas as it came in. He never neglected his families; he just neglected to pay them on time and in a manner that was appropriate to the courts, which according to Dr. Poussaint fits with the prototype of a mental disorder. Someone who suffers from mental illness may be impulsive. The mentally ill have trouble following through on things, even understanding sometimes what responsibility is. The mentally ill don't understand structure and guidelines or things like paying child support on time. Sometimes he'd give more than required, but it was always off the books. So Icelene marched on, prosecuting her husband on an almost yearly basis for child support.

Midway through 1998, the longest year of Russell Jones's life, Dirt was staying at his cousin's house in Brooklyn when there was a knock on the door. It turned out to be two burglars, who pushed their way inside, stole money and jewelry, and then shot Dirt once in the arm and once in the back. He was taken to Interfaith Medical Center, where he was treated and declared stable. Eight hours later, he walked out, paranoid from the attack and fearful of staying in the hospital (he had been shot a few years earlier in a street argument, and he believed the robbery was linked to an assassination attempt on his life). His distrust of doctors guided his feet away from the facility. The wounds were superficial and the hospital spokesperson mentioned in the press briefing that ODB "was quite a character."

A few days later, on July 4, ODB liberated a pair of fifty-dollar Nike sneakers from Sneaker Stadium, an athletic apparel store in a mall in Virginia Beach, Virginia. He was caught by a security guard walking out of the store with the size-11 sneakers laced to his feet. His back and his arm were still healing from the bullet wounds suffered just days earlier. ODB was charged with shoplifting. (Even as a celebrity, it was hard for Dirt to shake his childhood ways. His brother Shorty Shitstain was notorious for lifting forties from the corner store. "He and Shitty would go to the store and they had money, but they'd still steal beer. He'd have two pants under his pants and sneak out six bottles of Olde English," Buddha Monk said.)

Back in Virginia, Judge Robert L. Simpson Jr. issued two bench warrants for ODB's arrest and quadrupled the potential punishment, after he failed to appear in court to defend his shoplifting charges. He was back in New York recording *Nigga Please*. The judge's second warrant was an order for his arrest without bond, a bench warrant with no bail. If caught by the police, Dirty would be held in custody until his next scheduled court appearance. The fifty-dollar shoes, the damn shoes that he walked out with, that he could have paid for with the hundred-dollar bills in his pocket, those shoes were the first domino to drop. Back in LA, he went on a minor infraction spree. Dirt stepped to a bouncer at a Des'ree concert when he was asked to leave for disorderly conduct, according to the police report. Dirt, who was "drunk, disorderly and annoying patrons," threatened to "return to the club and kill" security personnel after they expelled him, according to the Los Angeles County sheriff's department deputy Boris Nikolof. The threat to kill someone with intent is treated as a felony and at the time was classified as a terrorist threat in California. A spokesperson for the House of Blues said that the incident involving Dirt was minor. The police felt differently. Dirt wasn't alone in his convictions. Rappers build credibility through rap sheets and police aren't shy about racial profiling. The same night as Dirt's terrorism threat, and not far from Hollywood, Artis Ivey, aka Coolio, was arrested in Lawndale, California, for driving his Humvee on the wrong side of the street. When the sheriffs pulled Coolio over for the traffic violation, they discovered that he was driving with an expired California license. They searched the car and found a small baggie of marijuana. And during questioning, Coolio told the officers that he had a semi-automatic handgun in the vehicle with a magazine loaded with 9mm ammunition. So, for perspective, ODB wasn't the only rapper misbehaving. If anything, Coolio's semi makes ODB's idle threats and sneaker theft seem downright charming.

Coincidentally, Coolio and ODB had just recorded a track for the soundtrack to *Slam*. On it they covered everything from government conspiracies to *The Warriors* to jail push-ups, but the most striking exchange is a call to power. Coolio says, "We want knowledge, we want wisdom / Y'all want bars, Cristal, bitches." And ODB responds with: "We want offshore bank accounts, property / We wanna show you how to do it, properly." Even with their public lives crumbling, if you read between the lines, they're both trying to get a pure message out there—control your life, control yourself. It was advice they both failed to follow.

Sometime after ODB's reign of terror, he traveled to Berlin and was kicked out of his hotel for lounging on his balcony . . . naked. German police don't take kindly to public nudity, and though no charges were brought, several of his hotel neighbors did complain about his indecent exposure and their consequent view. He returned to Los Angeles and once again was apprehended by the LAPD, this time in Carson, where he was attempting to scale a fence outside the workplace of his former girlfriend Krishana Ruckers (mother of Ashana). He was booked November 6 on his second charge of terrorist threats in three months for harassing his ex-girlfriend, who was likely pressing charges for money to support their child. On Christmas Eve 1998, Dirt was asked if he had any plans to fly to Virginia to face the shoplifting charges (really, at this point, the least of his worries), and ODB said, "Not today. I love it in L.A. The girls' ass look tight. Not a lot of cellulite . . . And I've got shows to do. I'm just chillin'."

It was a banner year by any standard and one that almost singlehandedly kept the cops, the courts, and the reporters in business. His arrests were nothing compared to the safe full of semis in T.I.'s closet or Snoop's murder charges, but Dirt's minor infractions and strange choices managed to sprawl across two countries and three states. All this—larceny, harassment, flesh wounds, rushing the stage at the Grammys, saving a girl from a combustible engine fire, traffic violations, drug busts—and he continued to record his second album with bursts of inspiration. And to top all that (and possibly explain it), ODB was nursing a crack addiction to full-fledged fruition. You'd think the only place to go from a year of "terrorist threats" and fence scaling would be up; you'd think it could only get easier, and that maybe ODB would have found reason, direction, boundaries, limits. And you'd be wrong.

On January 14, 1999, the eve of Martin Luther King Jr.'s birthday, ODB and his cousin Frederick Cuffie (60 Second Assassin from the Sunz of Man) were driving his 1999 Chevy Tahoe on Dean Street in the Brownsville section of Brooklyn when an unmarked police car set its siren wailing. ODB, wearing a bulletproof vest out of justifiable paranoia, his body still riddled with scars from the three bullet wounds of the past five years, waited impatiently for the officer to approach the car. According to an article by Peter Noel that ran in *The Village Voice*, the officers approached, one pointing a gun directly at 60's head, the other demanding that ODB get out of the car. Dirt rolled down his window saying, "Yo, man, it's me, man. It's me! It's Ol' Dirty!" The cops, not impressed or even aware of what Dirty meant, pressed for Cuffie and Jones to get out of the vehicle. Feeling that they were in danger, they refused. The same reporter worked on a crime-beat series that dealt with officers looking to meet quotas, noting that more times than not the officers were targeting black men. On top of the deck already stacked against them—being black in a new car in a neighborhood known for its corners—ODB had been on a tear all day about his impending death, claiming that the CIA was trying to kill him. So he saw plainclothes cops, their guns raised and extended, pointed at his cousin's temple, and he floored it. The undercover officers shot a round toward the vehicle, unleashing eight bullets toward two innocent men who had done nothing to warrant being pulled over in the first place. But now, with a cop chase ensuing and bullets flying, Dirt guided the Tahoe onto the sidewalks, into opposing traffic, spinning on hairpin turns. The cousins stopped only when Dirt thought he had a safe haven to run to, which turned out to be 1341 East New York Avenue, a boarding home for women owned by the rappers' aunt, Cheryl Dixon. With the cops pointing their guns toward Dixon, Cuffie and Jones eventually surrendered and were taken to the Seventy-seventh Precinct. The cops interrogated the two men separately, trying to get one of them to roll, to reveal what the cops thought to be true: that the cousins had guns that they intended to shoot toward the unmarked cop car (for no compelling reason, except to shoot guns). Neither would admit to what was not true and the charges were dropped. It helped that no gun was found at the scene and no shells from a second gun were collected: just the eight casings from the cops' weapons.

In a criminal court complaint against Russell Jones, one of the two cops was identified as the Street Crimes Unit police officer Christopher Roche. Two months later, the Street Crimes Unit came under heavy public scrutiny after four of its officers shot forty-one bullets at and into Amadou Diallo, an unarmed West African man. Reporters bundled the two incidents together to indict a Giuliani-era police culture that was seemingly one-sided and racially motivated. The Street Crimes Unit was made up primarily of white men who worked in overwhelmingly black neighborhoods. The number of bullets fired by Street Crimes Unit cops in their only two shootings in 1999 almost matched the number of rounds the unit discharged in all of 1998, according to police records. And 1998 was significantly worse than 1997, when the plainclothes cops fired just twenty-two bullets in fifteen gun battles *all year*. Investigators found no ballistic evidence that matched the officers' claims that ODB was armed, and a grand jury declined to indict him. Despite the court victory, it was clear that racial profiling and police aggression were alive and well, only seven years after Rodney King's public beating by the LAPD horrified the country. If any good came out of the incidents, it was that ODB and Diallo, by no choice of their own, obviously, flushed out an aggressively racist squad that was trained to meet monthly quotas in gun recovery and arrests. The all-volunteer unit was known for its motto "We own the night," and for its custom T-shirts quoting Ernest Hemingway on the back: "Certainly there is no hunting like the hunting of man, and those who have hunted armed men long enough and liked it, never really care for anything else thereafter." Though it's already clear that ODB's paranoia stemmed from a combination of having been shot three times, his crack addiction, and his mental instability, there is a compelling argument to be made that these guys *were* after him. Not him in particular but him as a black man.

Days after, he and his cousin were returned to their homes. Dirt held a press conference to explain what had happened. Newspapers were still reporting that ODB and Cuffie shot at the officers—with no gun to speak of, no evidence of any shooting on their part. That week *Rolling Stone* ran a headline that declared ODB GIVES COPPERS TASTE OF HIS HOT LEAD!!! [*sic*]. As if the sexual pun, or the three exclamation points for that matter, was appropriate or necessary. The magazine managed to get the story entirely wrong. During his press conference, Dirt, flanked by his lawyer and his mom, said he was going to press charges, to get whatever money was coming to him. "No doubt, of course I'm filing a lawsuit, what you think, the money's here. Cops took shots at me, now I'm taking shots at y'all. As much money as I can get, I'm a gonna get it." By the end of the year and after the international outrage over the Diallo shooting, including Springsteen's protest song "American Skin (41 Shots)," the Street Crimes Unit was ordered to wear uniforms and the 396 officers were disbanded and reassigned to other detective squads. Somehow, without intention, ODB had a part in this reformation. As he said in his press conference, "I thought the police were good guys, back in the days, until the motherfuckers started shooting guns and shit and I ain't really into guns, nah mean? I got a hole in my shirt this big and I don't play that shit. Of course I'll sue, if I don't sue I'm gonna look like an ass."

ODB had his own kind of decorum, repeatedly apologizing to reporters for swearing. "I'm the ghetto guy. I stay around the children, that way I can teach them whatever whatever . . . keep them calm. Fuck this, Wu-Tang don't be fuckin' with nobody so don't be fuckin' with us, that goes for FBI, CIA, that goes for all y'all motherfuckers, so stay the fuck off of my motherfuckin' back. I don't even own no gun, I don't own no gun period. I know a lot of officers in New York City, they pull me over, see that it's Ol' Dirty Bastard and say keep goin', get the fuck out of here. I been in the community, in Brooklyn, a long time and motherfuckers know I wouldn't do no shit like that. I whoop a nigga ass, 'cause I got to if I got to." A reporter then said "Um, you've got to make this easier on us to put this on TV." He said, "I talk the way I talk, I don't care if it's on TV. But you a cutie-pie, all right, I'll try to stop cursing, all right mama, I'm not gonna curse. I'm upset and shit. I'm tired of my girls messing with me. I don't want to talk about it. It's like this man, my name the Ol' Dirty Bastard, I'm a rapper-entertainer, I'm loved by a lot but a lot of people don't like me. That's tough, that's part of life. I ain't here to get on nobody's bad side, I'm here to make music, I take my time makin' music, don't rush me. I do what I want to do. I'm a good person at heart for real. I love women and automatically that makes me a good man. MTV, I just want to let you all know this is probably the last press you'll get from me for a while, 'cause you know, fuck that, you got to start paying me and shit if you want me to be in magazines. I'm too good-looking to be in magazines for free anymore. I'm crazy but I'm not too crazy. When I walk the streets I walk the streets as Dirt Dawg."

Despite his statements, ODB never pursued a lawsuit and never stopped talking to MTV. It wasn't exactly the kind of press conference that smoothed over his public image. And unfortunately, not much changes on the street if you're black and male, even if you go by Dirt Dawg. At the end of 2006, undercover NYPD officers, who were later acquitted, shot fifty bullets at an unarmed man named Sean Bell in Queens. How many times can Al Sharpton and Jesse Jackson hold press conferences in outrage, demanding change that hasn't historically happened and doesn't seem likely to happen anytime soon? Black communities were outraged, and the Brooklyn rapper Papoose responded the next day with a verse laid over Sam Cooke's "A Change Is Gonna Come." He half-rapped and half-spoke, like he recorded it in a hurry, and he got to the point real quick:

> *Mike Oliver said his gun jammed, he the main one*
> *Twelve-year veteran and don't know how to use a gun,*
> *think we dumb?*

Or you know, without being righteous or to the point, as ODB said in his press conference, "Hell yeah, I was wearing a vest. I'm scared like a motherfucker. Dirty don't pull no guns on cops, not saying I'm a soft-ass nigger but I don't want no grandmothers and shit thinking this crazy shit about me." Why are you scared? "For one thing he's been shot twice," his lawyer responded. "Na, na, let me answer that question my damn self. First of all I'm scared because the word *scared* exists. I'm scared like a motherfucker and you got rappers and shit and it's in my blood," ODB said.

A little more than a month after dodging those eight unwarranted bullets, ODB was the first person ever arrested in California for wearing a bulletproof vest inside his car. The police officers who found ODB double-parked on Yucca Street, one block north of Hollywood Boulevard, were enforcing a month-old law that forbids convicted felons from wearing protective vests. (In 1993 ODB pled guilty to aggravated assault in Brooklyn when he was charged after a bar fight for brandishing weapons.) He was charged with possessing body armor and released after posting $115,000 in bail. The idea behind the law was that felons shouldn't be able to wear protective gear comparable to that of the police, because they would feel emboldened in shootouts or would be more likely to act recklessly. But in the case of ODB, who at this point was more likely to be shot at than (and had probably already been shot at just as many times as) his arresting officers, the charges seemed absurd. The law itself appears misguided, especially when you consider that a study from 1998–2001 showed that across a two-and-a-half-year period, at least 9,976 convicted felons were able to obtain guns, which seems a far more immediate threat to keeping the peace than wearing body armor.

As if it's not painfully clear, ODB could not operate in this system and this system did not know what to do with ODB. To be fair, he didn't follow the law, he never seemed to have his driver's license (suspended or not), he almost always had drugs stashed in the glove compartment, and was ghetto enough to get caught, but not enough to know how to use the law. On "99 Problems," Jay-Z rapped, "I haven't passed the bar, but I know a little bit, enough that you can't illegally search my shit. So the glove compartment's locked, so's the trunk in the back. I know my rights so you'll need a warrant for that." ODB's response when pulled over in Queens with twenty vials of crack in the glove compartment and a baggie of marijuana was, "Officer, can you please make the rocks disappear? The kids, they look up to me." He assumed that by announcing that he was ODB, he could just be ODB. And of course, he was concerned about the children.

He may have been a ghetto superstar, but most of the people on the other side of the fence, the ones who decided his fate, the ones who wore robes and badges and fine wool suits, had no idea who he was. On March 10, during ODB's bail hearing, Deputy District Attorney Mary Ganahl requested that Judge Kevin Brown take into consideration Jones's status as head of a "street gang" named Wu-Tang Clan. *Seriously?*

10.

ROBERT SHAPIRO, ESQ., REPRESENTS, 1999

I'm still going through it, the pain and the hurt / Soaking
up trouble like rain in the dirt.
—DMX

At some point (perhaps when it was clear that prosecuting attorneys were unable to distinguish between gang members and rappers), ODB figured he could use a lawyer. With his rap sheet accumulating hits daily, he needed good legal counsel. So his manager, who for good reason kept a low profile, called Robert Shapiro. I remember Robert Shapiro, as does anyone who watched TV in the early nineties, from the O.J. Simpson trial. He was the one lawyer on the defense team whose head hung low (way low) when his client was found not guilty. There was something in his consequent silence that spoke volumes.

His corner office, in the MGM building on Constellation Boulevard in West L.A., was blocks from the apartment I grew up in. The building with the lion in mid-roar towered over a mall I once scooped ice cream at and shoplifted training bras from, and was the site of a back room at a boutique where I wrapped presents for twelve hours a day, fringing raffia paper to look like it had been unearthed from a burial site just outside Santa Fe. This particular back room at Jumping Dog (the store's quasi–Native American name) was where I got paper cuts and blisters on my fingertips, arranged dried flowers, and smoked pot with the part-time sales girl Wendy, who was having an affair with her other boss in a tall building behind the mall. This place, Century City, was where I grew up. It's since turned into a luxury mall with Louis Vuitton and Gucci boutiques, but during high school I spent more days there than I did in class, listening to my Walkman, killing time until I could arrive home as if I had actually gone to school. I was nervous as I approached Shapiro's building. I wasn't sure why Shapiro had agreed to talk with me. He was known as a shark and I could imagine him guarding former clients' secrets vehemently, plus legally I knew he couldn't say much. His office on the nineteenth floor was bigger than my apartment and it overlooked the mountains that separate the Valley from L.A. proper. A hazy cluster of buildings downtown was nestled at the eastern horizon, grayish brown from the smog. A crystal ball sat in a pewter stand on the coffee table. "Ah, that. A Gypsy client gave that to me," Shapiro said as he pointed to the chair opposite his desk, the place where I was supposed to sit. "What can I help you with?"

The last I time I had tried to contact Shapiro was as a high school intern for *Hard Copy*. I was supposed to spend the summer taking notes on *Inside Edition* (their direct competitor), logging hour after hour of Tonya Harding and her fake tears and her bad-luck white-trash knee-bashing ways—that is, until O.J. broke and then all of a sudden my internship turned into an all O.J., all the time affair. I went to Kato Kaelin's press conference. I worked with crews to tape the blood still staining sidewalks in

Brentwood. I knew every detail of every press conference and shelved my Tonya logs, happily. I was moving around doing something that felt so dirty: O.J. may have been a murderer, but *Hard Copy* was bloodthirsty, feeding off the gory runoff of the deaths of Ron and Nicole (because we all knew them by their first names then).

I was struck, now, by how quickly Robert Shapiro responded to my e-mail request for an interview: immediately. So, here we were, face to face, and I told him I was trying to find out who ODB really was and that he, as his lawyer, was probably around him during the beginning of the end. "I've represented a lot of people in the music business, but he just had an unusual aspect to his persona, about the way he dressed, his manner of speech. He would talk in jive talk except when I asked him to get really serious," Shapiro said. Even when ODB was supposed to be serious, he came off as a clown. His manner was his own but certainly not appropriate or understood in court. "He'd come into court with two different shoes, labels with price tags attached, but still looking neat and clean. The judge actually liked him. I mean, some days he showed up to court so loaded, with his hand up to his ear and talking to himself, just having a full conversation by himself. It's possible his behavior was a result of mental illness. One time he had his hat on backward, had on two different shoes, and he stood with his back to the judge with his hat facing the judge as if he was looking at the judge. And the judge, I think it was Judge Martha Revel, *still* liked him. She got a kick out of him because he was a harmless guy." Shapiro went on to talk about ODB's intelligence, about how RZA would call every day trying to figure out what to do, how to help. "I'm not an expert but he definitely had some mental health issues that would be apparent to the layperson. Whether they were the result of drug abuse or genetic disposition, I don't know. I generally think it was a combination of both. My whole interest with Russell, that's what I called him because I didn't want to call him old or dirty or bastard, was that I wanted to get him help. He was always affable, always nice, really just a very charming guy. I drove him home once because he had no transportation, and in his words he was totally broke and while we were driving home he saw a homeless man and asked me to stop, and he got out and gave the homeless guy everything in his wallet." ODB is the kind of person that people relate to mostly because he embodies so many problems that inevitably, they see their own. "But he was this compassionate guy who had a great heart, a great soul, and his brain suffered greatly from drug abuse," Shapiro said.

"When asked by the judge how many chances a person affected by drug addiction should get, my feeling is as many as it takes. If it's coupled with violence? That's something else. If it's coupled with dealing? That's something else. Or coupled with serious criminal behavior. That's something else entirely. But addicts suffering from a drug disease are not going to benefit from any type of incarceration. *Incarcerated addicts do not benefit anybody*—the individual or society. If anything it creates more problems."

At the time I was surprised by how openly Shapiro wanted to talk about addiction. It was obvious that ODB's arrests stemmed from drug problems, but there was something else in the way Shapiro talked about it. At the time that he represented ODB, Shapiro's oldest son, Brent, had already been in and out of rehab a handful of times. "ODB is one of those sad stories of someone who worked his way up from nothing, became a force in the music industry, and separated himself from the crowd by design. But you know, he suffered from a horrible illness and as a result he lost his life and I don't even know how he died."

I told him that the autopsy report classified his death as an accidental overdose. Shapiro sat silenced and a wave of sadness seemed to pass over him. He snapped out of it and held up a script that was highlighted and adjusted his reading glasses so that they were propped just at the tip of his nose. He told me he was shooting a scene with Jimmy Woods for the pilot of his new TV show, *Shark*. We ran a couple of lines that have him playing poker in the opening shot. "Yeah, it's my big break. Ah, shoot, I fold right in the beginning, I'm gonna have to rewrite this." And then we talked about boxing, because it turned out we worked with the same trainer, Freddie Roach. I also couldn't leave without asking him about O.J. I asked if they kept in touch and his face tightened, his brow lined with anger. "I do not. I never talk to him. That whole thing just got me better seats and better reservations." He asked me about my writing; he's authored half a dozen books and as I was leaving, he ran to the shelf to inscribe one for me. "Keep your guard up," he wrote. I thanked him, and as I turned to leave he grabbed my wrist and slipped on one of those elastic Lance Armstrong–style bracelets. It was black, and on one side it read "What's Your Story?" and on the other side it read www.brentshapiro.org.

I went to the website later and saw why Shapiro was so invested in helping ODB with his addiction. His son had died in the fall of 2005 from an accidental overdose.

After ODB employed Shapiro, he still couldn't quite keep his life controlled. The next three months were a blur of quickie jail stints, traffic violations, drug possession charges, and failure to pay child support (again). Overall, in the summer of 1999, he was pulled over at least four times in the five boroughs of New York and six times in two other states, each time producing small bags of marijuana or crack or both. (Once he was carrying twenty glassine bags of crack, which is more than enough to charge him with intent to sell.) Usually he was found speeding through red lights in a convertible red Mercedes with no plates.

Keeping his bicoastal court schedule straight was a seriously arduous task. On one particularly bad day in L.A., Ol' Dirty Bastard went to Santa Monica Superior Court on May 18 to address the charges of illegally wearing a bulletproof vest when he should have gone to Los Angeles Superior Court downtown. Judge Richard Berry postponed the hearing for a month, but Dirt was still scheduled to appear in Santa Monica two days later on May 20 to defend the House of Blues terrorist threat charges. By August 12, 1999, he had failed to appear at the postponed Los Angeles Superior Court date, and the judge issued a warrant for his arrest. He had enough names and personas to cover his almost weekly appearances, but they were all trapped in one body. That same week, he was scheduled to appear in a Queens court and a Brooklyn court to defend separate charges of drug possession, and he had checked into a rehab facility in Carmel, New York. He didn't stay, but he was there long enough to miss several more court dates.

II.

WHAT WOULD BIG BABY JESUS DO?, 1999

If God hadn't meant me to get high, he wouldn't have made gettin' high so much like perfect.
—The Wire

And somehow, between court appointments and traffic violations (and probably inspired by the events around him; how else would you explain the lyric "My words can't be held against me, I'm not caught up in your law"?), ODB managed to record one of the best hip-hop albums to date. On September 12 Elektra released his sophomore solo album, *Nigga Please*, which entered the charts as the tenth highest-selling album and spent the next six months on the Billboard Top Ten—all without any promotion from its artist, who was sequestered in rehab. ODB's vocals are arrhythmic, his rhymes are transcendental in their Joycean abstraction, and the album itself was aggressively profane and so vulgar that it could only be funny. Like ODB's unintentionally obscenity-laced press conference, the album's curse words are so excessive that their meaning is numbed with familiarity. *Nigga*

Please was also the album that officially birthed Big Baby Jesus. It wasn't so much a different persona but one more layer of *What the fuck?*

It peaked in November as the second highest-selling album, aided by the infectious single "Got Your Money," a track that introduced Pharrell Williams's falsetto, the Neptunes' production, and Kelis's rainbow Afro to the world. ODB begins the song with an objective: "You give me your number, I call you up / You act like your pussy don't interrupt / I don't have no problem with you fucking me / But I have a little problem wit you not fucking me." He paints the Ol' Dirty scenario, that the exchange of digits is a contract for sex. It's playful, and it's flattering that he's willing to engage in a verbal three-card monte (wait, is he OK with having sex, not having sex, or not not having sex?) and before you know it, the sex has probably already been had. After that he boasts of his incomparable prowess in bed: "You couldn't get another nigga, hoochie won't get moist." Then ODB nullifies his sexual intensity by claiming that he's a self-proclaimed, self-fulfilled fool. "Recognize I'm a fool and you looove me," he rapped while Pharrell hissed *sexysexysexy* on loop. But if ODB's a fool, then he's a fool for hire, one who knows how to sell foolishness to DJs, to the masses, to the labels. "Just dance! if you caught up in the holy ghost trance / If you stop! Ima put the killer ants in your pants." Here he assumes his Big Baby Jesus persona and uses his deity for good—in this case, for dancing. He was attached to a seventies aesthetic, entrenched in a Richard Pryor comedy moment, and always working the sound of reality into his lyrical flow. He layered beats and choruses and da-da-da and then stripped a song bare with one last, lazy verse: "You can call me dirty and then lift up your skirt, and you want some of this di-irty, God made Dirt and Dirt bust yo' ass. Stop annoying me, yeah, I play my music loud but it takes the Bastard Ol' Dirty to move the crowd." The lyrics are playful and sexual and full of braggadocio, nothing new to the art form, but it's the *way* he says them, the way he punctuates his words and trips over syllables and works each letter like an oral sex champ. Each song is infused with urgency and hilarity and *him*. That's why hip-hop misses ODB so goddamn much: he put all of himself into his work. So much so that there wasn't much left over.

In fact, there wasn't much ODB left to film the video; he was still in rehab and the label cut a bizarre yet totally appropriate video for "Got Your Money" by stringing together a montage of Rudy Ray Moore's *Dolemite* and leftover footage from ODB's video for "Shimmy Shimmy Ya." In the video, blaxploitation finds its natural successor: ODB. His head is sloppily Photoshopped onto the body of a shaky homeless person ordering a hot dog and the words *Ol' Dirty Bastard* are scrawled on the back of his white T. The Photoshopped head kind of shimmies and gurgles and he walks with an incredible bounce, like there are actually ants in his pants. (Bubbles from *The Wire* comes to mind.) He's a quintessential descendant of a Dolemite character—the misunderstood menace with swagger and style to spare. One of the best lines in *Dolemite* occurs when he's let out of jail and the Dolemite girls bring him a polyester suit because "You know, I don't wear no goddamn cotton." (A fashion statement? A statement on slavery?) In the video Queen Bee announces, "We are here to honor this man this evening who has done more for the blacks than anyone." She's introducing Dolemite, but clearly the video is also referencing ODB. The directors insert his face in each scene, in pictures, on T-shirts. It's a rude rendering, but a fitting tribute considering Dolemite is a predecessor to ODB's style. They are hyperbolic men celebrating the grossest stereotypes of black maleness.

ODB's urgency, his need, was clear. All you have to do is listen to the second track of *Nigga Please*, when he repeats and repeats at least thirty times to infinity "Big Baby Jesus, I can't wait, nigga, fuck that, I can't wait, Big Baby Jesus, I can't wait. . . ." *He can't wait for the cops, he can't wait for red lights to turn, he can't wait for a spotlight, he can't wait for anything, he can't wait for the rock, he can't wait his turn.* It's a drug-fueled mantra, interrupted only to force a laugh and to shout his way through some lyrics, and then he's back, warped inside that frantic insistence, until his voice is small and shrill and breathless. He really can't wait. He really is Big Baby Jesus. It's as if the repetition and trance have made it so. Then he calms down to give a shout-out to the Eskimos and the Marines and "all the woman [*sic*]" and school-teachers and basically anyone whose name he can remember.

It is in this circuitous rabbit hole that Big Baby Jesus came to be. Fuck his press announcements on Vibe TV and to MTV in 1998 when he announced that "there's no more ODB . . . no more Osiris . . . My name is Big Baby Jesus . . . don't kill me, because I know that y'all love me." He expected to be bigger than Jesus and brand-spanking-new and so good that he was beyond crucifixion. This album was the anthem for his new persona. He had an announcement and *it couldn't wait.* His cycling, tribal repetition is like Lamaze breathing, coaxing and welcoming this new persona to earth. The more he said his new name, the more real he became, the closer he got to rebirth. Maybe he was born again as Big Baby Jesus. Maybe with this album, he was finally going to put the legal woes and life hassles behind. If he heard that, you know he'd say . . . Nigga please. ODB's album title was as incendiary as his *Dolemite* video. The word is still controversial—Nas changed the title of his 2008 release from *Nigger* to *Untitled* after his label pressured him. ODB was making fun of himself, desensitizing the most controversial word in racial politics, and referencing Richard Pryor's album *That Nigger's Crazy* in three short syllables.

One sign of mental instability is a sense of deep religious fervor. Renaming yourself after a messiah would certainly qualify. Renaming yourself after a messiah and adding the words *big* and *baby* to the title—well, that's something else. Big Baby Jesus is a joke, but in some ways, ODB thought he was the second coming, and to some, he was. He walked the earth seemingly free from burden (police and judges and lawyers didn't necessarily agree, but ODB lived life in spite of and outside of them). In some ways ODB's career was a miracle—Jesus may have turned water into wine, but ODB turned a broke voice into gold records. That's much harder than stigmata. (Sure, spontaneous bleeding is difficult, but breaking into the record industry?) Interestingly, many religious leaders, prophets, and saints seem to exhibit behavior that today would be more likely categorized as some degree of mental illness. St. Francis of Assisi, for example, devoted himself to the poverty-stricken, living among them in beggar's clothes, often completely naked or covered only with a threadbare cloth, despite an upbringing of privilege. In his later years, when Francis lived on a branch in solitary confinement in the forest, he prayed each morning, and one morning awoke to see a seraph holding Jesus between its two wings. The fact that Francis was blind and had a vision of anything is one miracle, but after his visit with the angel, Francis's hands, feet, and sides bore five wounds, the marks of the stigmata. What if that vision was just a hallucination brought on by the extremes of living in the wilderness? How does anyone verify if a blind person sees a vision? If Francis staggered out of the woods today with stigmata, he'd be put in the nearest psych ward and likely given little Dixie cups of colorful antipsychotics.

Religious moments can come from manic people, just as

mania induces religiosity. In ODB's case it was a combination of both—he was freebasing and potentially manic depressive as a result of either the drugs or genetics. His mom told me there was no history of mental illness in her family and none that she knew of in her ex-husband's family. Regardless, the combination of addiction and illness was potent and public enough to warrant a very real messiah complex. In a manner of speaking, ODB *was* Big Baby Jesus. He believed it. I believe it. He was selfless in sacrificing his identity for the laugh and the evolution of his persona. He started out Ason Unique, a devout student of Allah; he morphed into Ol' Dirty Bastard, the black version of white trash; and now he unveiled another layer, the infant savior, the God of Gods and Earths. Listening to *Nigga Please*, I wonder how it took two months to get this man to rehab. On the title track he said, "I'm immune to all viruses / I get the cocaine it cleans out my sinuses."

But finally, on November 10, after Judge Revel sentenced ODB to three years' probation, a five-hundred-dollar fine, and twelve months in rehab, he actually entered treatment for an extended amount of time. Hallelujah. As ODB left the courtroom, he said to the judge, "Jesus loves you." Revel, smiling, responded by saying, "Thank you, I need all the love I can get." Whether or not ODB actually meant Jesus or himself as Big Baby Jesus is unclear, but for all the grief surrounding his body armor, getting no jail time seemed like a blessing. He checked into Impact House in Pasadena on Fair Oaks Avenue.

From their website description, Impact House sounds idyllic, like a drug facility that Lindsay Lohan would choose after declaring herself "exhausted." The facility sprawls over 3.5 acres of land, with a small creek and quasi-Asian bamboo bridges augmenting the landscape. When celebrities check themselves into rehab, what does that really mean? That they're trying to rehabilitate their image? That they need a few weeks secluded from the paparazzi to make lanyards and macaroni necklaces in occupational therapy? Does it mean they just need an out for a while? There are those who go to rehab because there is no other choice. ODB needed rehab desperately, so when he stepped into the facility voluntarily, it was in the hope that he'd get clean. The website shows three things—the bridge (over, I'm assuming, less-troubled waters), a beautiful wood-paneled library, and a room with a single bed simply appointed with clean white sheets. When I visited Impact House it felt a lot less cushy. The beige paint was chipping on the exterior, the windows were streaked, the interior of the main building was cream and gray like a hospital's, and the chairs were of the folding variety. The structure was nondescript and on a street wide enough that it might be considered a highway in small states.

One of the admissions specialists and counselors (she requested anonymity) agreed to meet with me and gave me a tour of the facilities. She disclosed that she was an addict and that she had been through the Impact House program more than once. She was very matter-of-fact in discussing her life, her addiction. She wore a loose T-shirt and comfortable jeans and had crimped Harley hair and eighties bangs. She said the first thing that happens after being admitted is that the patient is cut off from all outside influences. The next step is to ingrain the first three steps of a twelve-step Narcotics Anonymous program. *1. We admitted we were powerless over our addiction—that our lives had become unmanageable. 2. Came to believe that a Power greater than ourselves could restore us to sanity. 3. Made a decision to turn our will and our lives over to the care of God as we understood God.* "Over and over, we push those first three steps, just over and over."

Dirt would have been checked into one of the rooms from the brochure, but in reality, the room had four cots, not one. He had to share a room with others, and like everyone else, he woke up at seven a.m., made his bed, got dressed, ate breakfast. "Addiction is a lifestyle. It's such an automatic high to have that celebrity status and if your career goes down at any point, you need a different kind of high," the counselor said. So while ODB was holed up in Pasadena, embracing the shakes and sweats of detox, and while he was learning how to cook rice and beans for his fellow twelve-steppers, his album was still in the Billboard top ten and "Got Your Money" was a top-selling single. From Impact House, Dirt gave a one-off interview with yahoo.com to promote the album (the only interview he did to push *Nigga Please*) and said, "Look, Luther Vandross is good, Michael Jackson is good, Marvin Gaye is good. They all good. But Rick James, he is something out of the ordinary . . . the man is funky, I'm trying to tell you. This is the groove line that we grew up on. I feel that it's only a special dedication to say thanks to Rick James, and that's just how it is." His album, even its cover, was a nod to James. In fact, ODB's stint in rehab could be considered an emulation of Rick James, mirroring James's own struggle with addiction. "It's harder for celebrities and musicians; there's so much shit happening and people around you that say you're OK. It's a lot harder to hit bottom," the counselor said, noting that although ODB showed up before an official court mandate, he probably didn't come to treatment willingly. "Most people who are court-ordered end up in jail first, using, and then they have to come here." Most of the seventy people on staff at Impact have been through the program, so with each new arrival they're able to recognize the different stages of addiction. Before we moved from her office to the courtyard, the counselor shared her story with me. "I used to use whatever was around, acid, weed, cocaine. I was using coke for a while until I met Mr. Methamphetamine. And then it was over.

I was five years clean and I thought I'll just do a little, a little bit, and I'll be all right. Now I'm two years clean and it's hard to grow up at forty-six. It was just fun to get loaded." She got up and I followed her to the outdoor portion of the facility, where residents were standing, watching me curiously. There's a garage where residents are allowed to work on their cars, and above it she points to the bungalow where Dirt likely stayed. "He was probably moved upstairs. It's a nice place, a safe place. All clients have to go through the kitchen and work, over there." The yard is separated by gender. One of the strictest rules is that the female residents can't talk to the male residents and vice versa. "I've heard of patio weddings though, when people pass notes back and forth, and sometimes on the field trips to the beach and to the park they'll talk. But they're not supposed to." I couldn't find the river or the bridge from the brochure, but an orange tree and two grapefruit trees were bearing fruit in the yard. "His actions, at least what I heard after he left, showed that he didn't want to stay clean. But, you know, he was sick. And even here, you get the fuck-its. You say, Fuck this shit, I don't want to be here anymore. Fuck it. It's easier to go back to what we know. It's harder to face change."

12.

THE DIRTY VERSION: JAI-ALAI WITH BLOWFLY, 2007

Profanity represents just how real shit gets.
—R. Kelly

For me, ODB's work and his illness are about control. Up until ODB, MCs proved themselves on how fast, how tight, how interior their rhymes could be. It was about matching the syllable to the beat, pound for pound, inch for inch, within the parameters and structure of the DJs scratching and the instrumental backbeats. A freestyle was good, if the rhymes were clever and on the fly. Flow was skilled when it was fast and furious or at the very least on beat. ODB destroyed that foundation—his flow was when he felt like it, fast or elongated like molasses, each syllable dripping, slow. He teased meaning from the way he pronounced each word. He rapped when he felt something and he deconstructed words by pouring meaning into guttural sounds. His train of thought derailed from the minute he opened his mouth. His words rhymed sometimes, but most often did not.

He was like a hybrid improv comic–performance artist when he riffed; he created on the spot and teased each syllable with throaty trills. Nobody sounded like him. There was never a template for his style. Most of his idols were soul singers and comedians. He saw himself as Rick James or Blowfly or Richard Pryor; rap had never seen the bastardized character Ol' Dirty created. "No father to his style" was like his presidential slogan.

To say that ODB's work is lewd and obscene and particularly sexual is like identifying a puppy as cute. Other rappers such as Tupac spoke of women and sex behind a cloak of aggressive misogyny—ODB just celebrated the glory of sex. His name alone caused titters at the 1997 Grammy awards. If you tallied all the obscenities in his lyrics, you'd find he uses the word *pussy* 22 times, *fuck* 256 times, *kill* 55 times, and *dick* 19 times. The only time he uses the word *asshole* is in the lyric "Yo, I'm the cunt breath asshole eater / And if you let me physically eat it, it only get [burps]." *Asshole* is probably the least offensive thing about that lyric.

All anyone can do is laugh—it's ridiculous. In the song "Dog Shit," Dirt at first dedicates the verse to "all you bitch ass niggaz . . . And you bitch ass niggarettes," and promptly delves into some of the most sexually explicit and nasty metaphors a person could string together: Here comes Rover, sniffin at your ass / But pardon me bitch, as I shit on your grass / That means hoe, you been shit-ted on! / I'm not the first dog that's shitted on your lawn." ODB is permanently adolescent when it comes to language and boundaries—and it's true, shitting on women does push the boundaries of misogyny. He never claimed to be *Sesame Street*. He doesn't promote violence but he does use violent images to get his point across. Yet it's hard to take seriously because of how absurd his imagery is. More often than not it's cartoonish, kung fu–style action, his tongue the sword that cuts through an otherwise repressed society. His obscenity is so perverse, so wild that it becomes a new art form. *How outrageous can ODB be?* His sexuality is overt, a hyperbolic demonstration of what most people wish they could talk about freely. In fact, you might even call it progressive—it's possible there would be fewer STDs if sex weren't so stigmatized and bodily functions weren't given the Martha Stewart treatment. The ability to talk about these things openly would help people to be more aware and informed. I've always been bitter toward Joseph Lieberman and Al and Tipper Gore regarding their preposterous "decency" campaigns. Decency is when you let a free body of people decide what is and what is not decent.

Not surprisingly, the decency watchdogs eventually took notice, and there was a brief moment after his first album when Ol' Dirty Bastard was targeted with his first and only anti-obscenity campaign. The conservative advocacy group Empower America, led by William Bennett, made a cute mix tape of all the artists they deemed unfit for distribution. Bennett was flanked by two Democratic senators—Joseph Lieberman (Connecticut) and Sam Nunn (Georgia)—and C. DeLores Tucker of the National Political Congress of Black Women when he announced his campaign. Dirt was one of twenty artists targeted for violence or sexual obscenity and shockingly, the lyric they picked to protest *was* allegedly violent, but not sexual. They were offended by a freestyle duet between RZA and ODB. It's one of my favorite tracks because of how sweet and simple and playful it sounds. The recording is raw and the piano sample looped is a repetition of simple minor jazz chords. The song is clearly the cousins fucking around in the studio trying to one-up each other and work on a natural give and take, the kind of chemistry and camaraderie that comes from being kids together. RZA starts a sentence: "I won't stare at a ho, less I know that I'm going to the mo-" and Dirty finishes it: "T-t-tel, cause I'm lousy, technique is drowsy / Stop tryin to foul me." You can practically hear the smiles they had on their faces when they recorded that track. And toward the end, Dirty raps "snatch a kid by the braids," and both cousins shout "cut his head off." And that line is what Empower America chose to protest. The group targeted Time Warner, then the parent company of Loud Records, with varying degrees of success. Content-based protest groups, the kind that claim to protect Americans from American liberties and protest Mapplethorpe and *Harry Potter* alike, operate from a position of ignorance. That line is a throwaway line—punctuation at best. Through the course of the song Dirty references everything from "Over the Rainbow" to the New York Giants to acid rain. This was not a violent diatribe or even a gangsta rap. In this instance RZA and ODB are evoking kung fu movies and applying scenes of violence to their neighborhood. They are not instructing their listeners to find a child and behead him. It's simply a lyrical battle. After all, Wu-Tang is *for* the children.

Obviously Joseph Lieberman doesn't realize this. From the fact that his decency group would target ODB for violence instead of profanity or sexual content, I would guess that Lieberman spent zero minutes actually listening to Wu-Tang (though I relish the thought that he might be dancing around his living room to "Protect Ya Neck"). ODB's fans loved him because he *was* indecent. He acted out a fantasy that our puritan society frowns upon. Or maybe politicians who promote a "decent" society are unaware of the First Amendment. We could easily slip, and likely already have, into totalitarian cultural rule. In 2005 an ad ran online calling for Western bands to participate in a four-day North Korean "Rock the Peace" concert. The only guidelines were that the songs could not show "admiration for war, sex, violence, murder, drugs, rape, non-governmental society, imperialism, colonialism, racism, and anti-socialism," which pretty much eliminates all songs. Is the United States that far behind? No—Wu-Tang, and particularly ODB, are products of American society and American values. They represent many who have no other outlet; they have triumphed in a classic rags-to-riches way. As absurd as ODB was, he spoke about issues that people could relate to. ODB's persona and Wu-Tang Clan's near-vigilante drive for success—it came from somewhere, it's reacting to something—are just as much a part of the American dream as the clownish morality of Joseph Lieberman and his attempts to shut them down.

Besides, sometimes indecency breeds excellent art. ODB found himself in soul music and owed a certain debt to the porno rapper Blowfly. He was the one soul man who spoke brazenly and loudly, the self-proclaimed original dirty rapper. In 1965 Blowfly, the alter ego of singer-songwriter Clarence Reid, recorded an off-the-cuff ditty called "Rap Dirty," which pre-dated Sugarhill Gang's "Rapper's Delight" by sixteen years. The only problem? It was as profane as the title promised and barely made it out of the studio after Blowfly laid it to wax. His music was so offensive that he became the first American artist to ever be censored when his album *Porno Freak* was removed from record stores in Alabama on a court order.

In the second verse of a rambling introduction on *Return to the 36 Chambers*, ODB pays homage to his musical mentor. By way of self-identification, he sings, "I'm tired of this shit, remember the time I told y'all when I got burnt, gonorrhea, well this bitch, there's a new bitch goddamnit, ohh, bitch burnt me again with gonorrhea, so I didn't get burnt one time I got burnt actually two times . . . But the pussy was good! Yes the pussy was good! And here, ODB started aping a soul singer as best he could, crooning until he almost had you convinced, "The first time, ever you sucked my dick . . . I felt, the earth tremble, under my balls . . . First time . . . Nah I'm just kidding witch'all. How y'all feelin', listen to the album cuz it's BANGIN'." And that's how he chose to introduce himself on his first solo effort.

As often mentioned, there was *no father to ODB's style*—no soul singer matched his moanings and no performer could compete with his grip on an audience. But Blowfly inspired so much of his schtick—the blatant sexuality, the menacing laughter, the ease with which the show was comic reality. Lil' Wayne has co-opted some of his guttural renditions and free-spirited ways and Kool Keith certainly taps into the absurdist performance style. But Dirt has always had a little gonzo sideshow quality to him; he is after all a blood cousin to Flavor Flav (on the RZA side of his family). Dirt used the shock of obscenities as part of his hype-man schtick. It was as if he was trying to push the boundaries so far that even he'd be surprised at what he got away with. He also knew he wasn't the first performer to swear onstage or in the booth. He knew it because he modeled himself after figures like Blowfly and Dolemite, the kind of characters who got little to no airplay because they were too black and too blue for the mainstream to stomach.

But there ODB was, on his first album and on his first verse yelling a Blowfly song to an imagined girl who gave him gonorrhea twice. Fans assumed that ODB's STD soliloquy was the first of its kind. But in 1979 Blowfly released an album of astrology send-ups. The song that Dirt sang to his ex was from the "Taurus" track. And on the "Scorpio" track, Blowfly serenaded

Scorpio bitches by saying, "The reason I know, so much about this ho, because she gave syphilis to this dick of mine." If ever there was an influence on ODB's style, it would be Blowfly. A vessel for untamed sexuality, Blowfly was born from the bowels of Clarence Reid's nasty imagination. Yet ironically Reid is a grandfatherly figure offstage, prone to reciting long-winded passages from the Bible (not that dual obsessions with God and sex are unusual in the music world, just consider Prince and Madonna). Now, at sixty-eight, he continues to perform. Half curio, half history, he's paraded out to small rock venues and music festivals such as South by Southwest.

Reid was born in Alabama in another era, the product of Southern racism and the chitlin' circuit, of pure sexual demons erupting from an otherwise repressed career. (He happily claims that everything in his songs is tame compared to passages of the Good Book.) He's released at least twenty albums, each one of them more obscene than the next, under the guise of a glittery cape, a metallic wrestling mask, and a hand-stitched "BF" lovingly attached to his sequined track suit. In his early days, album covers depict him standing tall, like a superhero, in underpants over tights and knee-high wrestling boots. And maybe Blowfly is a superhero of sorts, one that has wrestled giggles from the dignified cultural elite. I defy anyone to not giggle at the profanity-laced parodies "Shittin' on the Dock of the Bay" or "I Believe My Dick Can Fly." And the image of this savior whom ODB aspired to be—a toothless Blowfly resplendent in his bedazzled caps and Mexican wrestling masks, extending his very long middle finger past the album cover, like he's going to stick the nail, which clocks in at a couple of inches long, in your nose.

Of ODB's predecessors, Rick James, sadly, is dead; James Brown, sadly, is also dead. But Blowfly is breathing, still recording, still getting onstage, and still pornographic as hell.

I met him at the Miami Jai-Alai a month before his Australian tour. Reid is to the Jai-Alai what Norm was to his barstool—committed. Reid shows up every day, noonish, gets a cup of sugar with a spoonful of coffee, and fills out a betting sheet, wagering modestly but mostly harassing the employees with grins and goading.

I arrived first in the cafeteria where we were meeting and got coffee. Three or four people were in the smokers' room watching the players warm up. I eyed the apple pie, but it looked like someone had stepped on it, so I returned to my table and folding chair. I was the youngest person in the facility by sixty years, not counting the Jai-Alai players. I had no idea what Jai-Alai was. It looked like a cross between racquetball and lacrosse, and seemed to be played with equipment designed by Edward Scissorhands. A player would torpedo a Ping-Pong-size solid ball against the wall at 120 miles per hour and an opposing player would catch the ball on the bounce and score a point. I think. The indoor court was at least as long as a football field and had a capacity of three hundred. There were eight people in the stands at noon on a Friday.

I was content with my coffee in the cafeteria, watching the warm-ups on the small screen broadcasting the action that was through two doors and maybe forty feet away. You could hear the referees' whistles sounding twice, in real time and on the TV delay. All of a sudden the two other people in the cafeteria, previously studying the day's betting sheets, rose. I saw a digital American flag waving in a liberated digital sun on the television. (It looked like a screen saver or a design for a Trapper Keeper.) But even the smokers stood, resting their butts in the Jai-Alai ashtrays. The elderly man to my left put his authentically worn trucker hat over his heart. I usually stay in my seat, but here, at the Miami Jai-Alai, I rose, feeling a pang of patriotism. And besides, the rough old man in the trucker hat looked like he could take me if he wanted. An electronic instrumental version of the national anthem that sounded like one of those musical greeting cards (angrily high-pitched) played. A few minutes later, Blowfly arrived, smiling his half-toothy smile to everyone in the room, greeting them by name and with a tender handshake. In person his middle fingernail was as long as pictured, thick and a little creepy. His manager, Tom, told me that during a show once, a girl leaped from the audience and bit one of Blowfly's fingernails off completely. "He was really freaked out by that."

A random friend of Blowfly's walked by without saying anything and dropped off a newspaper and a bag of chips, just like that. A minute later, taking a second lap around the room, the same friend dropped off a bag of M&M's. Blowfly thanked him and then said, "Wait, wait, take these back, I don't eat chocolate." Why not? "It's brown and it looks like shit. I don't eat that." He said it with a smile and his elderly friend hustled back to retrieve the candy. "See, what's your sign?" Scorpio, I said. He leaned into the tape recorder and half-sang, half-rapped, "They come in, they like to be beaten, they don't like to be fucked but they like to be eaten, Scorpio," then broke into a well-practiced and hysterical Dracula laugh. Then Blowfly pointed to the woman at the counter and whispered, "See that lady there, all I know was Saddam Hussein, Bin Laden was angels compared to her."

Blowfly, beyond his character, is a rap legend, sampled by Wu-Tang, NWA, and Snoop Dogg, and most famously by Ol' Dirty, who practically sampled his persona. "ODB was a good guy. I got a check in the mail for seven grand and I didn't have no idea where in the hell it was from. But my song was on *Return to the 36 Chambers*. Ice Cube is good—I got money from him.

Snoop Dogg, well they do shit slick and you don't never get no money from him."

Not enough people know that beneath his porno raps and caped persona, Blowfly orchestrates some outsize funk bass lines and beats that have been cherry-picked through the years. "All of my stuff, a lot of that, he got from me. I didn't want to take any credit but Ol' Dirty said, 'Yes you did, that come from that album you did with Curtis Mayfield.' I had forgotten that anything come from there. I think the song was 'Freddie's Dick Is Dead.' And he said, 'Yeah, it comes from "I got to keep on pussy, can't stop grinding, I got on my wand, it's on hard, keep on fucking." ' " Dirty sampled Blowfly and early on they performed together during Fishbone's weekly residency at Club Lingerie in Hollywood. "We met in 1992, after Hurricane Andrew. My house wasn't paid for then and I got a call from Jimmy Maslon and he said, 'You want to come out to California on Friday?' I said, 'Sure, so, when do I fly out?' He said, 'Friday.'

"Now, ordinarily, with James Brown you have to have four or five rehearsals. And I said, 'If I fuck up I'm going to make the biggest scene you ever seen. And when I'm pissed off I get real red.' He picked me up at the airport and we went to the club and all these motherfuckers are lined up like soldiers. And I thought, All right, let's get it over with. And I hear ba-da-da-du-duh and someone said, 'Who the fuck are y'all?' And Isaac Hayes was there and the Chili Peppers, and Flea and ODB, and I had never heard of Chili Peppers or ODB at this point, and Angelo Moore was there and we played the show." I looked at Blowfly and tried to match his gaze. That show in Hollywood would have been when I was in tenth grade and obsessed with Fishbone, before they started playing benefit shows to pay for the legal cost of defending John Norwood Fisher, who tried to abduct Fishbone's lead vocalist Kendall Jones after he quit the band and joined a religious cult. I started to wonder about Blowfly, still performing at post–retirement age, and how he survived in this volatile environment of entertainment and selling himself, when so many others couldn't. Blowfly has a tortured relationship to rap; as one of its uncelebrated founders, he's understandably a little bitter. Samples of his songs that appeared in Beyonce and DMX tracks earned $75,000 in royalties in the last quarter of 2006 alone, but Blowfly saw next to nothing in payment because he'd sold the publishing rights in a deal to pay off tax debts. He likes making fun of things; that's what his songs do. It's how he survives, by making light of shitty situations. "All those guys from N.W.A. used my shit and they never sent any money. I'd pull out my old records back from when we had men first walking on the moon and I'd say, 'See this shit niggers, this is rap.' I used to call N.W.A. 'Niggers Without Asses' 'cause all of them was skinny." Blowfly peppered our conversation with names of artists and producers from the sixties, dropping Gwen McCrae, Sam and Dave, Elvis, and James Brown. He'd name-check, then look at me and say, "You remember them, don't you?," and I'd shake my head.

The way Reid tells it, Blowfly emerged when he was just a babe in diapers, the first of eleven children born in Cochran, Georgia, the only incorporated city in what was mainly timber country; some local farmers grew cotton, soy, and winter wheat. The town's population was 3,500—half white, half black. By his account (which is clearly questionable) Baby Reid, unsatisfied with his Cochran setting, started chanting, "Fuck you, fuck you," at four months old from his high chair. When his grandmother Lucinda Bryant got wind of the infant's obscenities, she supposedly said, "Boy, you're disgusting, you're nothing better than a blowfly." When Reid tells the story, he adopts a high Southern, squeaky voice, something like a polite demon on helium.

The name stuck. Reid traded nasty songs for laughs with a diligent irreverence, but he also realized he could entertain and make more than he was making as a teen harnessing donkeys (a task he describes as punching mules at five a.m., because in Georgia the donkeys are stubborn and you had to slap them around to get them to concede to a bridle). "If your brother dated four girls at once, he was Casanova, but if girls did that they was whores, and I could never understand that." The way Reid tells it, you'd think his songs about fucking fat chicks and spooge were feminist anthems. "So I made up a song, 'Girls, You Can't Do What the Boys Do,' " and this white girl named Missy heard it and said it was real good and told her father. Now, he thought I was banging his daughter. I didn't even know what banging was, but he said to sing the song anyway and he was on the floor laughing. He sent me to Miami to record more. I was supposed to look up Henry Stone and I worked out a deal at the Criterion where I'd clean and record for a week, work two months and then get free sessions. Dizzy Jones wanted my material, he wanted me to write for him, so he let me use his band and we recorded something."

Reid separated his straight songwriting from Blowfly. He penned hit songs for Betty Wright, Gwen McCrae (he wrote the top-selling single "Rockin' Chair"), fronted the R&B group the Delmiras, and started touring with Big Maybelle, James Brown, and Sam and Dave. In casual conversations Reid can't help but slip into stories of his long life, one that existed outside the Jai-Alai bleachers. "Even when I was touring with James Brown, I used to change the lyrics. I said, 'James, that's not the right lyric, "You want to fuck a boy, doo doo doo doo," that ain't right, you want to fuck a sister? "She ain't got nothing tight, da da da, you want to suck me off but you can't change, you and Liberace had it all arranged." ' James and I, we were from the South, we knew how to fight, but Jackie Wilson, he kept his hands soft for the women. So when we got into it about money, Jackie hit James dat-dat-dat and James just knocked like duh. We from Georgia, he said. I used to fight bears in the woods in Georgia. They called me Bear Rug after that."

It's impossible to follow exactly what happens in Reid's stories. There's a sense of the fantastic, of history, and of resigned distance, but mostly he entertains with the absurd and the distinct possibility that 10 percent of what he's saying is true. "James Brown performed with Mick Jagger on *The Ed Sullivan Show*. It was the first time he wasn't the star of the show and he wasn't gonna do it. And he went out and did that old-school *please please please* that made the white girls pull they panties off. And Mick Jagger wouldn't go onstage afterward."

Hip-hop doesn't exactly make room for old-timers and it's unfortunate, because Blowfly deserves the Dirty South, the Neptunes, and anyone rhyming to sit at his feet and listen. His stories are bizarre combinations of biblical references, fisting Diana Ross, and adolescent body fluid jokes, but between the lines is an unearthing of hip-hop's origins. "I could never do anything to make Diana Ross laugh. She'd tell me, 'Don't fuck with me.' The real meaning of the lyrics from 'You Keep Me Hangin' On,' oh that was about Berry Gordy's sex life. Do dod do do, my pussy free, why don't you Berry, get fists out of me, why don't you Berry? You don't want to make me come, you just keep my pussy hanging on? She used to fuck him fifty times and only come once." Blowfly is a delightful lunatic, but he's also out to say more than his schoolyard porno poems at first imply. When he initially started recording raps, mimicking the DJs of Georgia radio who spoke in between and right through the songs, he was not taken seriously. Part of his strategy was and is to desensitize the world from sexual stigmas by being as deviant, as repulsive, as silly as he can be. The sex is served with a wide smile. He breaks down every boundary, including his self-appointed nick-names. In one fell swoop, he said, "Everybody hated to be called nigger. I wouldn't respond unless you called me nigger, so I started crying because my grandma called me an insect that laid eggs on dead things and shit. Well, if it wasn't for blowflies, when the dinosaurs died, and comets took over the earth, the earth would have become nothing but germs, but blowflies came along and laid eggs on those dead dinosaurs and shit and those maggots ate up the diseases. So I started calling myself Blowfly. But that's not the only name I go by. Some girl was trying to get my attention and said, 'Boy, what is your problem?'

"And the sheriff said, 'Call him his favorite name, nigger.'

"She said, 'I don't like that word.'

"And he said, 'He loves it.'

"And she said, 'Nigger.'

"And I said, 'Now get it straight, I'm the world's baddest nigger.'" Before Richard Pryor or ODB or Dave Chappelle, Blowfly flipped linguistics and turned a bigoted word into one of empowerment. He barely realizes it's controversial and contin-ues. "I'm skinny, never eaten no rabbit, no chilis, and no seafood because it smells like undouched pussy." The way that he slips words into casual conversation that would never make it past the *New York Times* copy desk, it's as if he doesn't recognize the impact anymore. Arguments have been made that if you use a word enough the meaning is lost, the stigma removed. When I asked Reid how he felt about the title *Nigga Please*, he said, "It could have been better."

Reid's made it this far, this long out of tenacity, but also because he never did drugs and prides himself on staying alone while touring. "I was on the road with Fishbone. They were good but they used too much drugs, pipe and drugs. I didn't do that shit and I had to get a room by myself because of all the women. I don't fuck on the road. They had bitches inside and out of their room, girls that smell like juice from a polecat. You know, a skunk or weasel." After a creative and profanity-laced discussion about the Bible and that motherfucker Moses, Reid told me about the times he would call ODB and leave prank messages on his voice mail. "I'd say, 'I know that girl you fucked in the bathroom wasn't a girl, it was a man.' I'd just be fucking with him. He did a lot for his family. I'd call him and leave him messages on his phone. He was a good guy though."

We walked from the cafeteria to the actual arena, where the second round of Jai-Alai was ramping up. The small men in helmets pummeled strawberry-size balls against a hundred-foot-tall wall, waited for a bounce, and scooped up the ball in a basket attached to their forearms, each player taking a turn, throwing, scooping, angling for the best shot, the fastest throw, the ricochet of the pebble, the lights flashing and the elderly audience waning. Reid looked at me and said, "You're so cute. I can't believe an innocent like you did interviews like Tom [his manager] said you did, about sticking a butt plug up a cat's ass." (I smiled, thinking, Huh?) And with that, he took his half-toothy smile and his bag with his racing form and sat in the lower righthand corner, nodding at the players he knows from daily visits and filling in his betting sheet for the fifth time that week.

Blowfly did one thing ODB couldn't—he survived, but not necessarily without consequence. He lives in a simplistic universe of cartoons, his Jai-Alai time, and his stage time. He eats piles of sugar and bananas and vanilla wafers and would rather go hungry than sit at a table with a plate full of fish. It's as if his childlike obsession with naughtiness is simply a by-product of living life as a baby man. As an artist he's catered to and taken care of; he's allowed to live inside his own peculiar universe. His sanity is such that he can survive. He's figured out a way to live by pouring himself into his spangled jogging suits and sputtering dirty words. ODB may have been a crazed free spirit, trolling his own crooked path, but he was engaged in life. For Blowfly to survive, he had to turn himself into a cartoon, while ODB was all too real and real enough to die.

13.

ODB ESCAPES, WALKS FREELY INTO A JAIL SENTENCE, 2000

Drugs is all around you kids. Look at that Magic Marker cap.
What the hell you think that is, some kind of crayon?
Take it off and sniff it and get high.
—*Dave Chappelle as Tyrone Biggums*

After two months at Impact House, ODB was allowed to travel with an Impact-appointed counselor to New York for court appearances regarding his Queens arrest for drug possession. The court date was largely insignificant—a routine charge of drug possession—except Dirt's behavior in court was anything but routine. While his lawyer Peter Frankel attempted to tell the judge that Russell was "getting his life in order" at a rehabilitation facility in Pasadena, ODB was shifting restlessly in his chair. And it was tough to maintain a "not guilty" plea after ODB fell asleep, then stared blankly at a female prosecutor and asked her, "Do you find me horny?" and *then* shouted at the same prosecutor, "Sperm donor!" while he picked his nose. ODB had finally shown up for court and was found in contempt within minutes of opening his mouth. Naturally, the tabloids picked up on the story, filing twin reports on ODB's latest misstep. For a while it seemed like ODB filled weekly columns for the *New York Post* and the New York *Daily News*. Dirt played this up, addressing the tabs by name. According to the *Daily News*, upon leaving the courtroom, ODB shouted to a reporter, "Hey *Daily News*, tell New York, 'Fuck them' and tell the world, 'Fuck them.' " According to one of the prosecutors, ODB and his Impact House counselor were at odds throughout the court dates and traveled separately back to Los Angeles. When ODB landed he was—shocking no one—holding a bottle of booze. Impact House discharged him and he was sent to Biscaluz Recovery Center of Los Angeles County Jail for violating probation. To make matters worse, while he was in jail on the West Coast, ODB was also considered a fugitive on the East Coast for missing the second possession charge from the summer before. It's tough to appear in court when already locked behind bars on the other side of the country. In March 2000, ODB admitted to violating his probation by possessing alcohol. After serving six months in county jail, ODB was sentenced to six months in rehab following three months of court-ordered psychological tests. He headed back to Impact House (where they once again enrolled him in the program) to fulfill the remainder of his sentence. But on October 21, 2000, with just two months left on his twelve months, ODB walked out of rehab. It was an open facility and he left through the front door, same as he had entered, probably wearing those fifty-dollar Nikes he lifted a year earlier. ODB was officially on the lam. Bench warrants were issued. The courts considered him a fugitive.

The rumor was that ODB was stashed in a safe house, recording some vocals with RZA. But only one verse actually made the Wu-Tang album *The W*. According to RZA, the recordings not used on the album were held because of some "very, very peculiar" lyrics. The verse that ended up on the album is at best paranoid nonsense, saved only by Snoop Dogg picking up slack on the rest of the track: "Old Dirty corporata, splash, I'm up on the punanny flash / Bad gas, Macintosh, the light is red / Pee in the bed, I'm frustrated." It's possible Dirt was going for postmodern, but that's a stretch. The words just show that Dirty is in trouble, that he's over some edge and can't quite return. It's like someone gave him a mic and said go, and Dirt just free-associated in between sips of the pipe. He's desperately trying to be old Ol' Dirty, but falls short.

Then on November 21, the fugitive emerged backstage at the Hammerstein Ballroom in New York. Steve Rifkind was waiting for the Wu-Tang set to start. It was the record release party for *The W* and eight of nine MCs had already arrived. That's all anyone was expecting. "Whenever a Wu record came out I got nostalgic," Rifkind said. "And I remember sitting on the steps in the back of the dressing room and I saw this woman who looked just like Dirty and it actually was him and he came right over to me. He was wearing this wig and he kept saying. 'It's me, it's me,' and you know you can't miss the voice." He eventually replaced the wig with the fluffy fur-trimmed hood of an orange parka, pulled over his head until Dirt looked like Kenny from South Park, which is to say unrecognizable except to those who could peek into the porthole of his coat. Onstage, the show started, with the majority of Wu-Tang hyping the hell out of old material. In unfortunate foreshadowing, the stage was set like a prison camp, complete with barbed wire. A few songs into the set, RZA announced a "special guest" and threw down the martial arts sample—the sounds of flesh pounding into flesh—and with the beat, the hand-clapping drum machine, out popped Ol' Dirty gracing the stage for "Shame on a Nigga."

Dirt was a chorus man—he could really pick up a flow on a handful of words and define them with the leaps and twirls of twisted vocal chords. That night he attacked the chorus like it was his last. On "Shame on a Nigga," Dirt shines throughout the song. He introduces himself with a hyped up "HUT ONE, HUT TWO, HUT THREE, HUT! / Ol' Dirty Bastard, live and uncut!" Those words, on that night at the Hammerstein Ballroom, were incendiary. How much more live and uncut do you get than an MC on the run who makes one last stop onstage, just before the inevitable train wreck? And as he sang his verse "I come with that ol' loco / Style from my vocal / Couldn't peep it with a pair of bifocals / Crews be actin' like they gangs, anyway / Be like, 'Warriors! Come out and play-i-yay!' " it seemed like a fitting sound track. Dirt was rolling as if he was his own gang from *Warriors*, running from subway turnstile to sheltered underground safe house to a random woman's crib. I wouldn't be surprised if he was wearing a feathered headdress and bell-bottom jeans as a disguise. He told the audience, "Just like a fly on your windowpane, I'm here lookin' right at you. I can't stay on the stage too long tonight—the cops is after me." And RZA reminded the crowd that it was the first time in three years that all nine MCs were onstage together, and they only performed a handful of shows after that one, so ODB's unlawful cameo made *The W*'s release party a historic event. In between singing "Wu-Tang Clan Ain't Nuthing ta F' Wit" and "Shimmy Shimmy Ya," ODB took his stage time as an opportunity to vent. He'd been underground for a couple of months, but that's an eternity to someone who thrives in the hot club lights. "You know, the whole fuckin' world is after me. Y'all know, I'm still surrounded," he said, before telling the audience that he planned to become "like a bird" and to subsist on "birdseeds or whatever.

You'll see, motherfuckers, you'll see," he said. He stayed onstage for another few songs, sipping on a bottle of cognac. The four-thousand-capacity crowd was definitely stunned.

"I didn't kick it with him much that night at Hammerstein. I didn't even know he was gonna show up," GZA said. Like any family, the Wu-Tang Clan was fractured; there had been rumors of fights and difficulties in getting all the MCs together to record this album, and not just because of ODB's legal problems. ODB's presence was like a stunning temporary salve. "It was one of those moments. People in the audience were shocked to see him, they were buggin' out," GZA said. Just before the end of the set, ODB zipped up his parka and adjusted his skullcap with the tags still attached and left the stage. The writer Jeff Johnson was there and wrote in *McSweeney's*, "Outside, in front, in a giant orange parka, with a couple of thug handlers, Ol' Dirty Bastard walked by. He made it past all the cops. They had no idea who he was. I went to shake his hand but the handlers told us to get the hell away from him and stop drawing attention. Then he stopped and shook our hands and asked, 'Hey who loves you?' I said, 'ODB,' and he said, 'You goddamn right.' " Even in a fugitive state, ODB took time for his fans, spreading the love like a guru atop a mountain, hugging his disciples as they approached, spreading the gospel. The most glorious part of that story, though, is that ODB showed up intending to get caught. How else do you explain mounting a stage and telling four thousand rabid, drunk (there was an open bar that night) fans that you're running from the law? Are you really trying to keep shit on the down low? And yet there he went, evaporating into the night like a ghost, trailing birdseed from the window of a chauffeured SUV.

Six days later, when ODB was ordering food at the drive-through of a McDonald's in the Grays Ferry section of Philadelphia from a 1991 Mitsubishi Galant sedan, some fans approached him for an autograph, which he gladly gave them. The few fans turned into a dozen or so and the manager got worried about crowd control. She called the police, not knowing that she was phoning in a fugitive, let alone a famous one. Officers Rebecca Anderson and Charlene Joyner of the Seventeenth District recognized ODB. They were fans of his music. The officers approached his car to make an arrest and (at this point it must have been a gag reflex) he attempted to drive away. He was stopped and arrested on the corner of Thirty-first Street and Grays Ferry Avenue at four in the afternoon. A representative for the Philadelphia police department described the officers' connection to ODB: "They knew from media coverage that he was wanted. They were really interested to meet him," Detective Frank Wallace said. "It was a neat experience for them." ODB's response to the arrest was simply, "The government is trying to kill me," which he stated through one of his lawyers, Peter Frankel. According to published police reports, he was identified through fingerprinting. He had no identification on him. His second lawyer, Larry Charles, told the press that his client was "rather sad" about his present situation and "would rather be on the road somewhere, rapping." He was arraigned a few days later and extradited to New York, where he would once again face two charges of drug possession (Brooklyn and Queens) and petty larceny (Virginia) and two counts of terrorist threats (Compton, Beverly Hills). Individually and even bundled the charges were small time. (When ODB was charged with terrorism, it was more in the vein of wreaking havoc and creating terror in a victim than its current definition of flying planes into tall towers.) ODB wouldn't have gotten time had he not been a high-profile mess and chronically self-destructive. But it had been a long two years.

On the second day of the new year, a quiet and handcuffed Ol' Dirty Bastard pled not guilty to the drug possession charge in Kew Gardens Supreme Court. Frankel asked that Justice Joseph Grosso release him on bail. Not surprisingly, Grosso denied the request with the rationale that ODB was, in fact, a flight risk, having been apprehended as a fugitive just a month earlier. Then, in March, the prosecutor Ken Holder offered ODB a plea deal to serve two to four years for the twenty vials of crack and the marijuana found in his car a year earlier. He took a month to decide if he would stand trial or serve the time. He was increasingly paranoid and convinced that the government was trying to kill him. A state-run facility, particularly jail, held little appeal. Frankel told the *Daily News*, "[ODB's] mental health is bad. He's trying to get some mental health counseling, and trying to get some spiritual counseling." ODB, with three platinum albums under Wu-Tang and two gold records from his solo career, was about to don the same orange jumpsuit as rapists, murderers, and sociopaths. On July 18, a day after ODB was placed on suicide watch and appeared in court with white gauze wrapped around his wrists, ODB was sentenced officially to state prison and recommended for psychiatric and substance abuse treatment. To coincide with Dirty's imprisonment, Elektra announced a twelve-song ODB greatest-hits package called *Free Dirty*, released on August 21, a couple of months after ODB was locked up. It included "Shimmy Shimmy Ya," "Raw Hide," "Brooklyn Zoo," "Nigga Please," "Recognize" featuring Chris Rock, "I Can't Wait," and "Got Your Money." For the first time since suing him twice for child support back payments, Dirt's wife, Icelene, spoke to the press, saying, "His mentality is totally different, he's not himself anymore. He's scared to go back to jail because people are threatening to kill him there. Me and the children know that he's not doing well." Reports surfaced that he'd suffered a broken leg after being assaulted in a holding facility. After two years bingeing on misdemeanors, violating obscure body-armor laws, and missing court dates in three cities, it was clear Ol' Dirty Bastard was a spectacular wreck. A dime-store psychologist could see that he was hurting on multiple levels. One with slightly more refined perceptions could see that he was paranoid, erratic, and out of control, but miraculously still alive in spite of himself, in spite of it all. Frankel told me, "He went to jail because he opened his mouth in a way that someone was offended. Was it bad judgment? Yeah, but was he treated fairly? I don't think so." And so the rapper most known for his freedom of expression, freedom of thought, and freedom of spirit was stripped of the very freedom that brought him fame.

PART THREE

JAIL, RELEASE, PAROLE, DEATH, RELEASE

14.

DIN 01A4392: CLINTON CORRECTIONAL FACILITY, 2001

*Maybe I'm jus' trippin', maybe he jus' snitchin' / See
it a whole lot different from my cell in Clinton.*
—Shyne

Chuck D famously called hip-hop "Black CNN" because it
reflects the reality of the inner city. Like a little ticker of truth,
the anchors of Black CNN (rappers) reflected the world they
represented. Public Enemy's political empowerment rap almost
seems quaint. Chuck D and company angrily rapped, but their
words were optimistic, as if they alone could inspire change and
revolution, though now you're more likely to hear their songs at
cheerleading competitions then anarchist rallies. They hoped for
a change in the status quo. PE was fighting the police, the government, racism, poverty, indifference. PE challenged Ronald
Reagan's criminally racist "War on Drugs," a policy that dra-
matically increased prison populations in the mid-eighties while
funding was cut for addiction treatment. Reagan's strategy targeted poor people and minorities. An investigative series in the

San Jose Mercury News exposed the CIA's negligence in dealing with the contras' connection to inner-city drug running. PE was a megaphone for the unheard voices of poor black communities. But their revolution led to West Coast gangsta rap, to Dr. Dre and Snoop Dogg and to the voices of the Crips and Bloods. Suddenly, what once was angry protest turned to division and violence. Black Panthers evolved into red and blue bandannas, perpetuating a black-on-black war that continues to fester.

The streets of Compton are filled with drive-bys and dropped bodies and sawed-off shotguns, so it's no wonder that gangsta rap represented what was happening. Unfortunately, gang violence overshadowed the social epidemics that ravaged the black community, like AIDS and addiction. Eazy-E gripped Glocks in almost every publicity shot and rapped about indiscriminate sex as an MC with N.W.A., but shocked a nation in 1995 when he died of AIDS at age thirty-one. He wrote from his deathbed, "Young fans have to learn what's real when it comes to AIDS. I would like to turn my own problem into something good that will reach out to all my homeboys and their kin. Because I want to save their asses before it's too late. I have learned that this thing is real and it does not discriminate."

If Eazy-E represented the AIDS issue and Dre and Snoop and Tupac and Suge Knight covered gangs, then that left ODB to represent the crazy black man crouched on a corner searching for half-smoked cigarettes. He was the confluence of problems some black men had to deal with. He was an addict, a father seven times over, paranoid, mentally ill and untreated, unable to function in a society with rules—he was the poster child for a real black male stereotype. Gangsta rap was what Senate committees and C. DeLores Tucker got riled up over when they should have recognized a rapper who was a walking census report. He didn't say it; he lived it. He didn't go to prison for street cred; he went because he had problems that not only went unaddressed, but were often glorified. The number of blacks in prison has quadrupled since 1980 and mostly because the "War on Drugs" targeted black communities. A U.S. Department of Justice study estimates that, if recent trends continue and things don't improve, at least a third of the black males born in 2001 can expect to do time. Blacks were and continue to be arrested for minor infractions like drug possession or public intoxication and sentenced with a severity unknown by white offenders, as if the crimes committed were those that gangsta rappers sing of. It's funny that ODB was so lifted, so surreal, but so grounded in everyday struggles. He was one with the people; he was persecuted like his neighbors in Bed-Stuy and treated with as little dignity and empathy as anyone else in the system. Not to mention that according to a Justice Department study published in September 2007, more than 60 percent of inmates nationally reported mental health problems. And jail is no place for the insane.

ODB was trapped. In jail he was just another number, DIN 01A4392. He was transferred to Clinton Correctional Facility in upstate New York, a prison with one twenty-foot concrete wall skirting the town line of Dannemora. The locals affectionately called Clinton Little Siberia, with average winter temperatures of 18 degrees Farenheit, not counting the windchill factor. (Inmates say there are two seasons in Dannemora, winter and July.) The prison, built in 1845, was originally surrounded by frontier wilderness. The prisoners marched thirty miles in shackles to work in the local mines smelting iron, the core of the local economy. Clinton was one of the first prisons run under the Auburn system, an industrial concept that strove for factory efficiency and one of the first to use its prison population as a workforce. The revenues offset the costs of running the institution, but local labor rallied against the practice, fearing free prison workers would replace local jobs. It wasn't a concern for humanity that kept Clinton from utilizing free labor. It was unions. In 1877, the mining experiment was abandoned due to the protests. The mines were filled with water for reservoirs. Inmates previously trained in outdoor labor were put to work producing shoes, barrels, wood ware, brushes, brooms, and baskets. In an early act of self-sufficiency, all of the items made at the prison were used by the prisoners. The shift seemed to quell local labor and the warden even decided that twenty-four-hour shackles were unnecessary. By 1889 the prison medical staff noted an unusual number of tuberculosis cases that responded well to the upstate environment. The doctors felt that the cold fresh air 320 miles north of New York City was helpful in curing consumption. Other prisons sent their tuberculosis patients to Clinton. A special forty-bed ward was added to Clinton's hospital in 1901 and another hundred-bed ward opened in 1907. Eleven years later, construction of a separate TB hospital was completed on a high plateau at the rear of the prison.

During the early twentieth century, prisoners began deforesting and building roads, living in off-site correctional camps with forestry graduate students as guards. In 1977 the Assessment and Program Preparation Unit (APPU) was annexed for prisoners who had trouble adjusting to incarceration. The separate facility was built for inmates who feared fellow inmates, and to transition them into the general population. Naturally, this is where Ol' Dirty Bastard stayed for eighteen months, passing his time in a four-by-six cell alone, with a small desk, a toilet, and a single bed. He went to rehab and attended GED classes. Those eighteen months were probably the only time ODB was confined to such a small space and so isolated, so deprived of the attention he thrived on. He was alone and likely still suffering from psychotic and paranoid symptoms, which the infirmary addressed with medication.

As an inmate, you lose almost all your rights, regardless of the severity of your crime (unless you're Martha Stewart). Even phone rates are designed to gouge the prisoner, because who cares about consumer rights when the consumer is a convicted felon? Within a month of his gubernatorial inauguration in 2007, then newly elected governor Eliot Spitzer decreed it unfair for inmates to pay Verizon three dollars to make a call and sixteen cents a minute thereafter, with the Department of Correctional Services taking a substantial percentage of that money. The Department of Correctional Services received 57.5 percent of the exorbitant rates, with the rationale that the money would help pay the cost of inmates' health care. (A health care system that, at best, uses cardboard as bandages and Tylenol as a cure-all.) Prison populations have more than doubled since 1985, when prisons held 744,000 inmates; now prison populations top two million, according to a 2003 Department of Justice survey. And those two million inmates are captives of a $37 billion industry.

America, the land of freedom and justice and peace, incarcerates a higher percentage of its people than any other country. Likewise, a disproportionate number of blacks are serving prison sentences. In New York State, 15.9 percent of the general population is black, whereas in New York State prisons, 54.3 percent of the inmate population is black. It's a staggering disparity—the Sentencing Project estimates there are ten times the number of black inmates to white in New York State. Also, according to the Department of Justice, nearly 5 percent of all black men, compared to 0.6 percent of white men, are incarcerated. The "War on Drugs," which amounts to ongoing assault on inner cities through government negligence, is a major factor contributing to the almost automatic incarceration of black men. According to Human Rights Watch, "Drug offenses account for nearly two out of five of the blacks sent to state prison. More blacks are sent to state prison for drug offenses (38 percent) than for crimes of violence (27 percent). In contrast, drug offenders constitute 24 percent of whites admitted to prison and violent offenders constitute 27 percent." In New York State in 2003, 440 black men were imprisoned for drug-related charges, whereas 39 white men were imprisoned in the same category. The rate of incarceration for black men amounts to a contemporary form of slavery. But this time, it seems that appalling circumstances and the ripple effects on black families are mostly hidden. Black men aren't in the fields—they are behind bars. They aren't visible. They are sequestered and lawless within a subsociety that most of us barely acknowledge, unless we're related to someone stuck in the system. ODB was exceptional in every way but he couldn't avoid the inevitable, adding one more to the already stacked stats of black men and prison.

15.

PRISON POT ODDS: ELMIRA, 2006

Incarceration without rehabilitation really don't
mean shit / Little Ricky's home, he gotta serve probation
for six months / But Uncle Donnel and Ol' Dirty Bastard
still in the joint. Reset.
—*OutKast*

I tried to get up to Clinton to see where ODB was incarcerated. It's a prison that might as well be a recording studio. It could be a satellite of Death Row Records or, more accurately, a 2–4 with Good Behavior Records. Within a decade of each other, Tupac Shakur, Shyne (a P. Diddy protégé), and Ol' Dirty Bastard were jailed in the same facility. Tupac twice referenced Clinton in his lyrics. In the song "Picture Me Rollin'," from Tupac's 1996 album *All Eyez on Me*, he raps, "You know there's some muh'-fuckers out there I just could not forget about / I wanna make sure they can see me / Number one on my list: Clinton Correctional Facilities." And in "Hail Mary," from *The Don Killuminati: The 7 Day Theory*, he says, "To my homeboys in Clinton Max, doin their bid / Raise hell to this real shit, and feel this / When they turn out the lights, I'll be down in the dark / thuggin eternal through my heart." But Tupac, who served eleven and a half months on a sexual abuse conviction before he won on appeal, benefited from being in prison. He drew inspiration from it; he got cred to counter his pretty face and long Maybelline eyelashes. Shyne, who has since converted to Judaism and now goes by Moses Michael Leviy, recorded the track "For the Record" for his sophomore album from the jail phone at Clinton. The gritty lo-fi vocals just add to the intensity of his circumstances. You almost expect a corrections officer to intercede and end the call.

ODB described his time in jail as simply watching cartoons and watching his back. He talked of the inmates who wanted to kill him, the guards who wouldn't protect him, and the meds that couldn't help him. After RZA visited his cousin in prison at Kings County, before ODB was transferred upstate, he posted a note titled "Dirty in Danger" on the Clan's website. "Ol' Dirty Bastard fears his life is in jeopardy and that a conspiracy is in effect to kill him. These concerns have been presented to the DA and prison officials have been alerted to the threat to his life. None of these state officials have given any regard to this matter. If something happens while ODB is in the custody of these officials, his family, his thirteen children (the exact number has always been up for debate), and Wu-Tang will seek full retribution in a civil resolution." RZA told me, "It was the worst time. That's when Method Man and I went to see him and Meth couldn't even believe it 'cause he thought they were tearing this guy apart. The jail bars, the handcuffs, it didn't make sense. He was locked up with crazy people. When he was downstate, he was moving slow because of the medications they were giving him. He kept saying it was hell in there." RZA's assistant Tam Layton added in an interview with *The Village Voice* that ODB had gained a significant amount of weight and that the medication definitely made Dirt "overly lethargic, kind of like . . . 'They have him in that state of mind, like those mental patients who stare at the wall.' "

The closest I got to ODB in jail was to talk to the one inmate willing to write back. I sent out a dozen or so letters to prisoners that had been in APPU around the same time as ODB. The only response I got was from convicted murderer and club kid extraordinaire Michael Alig. He had been transferred to Elmira just before ODB arrived in Clinton, after having spent two years in the same facility that ODB was housed in. Alig was sent to a general population prison because he relapsed and started using heroin again while at APPU. APPU was a privilege. A New York State prison safety report described APPU as a 258-bed protective annex where "half the inmates are sex offenders. Others include former judges, police officers, informants, and transsexuals. Among other things, this discrete unit affords selected inmates an ample opportunity to adjust to prison life in a controlled but not unduly restrictive environment. The ultimate goal is to transition these offenders into general confinement placement." APPU's inmates are kept separate from the general population. After I made contact with Alig and got permission to visit him at Elmira, I drove from Brooklyn four hundred miles upstate—a six-hour journey surrounded by woods and air on a road so unpopulated that even when I wasn't lost, I thought I was. I picked up breakfast at a diner in town and ate with the local gaze burning a hole in my back. I wasn't about to pretend to be local and when I left I asked for directions to the prison.

"Which one?" the man behind the counter asked as cheerfully and helpfully as possible. "There are three within spitting distance."

I asked about Elmira and he pointed up the road, "You're practically already there."

Elmira Correctional Facility was originally a prison camp established during the Civil War. An archived description from a Southern inmate reads, "If there ever was a hell on Earth, Elmira Prison was that hell, but it was not a hot one, for the thermometer was often 40 degrees below zero." Approaching the visitor's entrance of the prison, it's impossible not to notice the congenial embrace of two naked men, depicted in copper, nine feet tall. The two men, each of their genitals covered with a fig leaf, stand, hugging each other, guarding the entrance in some kind of strange, ironic welcome. The sculpture took sixteen years to install after the artist Enfred Anderson was commissioned in 1935. Two inmates posed for the rendering and one can only imagine the prison yard backlash.

The waiting room, where I was searched and acknowledged as a journalist, was nondescript, lined with lockers for purses and personal items that weren't allowed past the visitors' gate. One mustachioed and seasoned correctional officer asked me to take a seat and wait. He said that because I was a journalist, I had to wait for an escort. Then he apologized, saying they were so busy that it might be impossible to get me in with Alig. He pointed to a chair as his coworker, a younger woman, continued working on a list of gifts she intended to buy for her in-laws. As I sat, women and children filtered through the metal detectors, stripping their belts, offering themselves for examination. One weathered white woman, wrinkled and bony beyond her years, had the letters H-A-T-E tattooed across her knuckles. Her granddaughter was with her, wearing a T-shirt that was tight enough to reveal newly forming breasts. The elder CO started a monologue about appropriate attire. "Do you even know where you are?" he asked, incredulous. The woman just apologized and said she'd run to the car to get her granddaughter a cover-up. The little girl clearly knew where she was. They'd been there before. I was told to arrive at Elmira right when visiting hours began, so that I'd have the best chance of getting an escort. I called the day before and was told I wasn't on the visiting list and that I'd have to make other arrangements. I had to call again and talk to the warden to reconfirm my visit. I thought it would be smooth.

The criminal system is guarded, literally and figuratively, and no one within its walls is encouraging or cooperative when an outside party is trying to understand what it's like on the inside. It's rigid and systematic and requires dogged persistence and great patience, and here I was at Elmira, waiting, quietly reading. I realized while I was sitting that the one thing I forgot in all the faxing and planning and corresponding it took to set up this visit was a pen. As I sidled up to the desk to sign in and fill out paperwork, I lifted the CO's Bic so that I would be prepared for the interview, or at least have something to hold. It was a small thrill to know that I was stealing *at a prison*. I also knew that if I had asked for the pen, they would have likely let me borrow it, because the COs were outwardly sweet, if inwardly smug. They knew the power dynamic and had no problem flexing what little muscle they had. I could be as polite and friendly as I wanted, but they were gonna make me wait as long as it was entertaining.

I watched three, maybe four cycles of visitors go in and then come out. I watched a small inmate, maybe five-foot-six, being escorted in shackles from the general population to the exit door with a piece of cardboard taped to his face in lieu of a bandage. He was all bones. There was still spit dripping from his frothing mouth and there were deep red stains around the collar of his jumpsuit. He was escorted by half a dozen COs. He didn't look older than fourteen. His eyes were wild, shifting back and forth like a trapped animal. I asked again about my escort and the

CO, playing dumb, smiled sweetly and nodded his head. "We just don't have any escorts right now. So much is going on."

Shortly after, I had almost completely lost patience, but a new batch of visitors arrived to keep me company: the conjugal wives. The first trotted in with at least twelve grocery bags filled with tin cooking pans, raw sides of beef, macaroni and cheese, cereal, chicken, BBQ sauce, Pringles, all the mundane items lining supermarket shelves that inmates don't usually get to enjoy. She sat down next to me, fussing with the bags and tittering about. It was her first conjugal visit, forty-eight hours of trailer life with her husband, who was serving twenty-five to life. She offered the name of her bus service, an easy way to get from the city to Elmira. My frustrations melted; the COs were pricks, and I was annoyed about waiting, but my life wasn't this. I didn't need the name of a bus service to visit my loved ones in prison.

The second conjugal wife, more seasoned, came in with just as many bags and a rolling suitcase and asked the COs if she could put the meat in their fridge, which they reluctantly allowed. She sat down and immediately began mentoring the first wife on what kind of activities she could plan. "Oh girl, once I got these little slip-on heels from Target that lit up whenever I stepped. The lights were so cool. So, I surprised my husband, he went out for roll call and I turned off all the lights and did this little strip tease and my shoes were all lit up while I was dancing on the bed. Oh, honey, he loved it. You can bring in all kinds of things to the trailers." The wives, when asking anything of the COs, were quiet, politely *yes ma'am-ing* and *yes sir-ing* every request. Wife One said to me under her breath, "They are not the people I need to be pissing off."

Every half hour or so, I'd inquire about an escort and the elder CO would look to his colleague, shrug, make a phone call, and shrug again. "I don't know what to tell you." The inmate with the cardboard stuck to his face came back through the entrance, this time with a large fresh piece of gauze attached to his cheek. His eyes were still racing back and forth and the guards held his shackled wrists with rubber gloves on their hands. There was still blood everywhere and his green jumpsuit was unbuttoned to the waist, exposing an equally bloody white undershirt. The lady CO looked up from her computer and screamed, "How many? I had thirty-three in the pool. How many did he get?"

The CO guiding him back to prison said, "Twenty-seven. Who won?"

"Damn. I think Rich had twenty-seven. I can't believe I missed that one. The pot was up to two hundred bucks." She shook her head and mumbled something about buying fishing equipment while the conjugal wives sat mute, stunned into silence after realizing the COs were referring to a pool they had going for how many stitches the inmate got after being sliced from chin to cheekbone. "Our husbands are in there. It could have been them," Wife One whispered.

One thing to remember about the COs is that they are as trapped as the prisoners. There aren't many job options in the local economy, and the COs have to spend the majority of their lives in prison as well. They may get to go home and hold the keys while they're here, but I can see how being a prison guard could warp a person's sense of humanity. It's a system that encourages blatant numbness to violence. COs participate in a hierarchical subsociety that treats inmates like cattle. It's about control and power. They are callous because there is no choice. Even the prisoners on good behavior, like the ones in green jumpsuits who swept the room I was waiting in, were barked at and ordered to repolish an already dazzling linoleum floor—and that was a privilege.

Four hours passed and I was still waiting for an escort when a CO showed up and asked the elder one if he needed anything. I looked on the verge of tears and he said, "You free to escort her for an interview? You'd have to wait until she was done, the whole time." The guy shrugged and said no problem. "I haven't been doing anything all day." I was so excited to finally get into jail that I forgot how frustrated I was. I gathered my tape recorder and had my hand stamped with invisible-ink numbers. The CO escorting me said, "I can't believe they had you waiting all day. I was literally just sitting here. It's been real quiet." I made a mental note that asking for a special reporter's pass is not actually useful when visiting prisons. It just makes you a sitting duck.

The visitor's room looked like a school. The adjoining room, empty of noise and chaos, was designated for reporters and populated by wooden desks and blue plastic chairs with metal frames. Michael Alig bounded into the room and exclaimed, "You're late." He was wearing a green T-shirt and a pair of wire-rimmed glasses that held only one lens. "Oh, that," he explained later. "They broke and they won't give me new ones." For most of the interview he placed them next to his arm, like a prop. I asked him about APPU and about ODB's claims that other inmates were trying to kill him. "APPU was the safest place in the world. I can't imagine anyone feeling threatened there or causing any trouble. It's such a totally laid back place. There's no fights or even the slightest of anything leading to a fight that they would tolerate. They would kick anyone out who even thought about it."

Alig talks like an excited teenager. I wanted to buy him food from the vending machines but the lobby COs had instructed me to leave my money and ID in the locker. My escort gave me a stack of quarters for Gatorade and Doritos and Alig continued, "So he must have had some problems if he thought people were trying to kill him in APPU. I mean, I can see how prison can send someone over the edge. I've seen people get more paranoid over time." Alig described APPU with the fondness of a vacation. "There are phones, a weight room, and a shower. People play cards and exercise and just hang out. If he was in for drug abuse, he'd be in group. They follow the twelve steps but the program isn't acknowledged by the twelve steps. You sit in a circle and act out skits in front of people. I can see how that would be kind of embarrassing for him. You have to talk about your crime and your history."

I asked Alig if he saw the attack earlier in the morning. "Yes, I did. He was right across from my block. I just woke up to the screams but I didn't see anything. My porter said they were cleaning up the blood downstairs." He didn't look shocked or appalled, more proud that he could report something heinous from inside his cell to the outside world, to his old world of clubs and costumes and chaos. It also seemed like the victim's facial cut requiring twenty-seven stitches wasn't so bad by comparison. Alig's Elmira stories are of suicide attempts, self-castration via tuna-can lids, random cutting; it makes APPU seem tame and safe, almost fun. "When I was in APPU, I was part of the committee that planned inmate functions. I wanted us to be able to dress up on Halloween and go cell-to-cell trick or treating. We'd have candy from the commissary and then the COs asked me where we would get costumes and I said we could put white sheets over our heads. And they said, 'Why would you be using white sheets?' I said, 'For ghosts, we'd be ghosts.' You know the first thing that comes to my mind during Halloween is ghosts, not white supremacy. Ha, but this is prison."

The last part of APPU that Alig described was the winter yard, the outside area built on a hill and used for recreation.

After a snowfall, inmates would shovel out a walking path and use the excess snow to build igloos. They would use the small ice palaces for sex and pay other inmates to stand guard. Alig regretted not having been there at the same time as ODB but did say that a nightclub owner he knew had produced one of the Wu-Tang albums and that at least there was that nominal connection. We hugged goodbye, and I walked through the lobby, smiling at the bored COs. I ran at a full trot, as fast as my feet could move, to the parking lot below. I'd been in jail for only six or seven hours, but I was struck by the fact that, CO or prisoner or visitor, within those maximum security fences, we were all trapped.

Pulling out of the parking lot, I watched the new, almost winter air push fall leaves from near-bald branches down to the asphalt, the passing of time floating in matter and in spirit.

ODB did his eighteen months—he did his time because he had to. Ironically, he was in jail for drug possession and terrorist threats while the World Trade Center fell on September 11, 2001. In the years leading up to his incarceration, ODB was pursued in three states for lifting a pair of shoes and being an addict. Osama Bin Laden, who was already responsible for a World Trade Center bombing and two embassy bombings in Africa, was free to issue "Declarations of War," and publicly taunt the American government with glimpses of terror. It made me think of the Immortal Technique song "Bin Laden," in which they blame Bush for the fall of the inner city projects and accuse him of using the twin towers as a distraction from real terror, the kind produced in inner cities. They rap: "They tell you to listen, but they don't really tell you they mission / They funded Al-Qaeda, and now they blame the Muslim religion / Even though Bin Laden was a CIA tactician." While ODB was in jail, Wu-Tang released its least praised album, *Iron Flag,* toward the end of 2001. Not one word is uttered by ODB and the absence of his voice is palpable. ODB told me that no one from the Wu-Tang Clan, including RZA, took the eight-hour bus to visit while he was away. He told William Shaw, a reporter for *Blender* magazine who published one of the only empathetic interviews with ODB, entitled "This Man Desperately Needs Help," that he didn't even realize his third album (*The Trials and Tribulations of Russell Jones*) had come out. Elektra backed off its crash-and-burn superstar and D3 Records stepped up to release eighteen tracks recorded while ODB was on the lam, pre-jail, in fifteen different studios. RZA produced the album, which included collaborations with the Insane Clown Posse, E-40, C-Murder, Mack 10, and Royal Flush. RZA, after seeing Dirt at Kings County and Downstate, thought Clinton grounded him, that he was better after he was transferred. ODB was stuck behind bars and those bars not only sequestered him from society, they also separated him from his Clan, his family.

16.

ENTER THE WEISFELD, 2002

It wasn't long until I was the highest paid slave in town.
—Billie Holiday

For the eighteen months that ODB was away, he had only a handful of visitors. His mom and his family went to see him, and at the beginning of his sentence RZA paid him a visit at Downstate. Then one weekend a scrawny white kid named Jarred Weisfeld showed up with Buddha Monk. They took a bus at 2:30 in the morning 320 miles north to Dannemora, to make it in time for visiting hours. Weisfeld was twenty-two, a recent college graduate with a penchant for wearing curled-bill baseball caps backward, the son and heir of the founder of the Mudd jeans empire. To say he was out of place in the visiting room would be an understatement. He was looking for a way out of traditional ladder-climbing. Weisfeld dabbled in music management while he attended Lynn University in Florida, where he represented John the Baptist, a beat maker Wu affiliate. John the Baptist also happened to be Ol' Dirty Bastard's cousin and mentioned the connection in passing to his manager. Weisfeld spent the fall of 2002 as a production assistant at VH1, and, looking for a way around the drudgery of making copies and logging tapes, he started thinking about how to get ahead. And one idea was a project involving Ol' Dirty Bastard. "Hell no. I didn't know what I was getting into," Weisfeld said about meeting ODB. "I wanted to do kids' television. I wanted to produce a Nickelodeon show that would be the kids' version of *Punk'd*. I don't know anything about hip-hop and I've been ridiculed by everybody for it." But in ODB, he saw a potentially viable product for his bosses— a reality show called *ODB on Parole*.

Weisfeld pitched the idea without ODB's permission or even having met ODB, but he thought that if there was interest, he could convince ODB to participate. There was and he did, with one catch, according to Weisfeld: ODB insisted that Weisfeld become his manager full-time. By March 2003, less than a year after he had graduated from college and more than a year after Dirt was incarcerated, Weisfeld sold the show concept to VH1 and signed on to be ODB's manager until 2008. Ol' Dirty Bastard spent his remaining sentence behind bars (his term was shortened for time served previously) head-down and minding his own business. His girth had expanded noticeably. He was bloated and unkempt, his teeth were rotting under his gold fronts, and his facial hair grew in patches along his expanding chin. The *Blender* writer William Shaw visited him and spoke with Dirt about the album *The Trials and Tribulations of Russell Jones*. He listed the guest artists on the album and ODB perked up at one name. "E-40 is on there? He has the same birthday as me." ODB turned thirty-four in jail on November 15, and to celebrate, he spent the day as always: passing time watching TV. As Shaw was leaving, ODB said, "You know, I don't know whether Ol' Dirty Bastard is even here any more. I think he's gone." It was impossible for Ol' Dirty Bastard to live in solitary confinement or simply behind bars. He was a character born from attention and attention seeking, born with no known limits, and so it would seem that ODB died, leaving Russell Jones alone with the remnants of what was. When Tupac Shakur was released from the Clinton Correctional Facility, he said, "When you're in jail, you don't think you're ever coming back." Slightly more optimistically, the drug dealers on *The Wire* describe doing time as two days, "the day you come in, and the day you get out."

On May 1, 2003, ODB was released from the Manhattan Psychiatric Center, where he went after getting out of Clinton Correctional Facility. He spent three months in the institution gathering medications and a diagnosis. Though Weisfeld denied it, several newspapers reported that ODB was diagnosed as schizophrenic. "He's not schizophrenic," Weisfeld told me. "The only thing he's crazy about is women. It's just an act. It's just a matter of comfort. The shows that I've been at, there's only been one Dirty." The *Daily News* published an item with one unidentified source claiming ODB was taking instructions from a voice in the sky, but his cousin Mitchell Biggs refuted any claims of unchecked insanity. "He finished his jail time and he's getting an evaluation and will be released soon," Biggs said, and toeing the party line on ODB's behavior, he added, "I've known him all my life, and he's always acted this way just to mess with people. So all of the behavior other people may think is strange is normal for him. He's just having fun. As soon as he gets home, he's going to work on his new album and go on tour." After all the chaos of drug busts and traffic violations, the tyranny of addiction, and the unqualified bizarre court murmurings, the people closest to Russell Jones were still claiming that it was all an act, part of the show. *Dirty being Dirty.* RZA told me that he never knew of any diagnosis but he hinted that there was something with ODB that wasn't quite normal. "[ODB] don't give a fuck and to our society, that might be dysfunctional. I think it's like that movie *A Beautiful Mind.* [John Nash] had an alternate reality like most hip-hop artists. You get this idea about life that is different from the average person." RZA did confirm ODB's whereabouts between parole and freedom. "ODB's livin', man. He's out of prison, but he's not allowed out of the hospital for three months. He's in something of a mental and medical situation. He's keepin' strong though, on the real. And when he's out, he's gonna drop the hottest shit." But RZA's optimism had a hollow ring—he was hyping a fallen hype man.

Finally, Russell Jones was free, sort of. He still had to be ODB. The first thing he did while the ink was drying on his prison paperwork was sign a million-dollar recording contract with Damon Dash at Roc-A-Fella Records. Hours after his release from an asylum, ODB, flanked by Mariah Carey, his mother, and Dash, announced the deal to an audience of journalists and photographers at Manhattan's Rihga Royal Hotel. Dash kicked off the press conference by listing and thanking every company he was involved in—it took almost three minutes. The non-Wu-approved Roc-A-Fella was a surprising choice, and one that both Raekwon and Inspectah Deck publicly spoke out against. Abandoning the Wu family was tantamount to treason. Inspectah Deck told MTV, "It was the equivalent of going to war in Iraq and fighting [on the] Iraqis' [side]. Me, I wouldn't do it." Method Man, looking on the bright side, thought the union meant Wu-Tang was, at the very least, relevant, because Roc boasted Jay-Z among others on its roster. But Meth opposed the immediate Roc branding. "The only thing [I have] a problem with is him rocking their flag like that, the Roc-A-Fella chain. Dirty is an entity within himself." Technically, RZA had to cosign whatever deal was made because ODB was still under contract through Wu-Tang Records. Originally RZA tried with a little less money to woo his cousin back to the Wu-Tang fold. At the urging of his mom and Weisfeld, ODB went with Roc-A-Fella, over RZA and even over Pharrell Williams's label Star Trak. It seemed like ODB was making the decision partly out of feeling abandoned by the Wu in jail. "RZA may not have been on the scene but they were together, they were family," Icelene said. "He dealt with Rakeem all the way to the end, he was his favorite cousin in the whole world." And yet, he shed the loyalty to Wu-Tang that once was stronger than a family bond. In fact, at the Roc-A-Fella press conference announcing the deal, there wasn't one Wu-Tang member present, except for ODB. Reporters shouted questions, flashes popped and reflected off a newly minted gold tooth, and ODB delivered answers as only he could, spontaneously and playing along. He was back, filling the niche he had left vacant.

Did you smoke crack in prison?
Absolutely.

Are you planning on having new baby mamas?
Yeah, I'm down with that.

Will Big Baby Jesus make an appearance on the album?
Well, if you see him, sure.

With a lot going on, how do you find time to jerk off?
I don't know man, I got to stretch my body out a little, maybe get a massage. You're looking pretty cute.

How did prison rape affect you mentally?
I'm all right physically and mentally, I feel good.

What was the first thing you did when you got out?
Hug my mom.

Who's that grinning, shady-looking white guy behind you?
That's my man Jarred, we're doing our thing, we're Roc-A-Fella.

Dash wove a thick gold chain with a Roc-A-Fella pendant around Dirt's hooded yellow velour tracksuit, which was a sample from his upcoming clothing line. It read "Dirt McGirt," the new moniker of ODB. Turning a new leaf warrants a new name and Weisfeld thought ODB would be more marketable sans the word *Bastard*. The press conference was a reintroduction to a life he used to lead. It was as if the past decade never existed. He held on to his mom for stability and reassurance. She grinned and looked like she had spent the week at the salon preparing for her child's return. Jarred slinked onstage looking like he had just been bar mitzvahed. He wore a button-down white shirt with a tie and his backward baseball cap. Dirt, when asked, spat out his wish list for collaborators: "Jay-Z, 50 Cent, Ghostface, Mariah . . . I'm just happy to be here. I didn't think I was gonna touch no more microphones."

When Cherry Jones sat me down and told me her son died in jail, she was right. ODB was out and he was signed to a flashy label and he was being followed around by VH1 cameras and a hungry twenty-three-year-old manager who was now financially invested in his very being. His breath was 20 percent Jarred's, his face furthering a brand, and his crazy, well, it was amped up when necessary. The first and only episode of *On Parole* caught ODB coming home—to a party, to the Fulton Street Mall, to a manicure and pedicure, to his mama, and to a part-time job as a *Playboy* photographer.

It's one thing to ease back into civilian life, embracing the normalcy of a previous routine, but for ODB, life was never normal. So it seemed the invasion of VH1 camera crews was minimal, if not helpful in keeping his behavior in check. The show, in reality-TV tradition, played up the absurdity of Ol' Dirty Bastard existing in polite society. One of the first stops after his Roc-A-Fella press conference was a *King* magazine–sponsored spa treatment in SoHo. They dropped Ol' Dirty at Mezzanine Spa, an uppity facility described on its website as a "Zen-like wellness center," where a bikini-clad model coaxed Dirt into a manicure-pedicure package and held his hand as he skeptically looked at these new posh surroundings and wondered if the various seaweed-laced facial treatments would really be good for his image. "A nigga don't come out of jail and get his toes done," he said, fingering a feng shui–ed waterfall and earth-toned walls. "How are the kids gonna feel about this?"

17.

ODB ON PAROLE, 2003

*Open my mouth 'n' show you da fronts / Diamonds got
more carrots than Bugs Bunny's lunch.*
—*Paul Wall*

Weisfeld set up a celebrity guest stint as a *Playboy* photographer
for the newly minted Dirt McGirt within a week of his release.
With tightly pulled cornrows striating his scalp and a Roc-A-
Wear jersey covering his bloated belly, he reservedly entered the
Chinatown loft. "He seemed like he had a little glaze to him
when he came in," said *Playboy*'s photo director, Chad Doering.
"We were expecting him to be all over the place and we were
warned by his management that he can go one of two ways and
it just depends who shows up that day." Dirt held a digital camera in one hand, framing a skinny blond filly of a model—all
knees and bob cut and white-pantied crotch flashes—and Dirt
kept muttering to himself, "Oh shit, shit, shit, shit." The model
tried to help him relax by smiling and keeping her distance and
arching her back when instructed. "He was definitely into it,"

Doering said. "I think he was fresh from the can. It may have been a week since he got out of jail. I don't think he'd been around a nude woman in a while, let alone a *Playboy* model. When he came in I think he was a little overwhelmed. He was actually really quiet at first." ODB directed the model to pose in certain ways, holding the camera in one hand and lopsided. It was a surreal moment in ODB's homecoming—he was shooting a scantily clad white girl, a white crew was shooting him for VH1, and *Playboy* was shooting the crew shooting ODB shooting the model for the magazine. If only someone had been making a documentary about the reality series covering the photo shoot. "A lot of people come in here and their whole crazy attitude is a persona that they put on, but I think that he had really legitimate issues," Doering said. "It did seem like there were a lot of people handling him, you know? If he had been in prison for eighteen months, I'm sure his people wanted to get him in the public eye and back in the game. Maybe they pushed him too soon? I don't know. We deal with a lot of artists and the majority of truly gifted and intelligent artists, I find, are manic on some level or bipolar, and when they're hitting those highs they are incredibly creative, like savants, but it's the kind of thing that can switch in a heartbeat." When I talked with Doering a couple of years after the shoot, he mentioned more than once that Dirt seemed *really mellow*. "My gut when he left was that he was on some kind of medication. I know he was on probation and we couldn't have any alcohol on set. I anticipated a wild man and he was pretty sedate, almost sedated." It was as if Weisfeld was orchestrating the situation intentionally to set off ODB's personality quirks. He worked hard to highlight Dirt's ghetto roots by sending him to seemingly incongruous scenarios—such as a high-ceilinged loft on Canal Street with a completely naked and coifed apple-pie white girl. Dirt surprised everyone by just showing up and trying hard. "He was a lovable guy. He seemed like a dude that despite our different upbringings—I'm from the Midwest—we could hang out. He definitely took the photography seriously. I mean, he wanted a good product," Doering said of the day. And more than ever, ODB was aware of what sold and what he was selling, and he knew how to sell himself and now he even knew how to deliver a proper shout-out. When asked why he wanted to be a *Playboy* photographer, he answered, "Because I'm nasty like *Playboy*. You know what I'm sayin'? I'm a Scorpio and I just love nasty things. Whatever freaks me out, freaks me out. I love *Playboy*. *Playboy* is the shit. It's dynamite. And that's why I wanted to get down. You know what I mean? *Playboy* gets down forever." He smiled a toothy smile for the reporter, the cameras, and anyone else watching. ODB was fine, for today. He was a well-manicured photographer, enjoying his afternoon apprenticeship with models aiming to please him, but is it life if it's lived for the benefit of a VH1 series, or are these staged moments extended photo ops that market a staged reality? And if you're ODB, is it really in your best interest to have the producer of that series, which would in turn benefit from antics and misbehavior, double as your manager?

The VH1 pilot aired as a stand-alone show, with no follow-up series. The network could have been frightened of the reality of ODB's reality show, or the whole thing could have been just too depressing. Either way, the one episode caught Jarred on camera in action, sparring with Dame Dash. Weisfeld was knee-deep in one of the most psychologically and physically demanding jobs in history; stronger people bailed, lesser people failed. Weisfeld was somewhere in between, transparently self-serving but also naive enough to truly care about ODB, which I believe he did. I asked Dante Ross what he thought about Weisfeld and if he ever met him. "No, no I never knew him, but I saw him on

TV and I felt bad for my man. That was a fucked-up-looking gig. It looked like he was in a little over his head," Ross said. Another former manager of a Wu-Tang member stated it pretty simply: "Jarred was all about Jarred. And that's it." At this point Wu-Tang hadn't performed together since the release of *Iron Flag*, and each member operated on his own. Weisfeld quickly alienated most of the other members' managers, to the point of icy silence. A lot of them wondered in retrospect if Weisfeld's plan of a clothing line, heavy tour schedule, and album recording blitz was really the best thing for a fresh-out-of-jail addict, especially when the addict in question was only marginally functional. But Weisfeld was maybe too schooled in the Wu-Tang ethic of Cash Rules Everything Around Me, Get the Money, Dolla Dolla Bill Y'All. After all, ODB and his instability were proven moneymakers—and Dirt owed back child-support payments and alimony, plus he had to feed his sushi addiction. But for anyone who was keeping track, ODB was back. Within a week and a day of his release, ODB had two singles in rotation via the Roc-A-Fella machine. Dash released Dirty's "Welcome Home" with Nicole Wray, and a remake of KRS-One's "Sound of Da Police," which featured ODB, Beanie Sigel, and Peedi Crakk. Neither track was particularly notable for rhymes or even ingenious beats, but Dirt was out there getting airplay.

He did indulge in the things he had missed—that first week he was home ODB went down to Coney Island with Buddha Monk and fulfilled some seafood cravings. "He went for his oysters. He had 'em steamed and he had about twenty of them. Sushi was his number-one dish, though. He loved all the rolls but we used to tear up the shrimp tempura. He took me to another level of trying sushi. He'd say, 'Don't eat it like that, put this on there, try that on it, eat it like that.' It was always—'What are we doing tonight? Let's get sushi dawg. I need some sushi in my life right now,' " Buddha Monk said.

He was also found bobbing up and down in the recording booth at Right Track Studios, laying down verses for Pharrell Williams. He came home to ghetto celebrity status. On paper, he was back, and for his first stint onstage, ODB headlined a welcome-home party thrown by the hipster magazine *Vice*. The party at Plaid was to celebrate his return and their latest issue. The union of Ol' Dirty Bastard as icon and *Vice* as a movement made sense—the magazine known for its contrarian views and provocation was the perfect launch for ODB's rebranding, and ODB was the perfect mascot for a publication that celebrates dysfunction and freedom and the conjunctive bliss and tyranny of addiction. Their choice to celebrate ODB was a mix of admiration and admonishment. It was the perfect example of ODB's white audience—listeners who wished that they could live wild and big and ghetto fabulous but who had the option to turn his music off and walk away. One of his former managers, who chastised Weisfeld for booking ODB so soon and so often, said, "Those guys, they listen to him and wish that they were him, that they could live so out of control and be free. But they don't invite him to dinner, they don't date him, they don't try to know him. They just take the character and live through ODB's actions."

Vice magazine is controversial by nature. It made headlines with articles like "The Vice Guide to Shagging Muslims" and "Bukkake on My Face: Welcome to the Ancient Tradition of the Japanese Facial." One of its founders, Gavin McInnes, was quoted in *The New York Times* saying, "I love being white and I think it's something to be very proud of . . . I don't want our culture diluted. We need to close the borders now and let everyone assimilate to a Western, white, English-speaking way of life." He claimed he was being ironic, intentionally pushing buttons to prank the reporter and mainstream media. But in truth, *Vice*, like every other lifestyle magazine, with its American Apparel branding and Spike Jonze videos and effort to chronicle the hipsters of the world living large with cocaine-caked bloody noses and inexplicable bruises, is selling a fantasy. The founders of *Vice* idolize the ODBs of the world for actually living the life they only aspire to.

And it wasn't without genuine admiration that they booked him. "We loved his music. He was an inspiration to us. Our magazine was starting at the heyday of Wu-Tang," *Vice*'s editor in chief, Jesse Pearson, said. "Wu-Tang was so special and they were the kind of group that was so mysterious and gritty and had a sense of humor, and they were fascinating. They were like literary figures. We had heard rumblings that he was getting out of jail. And we never thought it was gonna happen, but we booked him for our party at Plaid." And so a concert celebrating ODB's freedom at a downtown hipster venue full of middle-class white kids with pouty lips and wife-beaters and trucker hats and layers of ironic pretense made sense. "He was two or three hours late. We put them in the artist lounge at Plaid and got them hooked up with food. Jarred [Weisfeld] just kept saying ten minutes, ten minutes, he's right around the corner. He'll be here soon, put us up there. So we put the Brooklyn Zoo up onstage and they were terrible and it became a really antagonistic thing with the audience and it was getting really tense." The three or four hundred guests were restless and Pearson went out front to get out of the way. "I went outside and was pacing. It was chaos and I didn't want to be there when the first bottle gets thrown. All of a sudden a huge SUV pulls up. He was really big, kind of lumbering, and he seemed really out of it and Jarred walked up to him and grabbed him," Pearson said, to guide ODB toward the stage.

In his first post-jail performance, ODB, looking four times the size of his former self, was recognizable only through his wild eyes and spit-shined teeth. "He was really nervous and his parole officer extended the time he could stay out," *Vice*'s founder Suroosh Alvi said, describing the party. "When he finally warmed up, and loosened up, he was incredible. And he was totally into three different girls in the front row and he left with those three girls, and I was like damn, he still has it." ODB got onstage with Buddha Monk and worked the room until the audience was a sea of dropped jaws. He was a couple of hours late getting onstage and only vaguely present when he was up there, running through a battery of hits, remembering 70 percent of the lyrics, which was more than expected. The club owner explained the delay by telling the audience, "Give us a few minutes and we'll get this boy onstage . . . He's not fit to get onstage right now. We're gonna clean him up. He has to leak." If that wasn't a bizarre enough introduction, ODB strolled onstage and said, "Nothin' like Friday the thirteenth. I feel like Elton John in this muthafucka. I been locked down for a while so y'all gotta excuse me. Let's see if I remember how to do this shit." Why he felt like Elton John we'll never know, but it turned out, to everyone's surprise, including those who had commissioned the show, that ODB did remember how to rap. "He seemed like he had that thousand-yard stare. In retrospect he was very disconnected and a lot like mentally ill people I've met before. He walked directly onstage. I think the mentality was that he just wanted to get it done and get out of there. Everybody freaked the fuck out. He did the hits, like a six-song set. He was semi-engaged and pretty disconnected but it was a fun show," Pearson said. He conjured up that indistinguishable, irrefutable, irra-

tional, rules-be-damned way he had with words, bringing syllables up from his guts and birthing them into a pulsating audience. The noise rock band that played after ODB's set was an
art-school Williamsburg duo named Japanther. To say that it was
an odd billing is to understate the case—it was another entirely
inappropriate welcome-home-from-jail show. But up until the
end, ODB's career hit entirely inappropriate notes, and though
his presence seemed like a contrivance, he was truly surrounded
by admirers. "We're all drug addicts. Recovered or not, dead or
not, we all have that in common, we have the fun and pain from
that experience. Coming from being scumbags as a punk or a
rapper from a disadvantaged environment, you are more able to
laugh at stuff. We loved his music. He was an inspiration to us,"
Pearson said.

The CMJ show where I saw him perform followed the *Vice*
gig and was an equally odd-seeming booking. Essentially, he was
playing white venues to hipped-out white audiences who lauded
him for showing up. ODB had become a modern-day, male version of the Hottentot Venus, an African woman with a large pos-
terior who was displayed on the nineteenth-century London
stage. ODB was also a curio put onstage and marveled at for his
physicality, his race, his muted sadness. He appeared to be completely estranged from his Wu brethren. Sure, he played a show
with RZA, but they were barely talking. He was barely talking to
anyone, in fact. He even moved out of his mama's house to the
apartment in Kensington, his first apartment on his own. He
recorded when time allowed—he was still on parole and had a
curfew that was hard to work with, considering he was not a particularly big fan of the daylight hours he was allotted. He got a
track, "Pop Shit," on *The Neptunes Present . . . Clones*, which was
the song he recorded during the taping of *ODB on Parole*. It was
lacking in almost every way, and it seemed like he'd never again

achieve the heights of the *Return to the 36 Chambers* days. Media outlets began to recognize what the *Blender* writer William Shaw had announced a year earlier; ODB was deteriorating, center stage, while some people watched in sick fascination or, even worse, didn't notice because it seemed like more of the same. Some were genuinely concerned. Piotr Orlov wrote in the *Phoenix New Times*, "When an infamous public life disintegrates, does anybody care to hear the moan? . . . If Dirty's primary commodity is as a personality that's a natural outgrowth of his musical popularity, it is quickly losing its value. Or should I say, the personality has outstripped the music."

To Jarred's credit, among these odd performances and rusty sets there was not one run-in with the police or parole violation in the first year of ODB's release, which is no small feat considering the years leading up to Dirt's incarceration. ODB may have been publicly dysfunctional and depressed, but he was getting arrested a hell of a lot less. He was making his curfew and staying out of trouble, seemingly. But then again, ODB woke up every day restless and confused. The last thing he said when we were sitting in his living room was "Life is boring, *my* life is boring." And when Ol' Dirty Bastard declares life a bore, something is wrong. ODB recorded a duet with JC Chasez (which probably didn't ease the boredom), for the 'N Sync-er's ironically titled solo debut *Schizophrenic*. He was also a judge with RZA on *America's Next Top Model*, in an episode that included riding in a limo and eating dinner with aspiring fashionistas. For something that should have been at least amusing, Dirt for the most part sat in bloated silence.

Then nine months later, on March 16, Dirt performed to forty or so people at Toad's Place in New Haven. The venue nearly canceled the show because of the foot and a half of snow that had dropped the afternoon before. But since a crew was there already shooting prep segments for a concert DVD entitled *Free to Be Dirty*, they soldiered on. The footage included a suspiciously skeletal ODB just six months after his post-jail girth; one could come to the conclusion that Dirt was back on drugs. He was wearing a trapper hat pulled low and answering questions as his name—DIRTY—was being assembled in lights onstage in the background. When Dirt talked, it looked like he had a severe case of coke jaw; he twitched and flinched and talked in circles and his head kept dipping back like his neck was made of gravy. His lower teeth were fighting with his upper molars, and at one point, mid-answer, it looked like his entire lower jaw was about to pop off and secede from his face. The interview feels candid and lucid by comparison to many of his previous interviews, with every third question having a relevant answer, but most of the time, Dirt seemed to be re-enacting his cracked-out days.

Never known to be particularly political, Dirty lashed out at President Bush—not for policy, but because the president was trying to kill ODB. "I think President Bush has a personal beef with the Ol' Dirty Bastard," he said, while his head bobbed up and down, dipping low toward the camera lens. "I think Bush is the most insane-ist motherfucker that ever motherfucking lived." The video cuts to ODB and an associate eating fast food as his friend says that he actually likes Bush because he stole the presidency and that's what America is really all about. "Steal your way to the top. I'll always be down with that." ODB, standing in the background, nodding, responded, "Yeah, we have that in common. As long as he back up the fuck off me, we'll be all right. All George Bush needs to do is get his dick sucked and he'll stop coming after me." The way he says it, his body language, his intensity, and the repetition of the claim—it's clear that ODB believes that President George Bush is trying to kill him. (For the record, I filed Freedom of Information Act requests with the CIA, FBI, DOJ, and ATF for the files on Ol' Dirty Bastard or the Wu-Tang Clan and got only a stack of form letters thanking me for my inquiry and letting me know no records were available.) In this interview ODB seems once again drugged out and mental, right back to where he was a few years earlier. Part of his reasoning for why he thought Bush wanted to kill him is that "he was a man-made product—you made me." That moment of self-awareness amid the rest of the interview's usual litany about women, sex, the aroma of various body parts, food, and jerking off was startling. He knew that his persona was a product. It was a commodity fueled by fan infatuation, and he made this declaration in spite or because of a boatload of narcotics. Later in the interview he also mentions in passing, "It's time for me to move on. It's time for there to not be an Ol' DB."

18.

LOCK THE DOORS, ROCK THE BELLS, 2004

*Wu-Tang went to Europe last month, but ODB's on parole, so
he couldn't go. Meth has a TV show, couldn't go, wanted
to go. But here it is now, there are no obstacles.*
—*RZA*

Amid rumors that ODB was quitting the Wu-Tang Clan, a July
2004 reunion was announced for the summer's Rock the Bells
festival in San Bernardino. Rock the Bells started the year before
as a homegrown effort to bring core, social, conscious, and independent hip-hop to anyone who would show up. The Wu-Tang
Clan hadn't performed together since ODB had been on the
lam and shrouded in his orange parka onstage at the Hammerstein Ballroom in 2001, and that was only for a few seconds.
They hadn't officially sold a show since 1999, five years before.
Getting the group to commit required countless calls to their
dozen or so managers individually. Chang Weisberg, who produced the show, had to refinance his house and borrow money
from his mom. He got each Wu in place, and finally asked an
incredulous RZA whether he would give the show his Wu-Tang

blessing. "I said, You got Mef? Yeah. You got Dirty? Yeah. You got everybody? All them?" RZA asked. "I said, You know what? Yeah. It's a Wu-Tang show."

Weisberg planned the festival for the NOS Events Center in San Bernardino, in an abandoned airplane hangar usually reserved for weddings that had a fire-marshal-approved capacity of 5,500 bodies. Weisberg sold closer to fifteen thousand tickets for the event and on a hot July day the hangar's indoor temperature hovered around 110 degrees Fahrenheit. There was no easy way to get the Wu-Tang together—Weisberg had to negotiate a separate contract with each of the ten MCs, which meant entirely different riders, payments, and conditions for each member. At the last minute, RZA sprung a film crew from his label Sanctuary to document the event (in addition to an independent documentary production already in the works). All the cameras set off an already paranoid Ol' Dirty Bastard. He had nixed any continued coverage for *ODB on Parole* because he hated being followed around by film crews and now he was being trailed by a dozen or so cameras, *which he did not like*.

But before he even arrived in L.A., ODB was in trouble. Weisberg said that when ODB landed, several police marshals greeted him on the tarmac because of an altercation with a stewardess. Weisberg brushed it off as a misunderstanding but told me when I visited the Rock the Bells offices, "You know he's done time and he's a convicted drug offender. The police will overreact to anything Dirty does." To top that off, Jarred Weisfeld wasn't traveling with him, not that he had any control over Dirt. He left managerial duties to Jerrome, ODB's bodyguard, and Buddha Monk, but stayed behind in New York. One of the Wu-Tang's managers speculated that Jarred stayed behind because he'd already alienated the rest of the Clan. The directors Denis Henry Hennelly and Casey Suchan documented the preshow Wu chaos in their film *Rock the Bells*. "The festival had been going on all day," Hennelly said. "By the time the other acts were done, there was still an hour and forty-five minutes of waiting until the Wu-Tang came onstage." The Wu-Tang were notoriously late arrivals and rarely made it onstage as one unit. So when the delay turned into a longer-than-expected drought of sound, Weisberg went out into the audience for crowd control and had various MCs spouting positive messages to keep the baked audience from erupting. Redman and MC Supernatural practically averted a fifteen-thousand-strong riot.

Backstage was another story. The delay was caused, unsurprisingly, by ODB, who refused to leave his hotel room. "Dirty didn't want to come out . . . Chang was trying to get his people to physically move him from the hotel room," Hennelly said. And so various people tried negotiating with the very stubborn MC. Jarred said via phone that Chang would sue Dirty if he didn't go onstage. And Dirty said to Jarred, "Word?" John "Mook" Gibbons, the very first Wu-Tang manager, went into the room and told Dirty his fans would be disappointed, that there were fifteen thousand people screaming his name. "Mook went to the hotel room and he left the hotel room thinking Dirty would come to the show," Suchan said. But Mook also remembered the first Wu-Tang show in Staten Island, when Dirty was AWOL and some guy walked by in the audience with a radio and Dirt was on air shouting out to the Wu-Tang from the Hot 97 studios. Not showing up was par for the course. It was rumored that ODB was doing drugs, that he was barricaded in his room because he was too fucked up to come out. "I was like, 'C'mon Dirty,' 'cause I knew I was gonna hear from RZA and sure enough when I picked up the phone I hear, 'Yo. Man, if y'all don't get him out of that room, y'all niggers can't say you're part of nothing no more.' And I was like, 'Yo, you can't use that on me no more because if I'm not a part of something because Dirty won't leave the room, then fuck it, so be it.' I said, 'That's a grown-ass man, I'm not gonna carry him and I'm not gonna let y'all carry him. He doesn't want you touching him,' " Buddha Monk said. It was also rumored that while various Wu members and producers of the show called, a couple of guys tried to wrap Dirty in his hotel sheets and carry him out of the room in a makeshift stretcher/straitjacket. Buddha Monk and Jerrome put a stop to that real quick. "His bodyguard kept saying if he doesn't want to come, he's not going to come. Chang and RZA didn't want to take the stage without Dirty," Hennelly said. And finally, with no particular provocation, Dirty relented and left the room. He got onstage and for most of the performance sat on top of a speaker swilling water and looking glum. "He was really retreated, but when he got up onstage, and his songs came on, he was pretty much in the moment," said Cherry, who told me in another interview that "when he was performing, he was himself." He remembered the words to his songs and gave the audience what they wanted—his presence and the totality of the Wu-Tang Clan on one stage for the very last time. "Finally, we got him out of the room and got him to the show," Buddha Monk said. "RZA looked like he was gonna give me the mic to do Dirty's parts and Method ended up giving me the mic instead. Raekwon was sitting in the back laughing cause RZA didn't really want to pass me the mic. Raekwon, I love him and his music, but he was not down with Buddha Monk being a part of Wu. Now, Raekwon knows, he has to give love, because every time Dirty didn't show up, I would do just like I did at that show." He sang the words, rapped the chorus in exactly the way Dirt would have, had he been willing. In keeping with the trajectory of ridiculous bills he'd been on in the past year, Dirty and his crew minus Jarred headed to Ohio after the show for a performance with Insane Clown Posse (ICP) and Vanilla Ice.

Jerrome the Colossus, Buddha Monk, and ODB drove to Nelson Ledges Quarry Park in Garrettsville, Ohio, for the annual Gathering of the Juggalos. (Juggalos are ICP fans—a face-painting motley crew of die-hard underground followers. They are like Deadheads but with rough edges and forties: less patchouli and tie-dye, more tit baring, bong huffing, and Wrestlemania. Juggalos will likely never have an eponymous Ben & Jerry's flavor.) The Gathering in 2004 was a couple of weeks after the Fourth of July, and the Methodist Church in town greeted concertgoers with a sign reading, "Welcome Back Juggalos. God Bless. Yard sale on August 4." Vanilla Ice was set to perform after ODB and before ICP on the third day of the Gathering. "My new following is sort of part of the Juggalo crowd," Robert Van Winkle, aka Vanilla Ice, told me. "They give respect to ODB and they don't give respect to much of anybody. Half of them at the show were giving ODB respect and half of them weren't. The half that weren't respecting him are really hardcore and they don't care that much about anything."

The Gathering, booked and attended by Jarred, was one of ODB's last shows. It was an odd booking, and the crowd knew it. An online photo journal from the event splayed titty shot after titty shot, baby oil wrestling, and what looked like a 90 percent white-male audience, most with wildly dreadded hair. The ladies seemed present solely for nipple baring and stripping. "The Juggalo Gathering, it definitely doesn't have anything to do with the music. When you say Juggalo, these guys are carny kids, they're Irish travelers, they're Gypsies," Van Winkle said. "They embraced what they feel is part of their culture and they didn't *fully* embrace him. I came out onstage with him that day because there definitely were some people throwing stuff at him because he was messing up a couple of his songs." Van Winkle noticed before the set that ODB would act completely normal and then have long spells of hazy silence. "He was like, 'Ice, you know, you gonna come back bigger than shit. I got your back, homie. We gonna do a track together.' He was just a great artist and I got mad respect for him. I got mad respect for Wu-Tang. I'm kind of in with the Wu-Tang." But Van Winkle saw ODB was off. "It took a couple tries to get him onstage. But other times he was completely normal. I don't know what he was doing or what was going on but I can assume . . . but I'm not gonna say anything one way or the other. Sometimes he was super cool and down-to-earth and knew what he was saying and was normal and other times he was not even there . . . I could tell something was going on but I didn't know what," Ice said. So, when ODB performed for the less-than-friendly audience, Ice decided to save him from the chorus of boos and the forty-ounce bombs. "It was during his unnormal moments, he just got lost in his verses. The people that respected him knew that he was in one of his moments. The other people just started throwing stuff at him. I came out and said this is ODB and I did a freestyle with him. I just cooled everybody down for a bit with some verses. Everybody gave respect," Ice said.

From that show in Ohio, Jarred set up some potential collaborations between ODB and Vanilla Ice. The pairing, though strange, seems almost fitting in retrospect. They both needed a boost. Ice had already laid down five tracks and, with ODB's input, he narrowed it down to three. "The tracks that I set up with him were a return to hardcore hip-hop, just mosh pit, banging hip-hop. He really liked 'em," Ice said. "He was feeling a lot of the tracks. We talked on the phone a few times and they were bad ass, and I'm so sad that we never got to do those tracks. He was a legend to me. I like to think that you should just erase the parts of someone you don't understand. You can't fill in the blanks, you just have to respect them for what they've done." The tracks that Ice produced were meant for ODB, ICP, and Vanilla Ice, a rehash of the Gathering lineup. Vanilla Ice recognized the instability and the talent and the broken-down nature of ODB—he'd been to disastrous places and back with his own career. But had ODB fallen so far from grace? What was he doing onstage at a hardcore Juggalo festival? Why was his comeback album going to include three songs with Vanilla Ice, a discredited rapper whose career had peaked in 1990? Where was the Wu-Tang? Where was RZA?

Two years after the historic Rock the Bells reunion and a year and a half after ODB's death, Rock the Bells once again united the Wu-Tang to memorialize ODB in front of as many fans as the NOS Events Center could hold. This time Weisberg staged the concert outdoors in an expansive field. On August 5, 2006, I drove out to San Bernardino with a backstage pass for the show. I arrived and was greeted by M-Eighty, a white MC of Think Differently Music (a label loosely affiliated with Wu-Tang Corp), who handed me a compilation before I could say hello and then told me that he really just wanted to go to law school. After that he asked if I wanted to smoke or if I could possibly call Chang and ask for another ticket, since he already sold his. I thanked him for the compilation, got my armband, and started to wander around the grounds. MC Supernatural was well into the first hour of his effort to get in the *Guinness Book of World Records* for longest freestyle rap. He ended up taking it nine hours and ten minutes later, with some seriously impressive flow of spontaneous rhyme. Though backstage was posh—a nice press area was set up for interviews, with a Hennessy backdrop—it didn't have the bodies, the sweat, the energy from behind the fences. A blanket of smoke hovered low, near the front of the stage, and some militant guards harassed people who stood too long in one place if it was the wrong place to stand.

At the beginning of the day the Visionaries performed, one of them clad in a T-shirt with a dodo bird on it and the label "hip-hop" below the bird, indicating the extinction of real hip-hop. I talked with two tiny girls—Annie and Annette—who were barely twenty but had been show friends since 1996 because "no one else that they knew would go to hip-hop shows." Annie had once seen ODB on Melrose getting a tattoo and together Annie and Annette saw him at the Glendale Galleria arguing with his girlfriend. She ended up storming off and Dirt got a ride with their friend, but before he left Annette took a picture with him on her disposable camera. These girls were underground hip-hop heads in a way I've never been, scheming to get a glimpse backstage at every show, recognizing the promoters, until eventually they were embedded backstage with actual jobs and two-ways, working logistics, directing the crowds.

It was mostly quiet backstage for the beginning of the show. Handfuls of people filtered in and out of the main room. For a while I sat next to Phife from A Tribe Called Quest. He was silent, with a small hand towel draped over his head. Talib Kweli filtered in quickly, answered a handful of questions, and ducked backstage. The college version of MTV, mtvU, was there recording interviews with just barely post-adolescent reporters, who would grimace and high-five every time they finished an "awesome" interview. Phife piped up from under his towel when I asked him about ODB. "I really miss him, despite not knowing him personally. I felt like I knew him personally 'cause I have all his albums. Just seeing him up there doing his lines and watching him get busy. When the lights go on, he knew it was time to perform. What I like most about ODB is that he was never afraid to push the envelope. Either you liked it or you didn't, but he didn't care because he liked it. A lot of people aren't willing to take chances, but that's the essence of a true genius and a true artist and he obviously was willing to take chances. A lot of people think ODB thought about what he was doing, but he didn't. That's what I've noticed about the creative process. It all starts when you're not thinking about it."

I went out to watch Supernatural in the VIP room. He was, in spite of being a gimmick and in spite of breaking a contrived record, seriously able to rhyme about anything for as long as he had breath and people in front of him. This dude was spitting rhymes and was going to be doing it all day long, without a break. I don't think I've ever done anything for nine hours straight, apart from being bored at work or watching basketball on the first two days of March Madness. But he was up there, glorious, words spilling, his dreads bobbing and weaving and dipping down into the audience. It really *was* something super-natural. He had so many words, and a dictionary next to him when he didn't. He'd rap and someone would hand him a picture or a banana and a hat or a key chain and he'd bring the freestyle back to the person in front of him and the object in his hands. It was like personalized rap, custom-tailored to the audience and the moment.

In the crowd I ran into an old friend, an underground MC named Busdriver, known for rapid-fire delivery and an expansive vocabulary and for performing with eclectic indie bands like Islands. We sat in the shade and caught up on small stuff and talked about the show, the Wu, the ODB. "It's a tough crowd for these guys—you've got a lot of entitled MCs. They are veterans, but nobody cares about the nineties anymore." We paused as the crowd went apeshit. "It's tough but whoever is up there right now [he pointed to the main stage], that guy has the crowd," Bus said. And just like that, fifteen thousand people cared about the nineties, or at least one of its catchphrases. Ramping it up to a volatile degree, DJ Kool announced that he was going to eh-huh-huh-huh, clear his throat. As antiquated as that song felt (it's been played at half time at least a million times in every arena, to revive lethargic basketball fans), to hear it performed in that big venue with that big reaction with the staccato punctuation between the words was overwhelming and fun as fuck. The gut-tural articulation of bodily function—it felt so ODB. It was as if each member of the crowd, with arms flying side to side, was doing the James Brown splits and hopping back to their feet, then running through a verse with an imaginary electric slide. Rock the Bells prides itself on activism, lyricism, and quality, but it also brings back the fun of hip-hop, the joy of screaming along with tens of thousands of people, voices and bodies mashed together. Dehydration as a sacrifice for good music, good show, good*ness*. It was the rare moment of live hip-hop living up to its promises of pure joy and acceleration. It was an ODB moment, or at least what he was like in the beginning, when the MC took his insides out onstage for the benefit of those watching and sali-vating and waiting desperately for something to happen. Some-thing earthquaking, mind-numbing, intoxicating, seemingly out of nowhere but performed on a stage between songs and time. He was something unexpected. He once stopped, midsyllable, and urinated onstage. He then hopped offstage, ordered a drink at the bar, got back onstage, and resumed the show. Jaws dropped. Busdriver was right—Wu-Tang had a lot to live up to, but right here, with this tired-out MC and the marathoner in the back area rapping for a title, hip-hop lived.

After DJ Kool's set, I walked back to the press area, where Phife was still sitting alone and shrouded in terry cloth. We got to talking about ODB again, and Phife said, "I remember the day he passed away, I had just landed in L.A. from Oakland for the Tribe Rock the Bells reunion. My friend called me on the phone and said, 'Yo, son, Dirty just passed.' We had a show with Tribe in Anaheim and we could barely do the show. We were just stunned. Me and Q-Tip did 'Brooklyn Zoo' a capella. We performed as if we were Wu-Tang, or we tried to anyway." DJ Kool and Redman bumped away on the main stage while twenty-foot speakers pulsated, leaving rectangular impressions in the Earth. After their set Redman came backstage and announced that his luggage was lost and that he needed clean boxers. He pulled out all the free Hennessy swag and tried to sell it, along with pink and red thongs that were hooked on his shoulders and draped all the way down to his wrists. "Fifteen dollars for the bags, two for twenty!" DJ Kool grabbed my hand and kissed the top of it and walked by. The press area was filling up with performers as they finished their sets. Booze was free-flowing and certain doors were breathing smoke. It had been quiet and air-conditioned all day. Annie and Annette traded stories of backstage infatuation, both of them scurrying to get pics for various blogs or school newspapers. As the night rolled on, the onstage wasn't nearly as entertaining as the company back-stage. It was like *Alice in Wonderland*: each door seemed to offer a different cloud of hallucinogens and endless bottled water. Supernatural was hitting his stride, about to cap the record with as many superstar DJs as the stage could hold, spinning him on his way to the nine hour, ten minute finish line. He hit it and said, "This right here is a God-given gift. I know that not too many cats out there can do what I just did." And with that he continued to rap without pause, to take the record and then some.

Black Star performed. Mos Def denied interview requests, explaining that his lyrics spoke for him. De La Soul, bookended by Black Sheep and Phife, rolled through a set that included

"Saturday" and "Me Myself and I." Immortal Technique chan-
neled his rage into riotous lyricism, telling the audience, "I'd
rather have you here than at a Minuteman or Republican con-
vention." Rumors floated around the back area that a special
guest was taking the stage. Chang was throwing out the name
Lauryn Hill, whispering it into his walkie-talkie. Some reporters
speculated that was a code name, that the show-shy femcee
couldn't possibly have agreed to perform. It was around eight or
nine and the Wu-Tang still hadn't made an appearance onstage
or backstage. Behind the stage facade (the real backstage) a
crowd of people, including Chang, cleared a path for "Lauryn
Hill," who ended up being the real Lauryn Hill. Her jazz band
had already taken over the stage and serenaded their muse front
and center. The crowd was waiting on Wu and was chanting for
their MCs. Her reception was lukewarm. For thirty minutes she
sang tracks to the audience from *The Miseducation of Lauryn Hill*
and ended her set with the Fugees classic "How Many Mics."
The crowd roared in return, won over finally. As she was finish-
ing her surprise spot, a bus with tinted windows pulled in behind
the backstage. And out poured the posses. Cappadonna lunged
toward the press, shaking hands and saying, "Yeah, we late, but
we got a good parking place." It was hard to tell if he was
responsible for the driving; he had been a cabdriver in Baltimore, so it wasn't out of the question.

At least two hundred strong, the Wu-Tang by sheer arrival
turned the backstage from sanctuary to mobbed hysteria. Scantily clad women appeared from seemingly out of nowhere; the
press who had been sedated all day long took their cameras off
tripods to run after shots. Bodyguards filled doorways entirely,
redirecting traffic at will. The most random assortment of entourage filled the room, demanding liquor, smoking cigarettes,
and flinging open doors that were previously off-limits. It was

glorious chaos. Among the Clan was a not-shockingly blotto Steve-O from *Jackass*; Sifu, the Shaolin monk whom RZA trained with; the monk's wife; a monk entourage; and a conspiracy theorist web producer. GZA, quiet and tall, chewed on a licorice branch in the corner, watching the melee he was already used to.

Method Man popped a purple toothbrush in his mouth and held a tube of toothpaste while he answered most of the questions, with RZA standing next to him, like his spine, for support. Meth spoke, RZA nodded, and they posed for pictures and listened to questions. "You know, we can't replace Ol' Dirty Bastard. He's up there onstage with us every time we get up there. We're just trying to keep his memory alive. He's one of the most original and aped MCs and not just on the East Coast," Meth said on loop, telling each camera crew the same story. When he was talking with mtvU, a buoyant Steve-O hugged Meth and drew a long breath from a collegiate glass pipe. He handed the pot pipe, still shrouded in swirling pot smoke, to Meth mid-interview, holding it for him while Meth sucked it in, paused, and then finished his answer in one exhale. And the exhale was the kind of smoke that moved like a dance, the kind of smoke that practiced puffers labor over and seductively release from moist lips like ether. It laced its way from Meth's mouth to the ceiling like a snake rising from a Gypsy's basket. GZA watched in the corner and we talked briefly about ODB after I asked him why he was eating bark. He explained, "It's a licorice stick." I recognized it as the same thing he chewed on throughout the Jim Jarmusch short he had filmed with Bill Murray and RZA. "One of the things I picked up from Dirt was that when he performed, he always sang every verse different. He sounded nothing like the record. He always changed his flow and he was so used to performing, he would just change everything he was doing," GZA said quietly.

Cherry walked by in white jeans and a white top, her hair done up for her stage time. When I had talked to Cherry a few months before the Rock the Bells shows, she had been livid. At first RZA didn't talk with her about the memorial shows. "RZA's family and my family was like this," she said, crossing her fingers. "I gave his family my bed. We were close when we lived on Linden Boulevard. RZA's mother was my niece, but she was like my sister. We were inseparable and when she died I couldn't handle it. I can handle my son's death 'cause I knew in my heart what was gonna happen to him, but for her I had to leave New York to get over the loss." Before Rock the Bells Wu-Tang had performed an eleven-show tour in ODB's honor—they traveled from New Haven to Boston to Philly to Baltimore to D.C. to New York to Florida. Cherry told me a few weeks prior to the first show in New Haven, "Now they're getting back together for a tour in the name of my son, what do you think about that? I'm not going to any of the shows, you know, except if Method Man's performing, I'll go because he really cared about Rusty, and GZA cared about Rusty too. I don't know about the other ones. I never seen RZA at any of Rusty's shows. Once RZA moved to L.A., he was gone." At the show in San Bernardino, I saw her in her clean crisp outfit and assumed that RZA had made it right, because she was smiling and thrilled for the attention and the opportunity to hear fifteen thousand people chanting her son's name. She and her two friends rushed by after she smiled and hugged me hello. There was no reason why she should remember me after the handful of times we met, but she pretended like she did remember, in a genuine way.

I stepped outside for some air onto the patio between the

backstage and the real backstage—the outdoor area was equally packed with spillover from the artist-designated bungalows. Groupies prowled, plastic cups littered the floor, and a few people stood waiting to run into cameras or someone with a tape recorder. I almost walked into Cappadonna, the unofficial tenth Wu, who looked dapper in silky pants and a shirt better suited for Havana. It's never been entirely revealed why RZA won't officially anoint Cappadonna as part of the Wu. It's rumored he went with a label that RZA didn't approve of, that he did time, that he was never going to be a Wu. But regardless he was always folded into the albums, with more verses on *The W* than ODB. Cappadonna also legendarily disappeared for a spell around the millennium—that was during his cabdriving phase. When I talked with him, it was like he was speaking in tongues, rhyming through his relationship with Dirt and explaining things to me in couplets and alliterative stream of consciousness. "The truth is the proof and the proof is all about coming together to perform as one body. As Christ, Allah, leka leka alm. ODB is with us, man, we don't mourn ODB. We celebrate and get things in place for the fact that we all a part of each other, including him, in the fact that we ate alike, be alike, and see alike. You know he ain't here in the physical but he will always be here in the mental and in the spiritual," Cappadonna said with his eyes half-closed. He opened them, looked at me, and explained that he met ODB in 1977. "I'm older than sun, moon, and stars. Did the dark come out of the light?" he asked. I nodded yes. "Negative. The light came out of the dark when God said, Let there be light, know what I'm sayin'? And we reflecting that same light and it's the same light that ODB projected to the people." I wasn't going to argue the possibility of nothingness, or what the absence of light and dark looks like; this was Cappadonna and we were bonding over the metaphysical and the hope that ODB's light touched us while he was alive and was touching us while we were standing in the artificial light of remembrance. "ODB was very outspoken and fast-forward and he wasn't afraid to step out and stand up for what he believed in. He was the one who got on the Arsenio show and told the world that the black man is God. How you like that? ODB, Baby Jesus, Unique Ason." I liked the way that Cappadonna remembered without thinking, that he was feeling through the times he had with Dirt and just sharing. "You know the thing I like best about ODB was that when I first met him, he hit me with a rhyme. He said, 'I'm the A-S the O-N the U-N,' what did he say? I'm trying to get in his voice."

At this point Cap started to actually rhyme and rap toward me in the way that ODB sounded, an almost perfect imitation of his growl. "The A-S, the O-N, the U-N, the I-Q, the U-E / yo you have nothing on me, I'm the maker, the owner, the cream of all things / rhyming is a small thing that make ladies scream, what's that shoutin' all aboutin'?" It was like he was channeling Dirt and I could picture him telling this same story driving in West Baltimore with a thick layer of glass between him and his fare. "He walked up to me with that verse and ever since then, he's been my boy. And we did a song together called 'Maria.' It's a real seductive rhyme. We were rhyming about trashy women who are subject to various conditions of body movements." I asked what body movements they were subject to and he carried on with his stories, either not hearing or too attached to what he wanted to say next. "ODB, we used to battle rhymes together, you know like I said I'll miss the guy but he'll always have a place in my heart. I feel like right now I've got to step up even more, 'cause I'm the last member and you know what they say, the last shall be first. Let ODB live through me and let me reflect that energy. We'll keep doing what we doing on a positive scale."

Cappadonna kind of bowed his head and thanked me for the chat; he seemed happy to talk to someone while the cameras crowded Meth and RZA. "ODB put everything out there, no secrets, he put everything out there for people to learn. It's good, it's bad, it's ugly, but we have to mourn his death and learn from his life."

As Cappadonna walked away, someone tapped my shoulder to bum a cigarette in a voice that sounded like sandpaper and truck exhaust and chewing tobacco rolled into audio. I turned to explain I don't smoke and Steve-O, eyes so glossy they made water look dry, said thanks and walked back to a corner where another girl handed him a smoke. I followed him, to try to find out what he was doing here as part of the Wu-Tang posse. I have heard Steve-O described as the white ODB and as far as public figures go, they do overlap. In some ways I think *Jackass* borrows a lot from ODB, in their partying and purposeful public humiliation and blatant, unapologetic sexuality and their self-flagellation and their wild abandon and their pure boldness. If the cashing of his welfare check on TV had included scrotum stapling and midgets, it could have been a segment on *Jackass*—*Ghetto Jackass* maybe. I think the link between Steve-O and ODB is blatant disregard for decorum and the need for an audience. "I was in the L.A. Correctional Facility and the correctional officer told me I was in the same cell that ODB stayed in. So, I figured ODB is kind of like my cell mate. They told me I was in his cell, and they said I was on Robert Downey Jr.'s block also," Steve-O said. He then proceeded to outline exactly why he was really there. He had a tribute planned and he was here to get onstage and remember ODB the only way he knew how. "I'm gonna get butt-dirty-ass naked, stick my balls and my dick behind my leg, and do a perfect standing backflip. Meth told me not to do it, but I thought Dirty would tell me *to* do it. I'd rather make people giggle than make people fight. So I don't care if I make an ass of myself."

Steve-O has a booming voice, one that echoes through the hills and the plains from miles away. I had already heard his plan, several times, about getting naked, making a mangina, and flipping backward. He'd explained it to half a dozen news outlets with every Wu-Tang member in earshot. I asked Steve-O if he'd met ODB at any point, aside from his cell mate–soul mate connection. "There was this rave in Manhattan on July 2, 2004," he started. I made a mental note that maybe Steve-O just acts fucked up—I was surprised he could name an exact date. "And I was opening for ODB. I was so excited to perform the same night that I went backstage to talk to him and he was already performing and I thought, ohmygod, Ol' Dirty's opening for me and I saw him onstage and he was just standing there with his pants down and his dick was out." He paused and said, "I'm telling you, he's uncircumcised. I have three photos from that night—one with his pants down, one of him holding a PCP pipe, and one of him completely passed out on the stage still holding the PCP pipe." ODB naked onstage is no shock. ODB with a pipe is no shock either.

But somehow the combination and Steve-O's retelling of the night made me uneasy and made me wish that Steve-O was remembering wrong or embellishing, as he is known to do.

Lauryn Hill's set wound down and though the crowd was satiated, the audience lifted their W's in the sky like a call for help. They chanted "Wu-Tang," they chanted "O-D-B," they waved their interlocked thumbs from side to side with erect fingers beckoning. Chang called for everyone backstage with a Wu bracelet to raise it in the air; hundreds of fists shot up and the nine posses plus family plus monks plus Steve-O plus Zack de la Rocha from Rage Against the Machine plus various performers who had already graced the stage were herded together and led from the fake backstage to the main backstage, where almost all of them ended up on the stage. The crowd roared with gratitude as the Wu-Tang flag unfurled and the beats got dirty and heavy and thick.

Method Man called the show a "Dirty-versary," dedicating it to the late Wu soldier, the Ol' Dirty Bastard. The fans waved and nodded to every beat and verse, as Black Eyed Peas' Will.i.am and de la Rocha joined in with the Wu-bangers. RZA asked the audience to chant ODB's name for his mom, Cherry, who nodded in gratitude. She looked pleased, smiling a sad smile and nodding in recognition of the moment—the loud peace that her son deserved, the chanting that made him human when he was really just an urn full of ashes.

Midway through the third song, Steve-O was somehow given a mic. He was onstage and shirtless and pacing, amping himself up. He revved the audience with more chanting, more cat-calling, more ODB appreciation, and he clearly still had the mangina backflip on his mind. As he was leading into his routine he said, "I'm here, as practically Dirty's cell mate, so I'm gonna Dirty it up a little more, not because Meth said so but because I think Ol' Dirty Bastard might like this." He ranted, trying to prep the crowd for his tribute. He was surrounded by Wu and affiliates and family who crowded around him in a halfmoon, silent save for the occasional *Steve-O* chant, which kind of missed the point. He stripped to his boxers, then ripped them off too so that it was just Steve-O, center stage, in his birthday suit. The MCs who previously surrounded him backed the fuck off. It must have been the gangly sight of Steve-O's bare-ass skinny naked self. He bounded around stage like a Labrador chasing a ball, penis flapping with every movement. He didn't seem embarrassed but he definitely was not comfortable. He thrust his pelvis in and out, bouncing his penis against his belly and thighs until he trapped it between his legs. And with his penis securely tucked in, Steve-O actually did a motherfucking backflip in ODB's honor while clenching a mangina.

Though odd, his dedication was kind of perfect in its meta nature. A four-story-tall banner of ODB's face hung in the back of the stage, ODB's giant wide eyes watching naked Steve-O. He didn't honor ODB with deep words and sorrow or pensive speeches or even sadness or a song; he honored him with action and absurdity. People do strange things in mourning. Raekwon clearly hadn't heard Steve-O backstage describing exactly what he was going to do (which seemed impossible to me, considering how many times Steve-O said it and how loud his voice is) and was outraged by the bizarre antic. But it's Steve-O, so you have to wonder what Raekwon was expecting. Don't let him onstage if you aren't prepared for the tasteless. Rae shouted, "This kid is a fucking crackhead or something, man." Someone else onstage said, "This kid's on heroin." But everyone laughed and hugged Steve-O as he pulled up his drawers. A couple of songs later an irate Rae brought Steve-O back onstage and demanded an apology, for ODB's fans, for his mother who was standing right there, next to this naked white man with odd tattoos crowding his pale skin. He demanded an apology or he was going to hurt Steve-O. It got ugly, mostly because his disapproval, while it made sense, was out of context. The audience had coaxed Steve-O into the act, and he'd been talking about his mangina backflip all day. So when Rae stormed off and the Wu hit "Triumph," all eight verses except for Raekwon's, the crowd filled in for the absent MC. It's not a Wu show unless someone's feelings get hurt.

They finished the night as a Clan, celebrating a missing

spirit, and ODB's absence was palpable, especially when the piano notes from "Shimmy Shimmy Ya" busted out and fifteen thousand lighters and cell phones dotted the landscape. Meth, in his magic way, leapt offstage, into the audience, freelancing with the crowd, shaking hands, giving himself over in a religious sense. Watching Meth's body while he's performing is like an exorcism; he opens his arms wide and collapses with each verse breathing in and out heavily and methodically. He is the performer, he is the ham, he is the one that you watch with ODB gone.

I drove up the next day to Oakland to catch the second Rock the Bells show. RZA never showed up; the crowd was tamed in stadium seating and the guest performer was Dave Chappelle, who darted onstage, froze, and then left as quickly as he came. During Mos Def's set, Mos sampled Gladys Knight and the Pips, referencing the "Old School" with the same song sampled on Wu-Tang's "Can It Be All So Simple." It had been a year and a half since ODB's death, and though these shows were set up to remember him, it didn't seem like anyone was willing to remember *all* of him—his loneliness, his drug problems, his failings as a father, his damaged body and mind. Part of the Gladys Knight song that Mos didn't sample goes: "Memories may be beautiful and yet / What's too painful to remember / We simply choose to forget / So it's the laughter we'll remember." It seems, that for our heroes, and ODB is one, they deserve to be remembered as a whole. They deserve to be honored by learning from their mistakes, by understanding what drove them, by not just emulating the good but choosing not to embrace the bad. With ODB, it seems so easy to graze past the tragic and the unfortunate and the sordid details that were made too public. Meth, once again, got out of his skin and traveled from the stage to the audience on the grass, rousing fans into ecstatic screams. As he passed, waves of the audience stood as tall as they could with their lighters up, saluting ODB and the Wu offspring now center stage. GZA's, ODB's, and Mastakilla's sons—L'il Masta Killa, L'il Osirus, and L'il Genius—bore out the ODB dream: that Wu-Tang is for the children. Indeed.

19.

THE LAST DAYS OF DIRTY, 2004

It's only one capable, breaks the unbreakable, / Melodies unmakable, pattern unescapable . . . / A matter of life and death, just like an Etch A Sketch, / Shake 'til you're clear, make it disappear, make the next
—Rakim

After locking himself backstage on more than one occasion, and after rampant speculation that his weight loss had little to do with diet, ODB seemed to be back in the good graces of chaos. Only this time he didn't spout charming phrases like "Sperm donor!" or "President Bush is trying to kill me." He was quiet and reserved, and he had moved back into his mama's house, a neighborhood away from the now-empty bachelor pad in Kensington. Frank, Cherry's new husband (they'd been married while VH1 was filming *ODB on Parole*), moved out because Dirt was afraid of him. Maybe not afraid, but Dirty thought Frank was a spy—a CIA agent plotting against his life, working for the government. Cherry Jones told me, "The things he was seeing were real to him. I couldn't see them. I just kept saying, 'Mommy's here.' He never slept. He always looked haggard like he'd been on a binge for two or three days."

When Dirt got back from Ohio, Jarred realized Dirt had relapsed, so he tried to isolate him. Weisfeld wanted to flush out the source that was feeding ODB drugs. "He was stuck in a house where he had no freedom. Jarred was keeping everybody away from him. Jarred thought the people around him were influencing his drug use. He didn't know who to trust or who to pinpoint in terms of the drug use," Buddha Monk said. But ODB, even in a staggering state of despair, could find his way to a dealer. Jarred kept everyone away and thought that would sort it out. But Dirty was getting drugs from any dealer he could. "Dirty was a mastermind. Everybody thought he was crazy but if he wanted to get something, he knew where, if he wanted to get somewhere, he knew how, if he wanted to go to the party, he knew where it was at. Jarred didn't know Dirty like his family knew Dirty," Buddha Monk said. And so, in the solitary confinement of his mother's brownstone and in defiance of Jarred's attempts to keep his addiction at bay, ODB found solace in crack, the one thing other than center stage that satiated him.

Buddha Monk, to this day, does not think that ODB's drug use was out of control. "In our lessons, it tells us, don't let things overtake you. If you're gonna do something, analyze if it was good for you. In my mind, Dirty taking drugs, it wasn't out of control, at least in my mind, it was just his way of freeing himself from the stress he experienced." But crack's not exactly a user-friendly drug. Buddha, the voice behind Dirt when Dirt's mouth was too numb to move, sat silently believing that Dirt could outrun the drugs, the paranoia, the decimated organs on the inside of a body that could tolerate no more. "There were times when I was sitting in the room and he was doing his thing and I said,

'Dirty, how long are we gonna be doing this?' and he'd say, 'We'll be doing this shit till we're seventy years old. We'll never stop rapping.' He could be high as hell and someone would ask him what's today's mathematics and he would know."

And so Buddha Monk would try to stave off ODB's complete destruction with small sacrifices. "There were nights that I got high because there were so many drugs in front of him that if I didn't do some, he would die. He liked cocaine, but really, he smoked crack. I'd have to hide drugs from him. He never meant to hurt anybody. But Dirty did what the fuck he wanted to do and that was just it."

And so, in his final days, ODB tried like hell to just be ODB, but he was tired of being ODB. "When Dirty wasn't being Dirty, Buddha was being Dirty. When he first came home, I did most of the shows. For me, my job was to not let Dirty fail at being Dirty. The fame recognition wasn't there for me. I didn't cry about it. Everybody knew who Buddha Monk was and that was enough for me. I needed to keep Ol' Dirty Bastard, ODB, even if he wanted to stray to the left I had to bring him back to the right," Buddha Monk said. But Buddha Monk is only one person and it would have taken several platoons to calm the one-man-army Ason. Although he devoted his life and love to Dirt, Buddha couldn't keep up. "After a while, I got tired. The last seven or eight shows we did, I got real tired and I didn't want to go on the road and I found out right around then that I developed congestive heart failure from all the buildup of stress and all that. I lost like five or six relationships for him," Buddha Monk said.

Buddha was so close to ODB, Cherry thought of him as a son, and Buddha Monk called her Mommy. He loved Dirt like a brother, like kin. So when Dirty asked him to stay home for a few shows, that he was switching up the crew and taking Popa

Chief instead, Buddha Monk took it as a sign. "He didn't talk to me right before he passed away, but I felt something was wrong. There were a couple shows he didn't want me to go on. I think he knew something was up and he kind of saved me from the blame. I feel like if I had been there, people would have looked at me and thought, 'Oh, Buddha how could you let that happen' or whatever. And I think he was saving me from that."

The last time ODB got onstage, he fell off. He'd been nursing a lame leg from a prison fight at Riker's for years and after only a few garbled renditions of his classics, ODB disappeared from the stage, and popped back up with an aggravated leg injury. He was in Fort Collins, Colorado, at the Aggie Theatre, where a sold-out crowd sat stunned but not surprised at the wreck on display. A camera caught him, crack pipe at his lips, a jeweled haze of smoky coke lifting him out of his misery. The lens also caught him rambling, confused, disoriented. He'd performed like this for the past year or so. This wasn't the Dirt who, in his prime, dug in and ripped verses from his bowels, vomiting his demons in a trancelike state of Santeria witchery.

No, this Dirt smoked onstage, fell off the stage, and for the few minutes he graced the stage, couldn't throw a rhyme together to save his life, a life that was desperately in need of saving. He limped in front of sound monitors, shouting at the walls, and gave every ticket-buying member of the audience a story. The sound engineer described the night as surreal. "He was so messed up. The crowd was going nuts and we just wanted to get through the night. ODB kept stalling. He ended up talking and most of what he said didn't make sense." At that point bookers were lucky if he showed up at all. He missed a show in Connecticut and the *Hartford Courant* wrote: "Booking Ol' Dirty Bastard is risky, in the way that playing Russian roulette with five bullets is risky." The sound engineer continued, "He didn't rap

at all. He just kept saying, 'Y'all don't know me. I'm crazy.' "
ODB asked that the room be cleared. He instructed the security
guards to empty the house. They didn't. Restless and rowdy, the
front row started launching full beer cans at the already injured
headliner. He talked for forty-five minutes. Popa Chief and DJ 2
Evil tried to goose a performance out of him. ODB was scheduled to meet Wu-Tang in New Jersey the following night for a
reunion show. "He felt bad because he tried so hard to get to the
plane to get to the show in Jersey but he missed it, and from
there it was downhill. No one knew what was going to happen,"
Buddha Monk said.

ODB missed his flight, and flew in the next day from Denver,
landing at JFK about the same time that Method Man was
announcing to ten thousand fans packed tightly into the Conti-
nental Arena, "There's no one bigger than the Wu-Tang Clan
and when you see Ol' Dirty Bastard, tell him that." ODB took a
car to his sister's house in Brooklyn, where he was staying. His
mom needed a break and Frank wanted to come home, so Dirt's
sister picked up the slack and took care of him. After the show in
Jersey, RZA took a car to Brooklyn to check in on Dirt and
ended up taking him up to the 36 Chambers Studio, Wu head-
quarters, a luxury loft on Thirty-fourth Street and Tenth Avenue
in a brick building with ivy crawling toward the sky. "When
RZA went and got him to go to the studio, they had to carry
him to the limo," Buddha Monk said, partially because of his leg
injury and partially because his body was destroyed, ravaged by
decades of abuse.

This last day at 36 Chambers Studio, when police found his
body, stalled from heart failure after cerebral hemorrhaging—
this last day was predicted. Before ODB left for his last short
tour, he stayed at his mom's house on Fourth Street. That night,
it was Rusty and his doting mom cuddled in a corner of an

upstairs bedroom. "I rubbed his feet and held his head because he had trouble sleeping," she told me. "Rusty said, 'This is the last time you're gonna see me, you're never gonna see me again.' He was going to Mexico or anywhere far from here. He said again, 'Mommy, this is the last time you're going to see me.' And I never saw him again and I got that call that he was dead." His mom wasn't the only one who was hearing Rusty's premonitions. ODB called RZA and told him. He was gonna die. "He had a couple of conversations with RZA and a couple other people," GZA said of ODB's last days. "He just felt like he wasn't gonna be around that long anyway. He thought he was gonna run into something; either it was gonna be a wake-up call or it was gonna be a wrap. That's what it was gonna come to." But ODB knew what he was doing. It wasn't about starting again, as much as everyone around him wanted to believe that. "If he would have made it known that he had swallowed something, that would have been something. It was in the autopsy report that he swallowed a bag and that it opened up," GZA said. But an addict doesn't swallow an entire bag without knowing what would happen next. On November 13, 2004, ODB was mute. RZA stayed at the studio with him, along with some members of the Brooklyn Zu who had watched him disintegrate in Fort Collins the night before. His fifteen-year-old son Barson was at the studio recording. According to Buddha Monk, "He was laying on the floor sleeping. He stayed there overnight; some of the Zu was with him but they left. RZA sent them home. They said he woke up and had a bowl of cereal and knowing Dirty, it was cereal that had a lot of sugar in it. 12 O'Clock said they was leaving and he lifted his head up and said OK like everything was cool, and he went to sleep and three hours later he was dead."

Paramedics found him curled up in the fetal position on the floor. Barson and ODB's two daughters Teniqua and Shaquita had been sent home in a limo hours before, around the same time the Zu members were dismissed. Bar-son told the *Daily News* later that his father "had been acting anxious and unsteady—at one point scratching his head and panting so heavily that he removed his shirt and asked for cold water. I already knew something was going to happen. He was shaky and mad paranoid." Barson called Icelene and said, "Daddy passed away." Icelene made her way to the studio. "People were trying to revive him and we thought he was just in a coma because I thought nothing was gonna take him out. I just couldn't believe it. He was just lying flat on the ground."

A photographer for the *New York Post* was sent to shoot whatever vigil emerged. No candles were lit, no flowers placed; Ghostface and GZA talked with the handful of fans who materialized. "I arrived thirty minutes after he died," GZA said. "It's crazy because everything was moving so fast but at the same time it was moving so slow. You see people moving around. It was like a bugged-out moment in a crazy film. The police were asking questions and we didn't know what he took." The *New York Post* later reported that ODB swallowed a bag of cocaine. Jarred denied any drug use, saying Dirty was clean and sober up until the last minute. The New York medical examiner's office simply stated, "Accidental overdose from a lethal combination of Tramadol and cocaine." The Tramadol was a painkiller prescribed to ease the discomfort of his leg injury—it was the one drug that was approved by his parole officer. On November 13, two days shy of his thirty-sixth birthday, Russell Jones finally achieved the stillness of mind he'd been looking for his entire life. It was the suicide that was never talked about. Death silenced a voice that for ten years previously had been louder than sound. To Cherry, Dirty died when he went to prison. To Buddha Monk, Dirty died when he made it be known in an interview that it was time for another Ol' Dirty Bastard. To most of the Wu, Dirty never died; he lives in song and spirit and in the life they live for him. Cherry said: "How was I supposed to cry when I saw him for the first time in his life at peace? I saw him sleeping and he could never sleep. That's why he did so much drugs. The paranoia and the demons were keeping him up. But now, he could . . . And he had a smile on his face. And all I did was put him in my arms and hug him."

20.

STATE OF THE WUNION, 2006

You got to see his stage performance. It's something to behold.
He uplift the whole Clan at times, you know?
—Method Man

I'm not sure if there's a right way to mourn or to honor who ODB was, who he is in spirit. Shortly after his death, Wu-Tang announced six shows on the East Coast to remember him. I went to the first one in New Haven, at Toad's Place, the site of Dirt's DVD filming. On the train, pixilated bare winter branches breeze by. There's a Suit seated across the aisle, his blazer across his lap and his tie draped half-in, half-out of a beaten-down leather briefcase. He's got two Michelob Light plastic wide-mouthed bottles lined up next to his feet. I feel like I have to keep it a secret that I'm going to the Wu-Tang show. Everyone around me is commuting to wives and husbands and children and homes in Darien. As I was leaving the office, I told a coworker what I was doing and he said, "I can't think of anything sadder than going to a Wu-Tang Clan show, *alone*, in New Haven."

The Suit shuffles papers and greets people by name. He knows everyone in this car and several in the next one. Twisting his fists in the air miming a motorcycle ride, "Dave, didja get out this weekend?" says The Suit.

"Yeah, perfect weather for a ride," Dave answers.

"I wanted to get out. My brother-in-law just got a seventy-nine Honda, and he already has the Harley." The Suit seems particularly excited by the idea of getting his leathers on.

I can see him from the reflection of the window gesticulating and draining one of his Michelob Lights. I'm not sure what to expect in the audience tonight. Toad's Place is practically on Yale's campus and the audience will likely be the people who bought the "R.I.P.O.D.B." T-shirts the day after he died. I'd put a hundred bucks on the possibility that someone will be hawking freshly silk-screened T's.

At the New Haven train station, there are arrows and signs for shuttles to Foxwoods and I stop and think about what ODB would do. He would probably skip his memorial tour and jump on a bus, eat some sushi, throw some money away, and call it a night. I consider this option, pause, and turn toward the cab line.

A cabdriver, who is quite possibly an actor playing a cabdriver, tells me about the time he met Babe Ruth, Ty Cobb, and Ted Williams and curses himself for not having a pen and paper to get the now-requisite signature. He has rosy red cheeks, like he keeps a flask under the passenger seat, and his shtick feels rehearsed, removed, a little too cute. I'm convinced this cabdriver is driving in circles, which is my fear when I get into any cab in a strange city. He drops me at the Duncan Hotel after telling me about a passenger with an out-of-control parrot that clawed at his face, forcing him to establish a no-parrot rule. There's no way that this guy is a cabdriver.

The line outside Toad's Place is hundreds deep. It's below freezing and the crafty Wu fans have left jackets, scarves, and any other semblance of warm layers in the car so they won't have to worry about them later. If the scalpers and T-shirt vendors were smart they would be selling those hot packs that skiers put in their gloves and boots. The line is not moving. At all. The bouncers are frisking each person individually, and the crowd issues a violent collective shake. The fratty boys next to me start talking about how they were at the Jersey show the night ODB didn't show up and then later died. They say it with an air of historical righteousness—as if ODB never would have died had the parallel plan occurred. Had he not missed his plane, he wouldn't have gone to the studio and he wouldn't have swallowed that bag.

There's some frisky talk about whether or not *all* of Wu-Tang will represent. Two girls skip the fifty or so people behind me and sidle up. There aren't that many women around. Sherry, hunched over from the weight of gold nameplates, starts talking about how she borrowed her brother's car to get here from New Britain, Connecticut. We talk about speeding tickets and automatic versus manual transmission. She looks anywhere from sixteen to thirty-four, depending on how hard you interpret the valleys beneath her cheekbones. She talks a lot about the eighty bucks she shelled out just for tickets to wait in a freezing line to see a show that might not even happen. Her friend, coiffed and freshly permed, wearing a jean jacket shrug, keeps looking at the front of the line, like she doesn't have the time or inclination to wait.

Sherry tells her to go do her thing if she wants to check out the front and waits with me a few hundred yards from anywhere warm. I don't know how but we start talking about Sherry's husband, whom she married three years into his prison sentence just to show him she was serious and not fooling around. I keep trying to guess her age and I have no idea. She's hardened in a way that a prison wife has to be. We talk about the trouble with in-laws, and she describes her ceremony as brief. Marrying someone in jail has some serious advantages. The anxiety of dating and meeting and getting to know a person is automatically restricted by time, letters, and steel bars. You have to be committed to forgive the glass that's in between and to wait on call for conjugal visits in a dusty trailer.

There aren't many scalpers, but plenty of mix CDs, two for five dollars, are being hawked. Some are just instrumentals and some are straight copies of Wu-Tang albums and others are reinterpretations. The kid in front of me buys two and gives one to his girlfriend. He's white, looks fifteen, and has thin cornrows with unbraided sideburn fluff curling around his cheekbones. He looks like Brendan Sexton III. His girlfriend is black and he keeps stroking her ass and sweetly slobbering all over her face. We are forty-five minutes into the line and still nowhere near the front. We've bonded over hypothermia. Sherry followed her permed, shrug-wearing friend to the front. The couple behind me now is a big black woman and her tracksuit-wearing husband. He's in matching red velour and keeps talking about the hoodie he should have put on underneath and how bad he feels for the shorty in a tank top. ("Yo, frostbite ain't sexy.")

He smokes Newport menthols, which he gives to one person and sells to another. His wife has a flask between her breasts where she knows they won't frisk her and where she's got some storage space. She repeats loudly, "I'm about to turn into a black Popsicle," while her husband measures the distance to the door in football field lengths. "We're one down from the do'!" he says as we get closer. Once through the pat down, they rush to the bar for mixers.

Inside Toad's, it feels like a sauna, with pot burning instead of coal. It feels like paradise, that we are special, special people allowed indoors. There is rolling, there are jeweled blunts littering the dark space like Lite-Brites, and the secondhand fumes have me wishing that the glowing tips of each joint would combine into a Day-Glo W in the rafters. I note the fire exits; they are far from where I am and I'm pretty sure Toad's Place is already past capacity, clocking the crowd at somewhere north of six hundred.

The first act, an ethnic Limp Bizkit, is booed off the stage. He tries not to take offense, but he's wearing a do-rag and a porkpie hat, a tough combo to pull off in any crowd, let alone a frostbitten, ravenous one. The audience wants Wu and only Wu. Fists interlock to form W's along the horizon of the crowd. Chanting won't get it done. There are still naysayers claiming one if not several members won't show. It's a reasonable fear. Method Man, according to a new friend, is least likely to show. They are making us wait and wait. Nas is on the sound system in between. The girl behind me bitches about how she didn't pay forty dollars to go to a club to hear someone spin some songs she can listen to in her car.

A fog machine rages as the crowd's own fog continues to generate dense smoke. I feel like I might pass out if the show doesn't start very soon. I feel old. I think fondly about the bus to Foxwoods, where I could be enjoying free Coronas and losing money, one quarter at a time, to the digital slot machines. Somehow, that fantasy seems like a more authentic way to honor ODB. He wouldn't sit here and wait.

And then the club goes black. And I don't feel like ODB

would have skipped out. He could be here in the rafters, who knows. I scramble to see and am swept into a sea of limbs. One by one the lesser Wus appear, the little dude next to me announcing each name as they swagger onstage. *Inspectah Deck . . . Masta Killa . . . U-God.* They breathe out some solo joints; the audience does the same in tandem.

Left and right hands form the Wu in the sky, pulsating with the shaggy-ass sound system. Eight MCs make for a powerful presence and as they knock shoulders and grind aimlessly, the Wu-Tang Clan trip over one another lyrically, asthmatically, spitting rhymes and waging riots in the crowd below.

For the most part the audience leans in, doxologizing the gods onstage, chanting lyrics for them, tumbling to be near. Method Man stage-dives and GZA curtails the frenzy into a liquid silence that drips to a slow-building beat. He sermonizes and speaks to glories of Dirt Dawg. This is what I was waiting to hear. People tolerate it for maybe a second and start muttering, "Man, this is some ghetto-ass shit." GZA is practically in the fetal position, curled around his mic, talking of character and truth and that Ol' Dirty would want this to be a celebration. It's true, he would, but I don't think he lived his life imagining his death and certainly not the tour that would mark it.

GZA nails ODB with a kind of tribal ferocity. The beat is simple: eastern, the sound of a sitar winding on loop like a death march. His eulogy, a song named for the first incarnation of Wu, "All In Together Now," is simply a character portrait.

ODB was known for a few things and most of them circle back to crazy. There was a staggering segment on *Yo! MTV Raps* in which he's seemingly drunk or in a daze, reciting long blocks of nonsense that had to be truncated by Ed Lover or whoever else was hosting. He'd recite circuitous diatribes, bobbing in and out of the camera frame, tangent after tangent, spinning on something. And even after Ed would intercept with a pointed question—just to stop Dirt from talking—ODB would roll back his eyes, open his lids wide, and incredulously explain that he had no idea what he was saying. Laugh it off. And cut to commercial.

And though the newly reformed Wu are a powerful presence, something is missing. ODB was a man who was willing to be lost in his own world and share the journey blow for blow as it was happening—with words, with breathy sound, with body movement. He took you where he went, the whole way, warts and all. GZA precluded his eulogy by saying that this was a celebration, that ODB would want a celebration. Maybe ODB celebrated a little too much, maybe he was too celebrated in his lifetime, or maybe he was celebrated for the wrong things, but it's clear that he was a celebrity, capital C.

GZA concluded the night with his tribute, including this stanza:

From downstate, psychiatric
Who tried to put a code on his brain until he cracked it
Now the media wanna view him like they knew him
And his head nurse wanna sue him 'cause she blew him

GZA told me later, "When I perform that song, that's really him speaking through me. That's what he went through. That was what I saw. I didn't have to ask him every day what he saw, what he went through. I just had a vision of him."

21.

THE AFTERLIFE PARTY, 2004

Hey, Dirty, baby I got your money.
—ODB

Five days after ODB overdosed, Icelene Jones, who had been on
the periphery save for alimony demands the last six years of
ODB's life, instructed her lawyer Darryl Nicholas to inform
ODB's lawyer Mark Frey to freeze the estate's funds; she was
planning to challenge Cherry Jones's power of attorney. ODB
did not leave a will— he left thirteen children from four mothers,
and possibly more. Icelene was doing her part to keep the estate
in her immediate family, and by law, with no will, the estate is
rightfully hers. Even the funeral was a duel—Cherry made
arrangements and Icelene, struggling for control, made alternate arrangements. "She left the pictures of the other kids out of
the funeral," Cherry said. "She offended the other children. It
was evil. I don't even want Rusty's money. Anything Rusty got, I
told her, it's yours. She keeps telling the news media that we

were fighting over money and he didn't even have any money, not a penny. I never knew he had an estate."

The bickering over cash and control started before ODB was even laid to rest. "When he died, I felt like I was being attacked, so I moved to Georgia. Brooklyn just didn't make sense without him," Icelene said.

The service, held at the Brooklyn Christian Cultural Center for an audience of three thousand friends, family, and fans, included two commemorative programs—one said Russell Jones was the father of three, the other said seven; neither was accurate. ODB's music videos flashed on a big screen over the altar and a live band played his hits. In sudden bursts perforating the thick air around ODB's coffin, mourners stood up to sing along with verses that defined his career. His words, at least, lived on. He lay, unencumbered by his life's burden, in a white suit, clean and crisp and tailored to his withered limbs.

Before the funeral, Cherry released a statement to the press: "To the public he was known as Ol' Dirty Bastard but to me he was known as Rusty. The kindest, most generous soul on Earth. Russell was more than a rapper, he was a loving father, brother, uncle and most of all son." Mariah Carey showed up to pay respects in black couture and sunglasses; she left shortly after, bowing her head in front of Dirt's body and examining the collage of ODB propped on display tripods. "With our culture, people don't understand hell is what a man has to go through to really get right in his life," Popa Wu told an MTV reporter. "It's trials and tribulations you must go through. He did his. Everybody in this world has got some type of bullshit with them. I been around the world three times with [the Wu-Tang Clan]. Everybody in the world loved that man. That man is a legend, an icon. He used to leave his car parked at a light, jump out, and give all the kids money. Police used to be like, 'Dirty, you have to move your car.' He wouldn't move his car until he gave every-body money. He showed people love. He was so real."

ODB's death was equally real. As Jones lay silent for the first time, RZA eulogized his cousin, remembering their teenage years together and comparing his cousin as Ason Unique (radi-ant, beautiful, angelic, powerful) to his stage-born alter ego ODB (wild, unpredictable). Remorseful, RZA felt responsible for his cousin's decline. He admitted a distance between the two that was palpable. As Dirty inched closer to the end, he told RZA, "I'm dying." RZA said he thought Dirty was high. He warned the congregation that we all need to keep love in our hearts and never neglect family. Shaquita, ODB's daughter by Icelene, read a poem she'd written: "My heart is thrashing, my soul is break-ing, my father is freed, and now he has awakened." Obituaries highlighted his checkered life—the arrests, the Grammys, the welfare check—occasionally mentioning his music, his inescap-able flow.

Shortly after the funeral, Icelene, having won power of attor-ney and control of Dirt's estate, had ODB cremated. And before he became an urn full of ashes, Icelene had DNA samples taken just in case unknown offspring appeared. After the court deci-sion, Cherry—as she described it—ran Icelene out of town with her three kids in tow to Norcross, Georgia. "When Roc-A-Fella signed him, she thought all the money they gave him was for her to have and when there was no money, she turned on me," Cherry said, visibly disturbed just at the mere mention of ODB's wife. "And I haven't heard or seen from her since." In the mean-time Icelene appeared with her kids on Wendy Williams's Hot 97 radio program. (Williams later earned a place on the Wu enemy list by outing Method Man's wife as a cancer patient.) "Her kids went on the radio and said that they were gonna kill me, gonna stomp my brains out. I haven't heard anything from them but I have so many other grandchildren, I don't worry about it. It's just over money. I worked all my life. I worked when Rusty was famous and that's what he admired about his mom." Cherry's eyes narrowed and she said, "When they got on the radio and threatened my life, Icelene moved out of Brooklyn because she knew it wasn't right. I was born and raised in Brooklyn and she knew that going on the radio like that was the wrong move for her, so she got out."

Buddha Monk, who had known Icelene since she was a teenager named Shaquita, couldn't understand the baby-mama drama either. "As fast as he got money, he gave money. He was writing checks to the baby mamas for $250,000; that's why I don't understand why Shaquita is acting like this." Death has a funny way of bringing out the worst in people and Ol' Dirty Bastard's family was no different. "He loved Shaquita, whatever anybody might say now, through all of this madness, he loved Shaquita very much. He always provided for them. And now Shaquita is doing all this stuff, I can't believe she's doing Mommy like that 'cause Mommy was taking care of all of them," Buddha Monk said. But when Icelene and her family arrived in Georgia, she didn't have enough money to pay for the moving trucks. These were the kind of fights that ODB had no interest in.

ODB's life was chaos and predictably so was his death. On first glance, it seems illogical that someone who lived with a death wish and a rumored dozen babies would get out of jail, receive a high-profile contract, and not write a will. But this was Dirty and really the money he left behind was the least of his afterlife worries. His legacy was still under Jarred Weisfeld's management until 2008. Within a week of his death Jarred and Cherry announced the first posthumous record, an official mix tape titled *Osirus* that was scheduled for a December release.

They also jointly announced the airing of Weisfeld's second reality TV attempt, *Stuck on Dirty*. In the show, which finished filming just weeks before ODB's death, a man was challenged to hang out with the rapper for five days straight. The concept was for Bob, a mild-mannered Italian guy from Queens, to stay within ten feet of ODB over three half-hour episodes. He was electronically tethered to Dirty by a mechanism that beeped if he moved too far from the rapper. Each time the alarm sounded, Bob lost $5,000 of a $25,000 jackpot. According to a newspaper report, Dirt, true to name and reputation, didn't bathe the entire shoot. I guess it's a funny concept if you're throwing around ideas in a bar, but when you consider that these were his dying days, when he was least functional, least aware, least willing to live, it's not just sad, but offensive. This was a man on the brink of suicide and suffering from paranoid hallucinations, and yet he was filming a reality show with buzzers buzzing while a strange white guy shadowed his every move.

The years after his death have been riddled with lawsuits and press conferences that at best are tacky and at worst speak to the responsibilities and sufferings ODB was trying to avoid. Cherry Jones, along with Susie Wong and Cheryl McCall (the mothers of two of ODB's other children), filed civil charges against Icelene Jones for mismanagement of Dirt's estate and for depleting the $225,000 left to her and her children. But ODB is no Tupac or Biggie; his estate generated just $122,000 between June 2005 and August 2006, which would be split seven ways. Judge Margarita Lupez Torres overturned the previous ruling that granted Icelene power of attorney. To complicate matters, Damon Dash refuses to release ODB's last album, *A Son Unique*, because Weisfeld and Jones are demanding final payments to the tune of several hundred thousand dollars on the million-dollar contract negotiated when Dirt was alive. The court papers read, "If money is still owed to the estate . . . Mr. Dash does not intend to pay them and will drop his plans to release the record." The album that was set for release in early 2004 and again in the fall of 2006 and again in November 2007 has yet to materialize. And still the mudslinging between Icelene and Cherry continues. Icelene accused Cherry Jones of misusing $200,000 to $500,000 of the estate's funds, to which Weisfeld responded: "That's the most retarded allegation I've ever heard in my life. Icelene knows where all that money went—it went to Icelene. All Dirty did was take care of her."

So why is it that Tupac and Biggie can live eternally in our culture but ODB is lost in the ether? An album he finished while he was alive can't even get released, let alone a posthumous effort or a mash-up tribute or a *Best of* . . . Was it because Pac and Big died in a flurry of bullets when they were young and in their prime? Was it that ODB wasn't nearly as prolific? When Shakur died, he left a catalog of six studio albums and 153 unpublished songs, worth an estimated $60 million. Or was it because ODB suffered publicly and was broken by the time he died? His managers and family and Damon Dash just reflect the life Dirt led, and that life was a mess.

EPILOGUE: GROUNDED BY DIRT

What's the world without Dirt? Just a bunch of fucking water.
—Rhymefest

What defined ODB? What was his legacy? What should be his legacy? He lived a life of plurality and contradiction—he was expansive but down-to-earth, he'd hug strangers but lived in paranoid seclusion, he lived for children but was only marginally available to his own. *What ultimately defined ODB?* He did. At first, when he was young, he loved himself; later in life, he loathed himself; and in the end he simply quit on himself, leaving the world to wonder who he really was. In a lot of ways, he's defined by how he's remembered.

About a year after the Wu-Tang tribute in New Haven, ODB's family threw him a thirty-eighth birthday party at the Canal Room in Manhattan. I found out about the event for no other reason than because I had signed up for Google alert on ODB. The news was published on a British site called *Choco-*

late and announced the party with performances by Brooklyn
Zu and Wu-Tang, hosted by RZA and Ghost and GZA. I
RSVPed and got an immediate response asking me to forward
the invite to "colleagues and industry professionals." At which
point it was obvious that Wu-Tang had nothing to do with the
event. I knew Buddha Monk wasn't going to be there because he
was in Switzerland.

The line moved slow, but it was warm out. An elderly black
man in a proper hat with a feather tucked inside the band stood
next to me. He nodded occasionally to other people's conversations but was silent. He had a weathered face, lines striating his
cheeks like intricate tributaries, and though he looked, talked,
and walked content, those lines criss-crossed hard and deliberate
like the life he probably led. I wanted to talk to him, so I compli-
mented his turquoise chip necklace; it reminded me of one my
grandmother gave me. He said it was made of beaver teeth that
a friend in Chile had collected. It was clearly turquoise. He
introduced himself as Pops but *not* Popa Wu, whom he is consis-
tently mistaken for. He handed me a flyer for his film production
company—the flyer included a glossy group photo of big-assed
women in too-small bikinis. He talked about the beauty pageant
he was hosting off Franklin in Bed-Stuy that June, inviting me to
come along. Pops was ODB's uncle, Cherry's older brother. We
talked a bit about Dirt as a kid. He put his arms up like he was
cradling a spirit and said, "Oh, he was good baby. And when he
was fourteen or fifteen and just needed a place to get away, he
came to my house on Putnam. It was quiet there and he'd just
rest." We waited in line trading secrets about ODB and once
inside we watched the empty club fill slowly. Pops started explaining who each person was and introduced me as his writer
friend Jaime.

I went downstairs, heading to the VIP room, where I spotted

an MC whom Pops had pointed out earlier, Shorty Shitstain. He was manically making the rounds in an oversize kelly green velour hoodie with every NBA team icon. The sweatshirt went down to his knees and he donned a matching green baseball cap, flat-billed and backward. I cornered him and said, "You're Shorty, right?" He looked up and down, up and down, and smiled and said yeah and put his arm on the low side of my waist. "I'm Shorty, how'd you know that?" I said Pops told me and then I asked if he was Shorty Shitstain. He said, "Well, I was Shorty Shitstain but I changed it up, yo, I can't have that name always. How is it you know my full name?" I reminded him about Pops and asked how he was related to ODB.

"He's my brother!"

"You're Cherry's?"

"Yup, she's my moms. Dirt's my older brother."

"Is Bill your Dad?"

"That's not important, don't worry about that."

He looked up and down and up and down again.

"You should stick by my side. I'll take care of you."

I wandered away from the VIP room and upstairs to find 60 Second Assassin, who at forty-three looked spent. He roamed the club in a striped polo shirt and a beanie with tags still attached. I told him I'd been trying to reach him. He said he didn't have e-mail or a phone at the moment. I thought he was just trying to dodge me, but within a few minutes it became clear that he really didn't have a phone, he really didn't have access to e-mail. He took my number and held on to the piece of paper. I asked how he was holding up.

"I'm trying to be all right. Today, I'm a student."

"I feel like a student every day," I said.

"Well, yeah, there's that too. I'm just wanting to be all right. I'm just tryin' to make it through, you know?"

The music was loud—we couldn't hear each other. So we awkwardly prom-danced for a couple of rounds to the DJ's choice, Snoop and Tupac. I was aware of how offbeat and tentative I was and more aware of 60's subtle demise. He was too skinny, he was a little slow and subdued, and in this roomful of family and MCs and former collaborators he seemed to take some solace in the dance floor. Downstairs he had been arguing with another MC who challenged his legitimacy, basically asking what 60 had done lately. It seemed like surviving wasn't enough. Back and forth we swayed, aware of but not really in each other's company. He held the piece of paper with my phone number and gripped it like it meant something.

The stage looked like a lounge, with chairs and pillows lining the back area. The performances began slow. First out was Shyheim, a Staten Island Wu affiliate who was known for being the youngest Wu, but that was ages ago and you could see his baby face thinned out by time. He looked too put together, too cool to stand without swaying. He said at the beginning, "Yo, Dirty told me to do my thing, so I'm here doing it." He expected the crowd to be with him, just because he was up there. He was tentative and quiet and complained about the sound system.

Shy made the audience wish for the ODB interludes blasting between sets. I'd forgotten how good a song sounds when it's so loud your calves trill, your knees hurt, and your hips sway involuntarily. And there was that voice, alive in the system, alive in its urgency and yet very very dead in reality. Made me think of that old-world response to cameras, the fear that they steal your soul, yet how lucky we are that DAT took Dirty, that we have two albums of him raw and uncut.

Brooklyn Zu stormed in front of the audience and 60 Second Assassin, crowded by chaos, collected half-empty cups and bottles from the stage, like tidying up the space was his job. He moved the cups to the side and sat in one of the chairs to the left of the stage. A hooded MC tried audience participation, passing his mic from lip to lip encouraging folks to sing "It's a cold, cold world." He paused and placed the mic at my chin. I sang into it.

Outside, I met another ODB uncle, Cherry's other older brother, who was onstage with the Joneses and the cake and kept pumping his fists in the air like a geriatric hype man, just happy to grace the stage one last time for any reason at all. He had come in from Philly for the night and remembered Rusty as a kid with dew in his eyes. Everyone does, even neighbors from Bed-Stuy.

The neighborhood has changed since Dirt was a youth. Twenty-five years is an eternity in real estate, enough time to remake a ghetto with gentrification and architectural lofts. In 2006 ODB's brother Raison Allah commissioned an artist to paint a mural of ODB on the corner of Putnam and Franklin while he was working on a documentary about ODB. That his crazy face gets to watch over the corner that he hung out on when he was a kid is a sweet remembrance.

The mural is an exact replica of ODB's welfare card cover from *Return to the 36 Chambers*. The paint was fresh, the yellow and blue lines fuzzy from airbrushing. From across the street you can see ODB's Medusa hair, his wild eyes, and his crooked teeth. If you've seen the record cover, there's not much more to the mural; it's a backdrop for a bus stop and shares a wall with Lovell's corner store. Lovell sells soda, plantain chips, and little else. He looks to be pushing sixty but it's hard to tell behind the double-paned plastic wall that separates his cash and his body from his customers.

Lovell's been on the corner since before Dirty's day. He saw him come up as a youth, sold him soda, and knew his parents, who lived around the way at 112 Putnam. "His folks don't live down there anymore. They went different ways," he said, which is a touchingly accurate description of divorce. According to Lovell, ODB used to walk in the store saying, " 'Hey Lovell, how you doin'?' He was never a trouble to me but *they say* he was kickin' drugs and stuff." He described the young Russell Jones as polite, appreciative, and calm. Down the block from the mural, ODB's childhood apartment stands empty, save for a life-size cement poodle. The dog has a perm and guards the door in absurdity and with a faint smile. The damn statue has bows in its ears. And it almost seems fitting, more fitting than the welfare card, to memorialize the late Dirt Dawg with a bitch.

Russell Jones lived a loud life; his afterlife is shrouded in quiet recognition, and not from the people you expect. His last studio recording was commissioned by Sam Spiegel, aka DJ Squeak E. Clean (Spike Jonze's brother and fellow heir to the Spiegel catalog fortune). The track features Dirt rapping with Karen O from the Yeah Yeah Yeahs and Fatlip from the Pharcyde about self-destruction and creativity. "I bought *Enter the Wu Tang (36 Chambers)* the day it came out. I believe that Wu-Tang changed my life. It was a big part of my adolescence. I was obsessed with them. I had a lot of angst, I was really dissatisfied with where I was at, I was bored by my life. I think I was attracted to the violence and the anger in it, but also the humor and fun," says Spiegel. The Harvard radio station WHRB, better known for its classical programming, aired a twenty-four-hour tribute to ODB, playing every track he recorded and some he just breathed on. DJs Sam Jacoby and Darius Felton, both founders of the hip-hop show *The Darker Side*, sandwiched the spinning eulogy in between Bartok sessions. In Pittsburgh, Zane Leibowitz, a twenty-year-old piercing artist, had Dirty's face inked on his foot. When GZA saw it at a show, he told Leibowitz, "You've got a backstage pass for life." (Leibowitz has since tattooed the remaining members of the Wu-Tang Clan on his body.) Bucket-head, the ubiquitous shredder known for his mute mystery, posted a tribute on his website that is simply a zombie-masked Buckethead dancing and posturing to Dirt's "Shame on a Nigga," singing along to the verses and miming the words with severed masks attached to his flailing arms. He also posted a remix collage of "Shimmy Shimmy Ya." He posted both files next to a sweetly Photoshopped homage of ODB standing on his own tombstone with a forty, birds circling and Buckethead ominously crouching in the foreground with chickens and over-turned KFC buckets. The ode to ODB is a permanent fixture of Buckethead's website and he simply states, "Buckethead was deeply saddened by the death of ODB and did a tribute to ODB." He includes two ODB quotes above and below the imagined grave: "Never been tooken out, keeps MCs lookin out" and the quote from the Hammerstein Ballroom show when ODB, continuing his fugitive status, said, "Y'all know they had the ODB locked down, right? Well, I'm here to tell you that they can't keep me down. Now I'm free and I'm out there like a bird flying around, so y'all better leave some birdseed on your win-dowsills, because I may be flying by your house."

Murals popped up around the corner from ODB's Bed-Stuy childhood home and as far away as Amsterdam. There's even a Dutch cover band called Wu-Tang Brothers that features a Nordic ODB named Örn Alexander Ámundason. His face was stenciled and graffitied on bridges and billboards. Rap Snacks released a sour cream and onion edition of chips with Dirt's face on the bag; dj BC, on his *Wu Orleans* mash-up, remixed the most up-tempo brass band with a sped up Ol' Dirty singing "Got Your Money." The Dirty Dozen Brass Band sings between rau-cous horn sections and Dirt's voice, "My feet can't fail me now, my feet can't fail me now," almost as if in this life after death,

ODB has no need for feet, like he's in a permanent state of flight. Buddha Monk spends five hours a day maintaining the Ol' Dirty Bastard remembrance page; he has gotten 2,500 ad requests and the songs posted have all been played more than a million times, even the little-known recording "Thirsty" from the *Blade 3* soundtrack. His son Young Dirty and GZA's son L'il Genius perform at various Wu shows, hopping onstage to continue the legacy into the next generation. And Wu-Tang always remembers, with a track dedicated to Dirt on *8 Diagrams* and various MCs leading audiences in ODB's hits. Ghostface once had a crowd under the Manhattan Bridge singing the entirety of "Shimmy Shimmy Ya" in Dirt's honor.

And that's what separates Wu-Tang from other hip-hop acts. They've managed to stay underground for almost two decades and have attracted a teenage following now without even trying. Their shows are equal parts old-timers remembering back-in-the-day and young'ins who weren't even born when RZA and GZA and ODB went by All In Together Now. At first the Wu-Tang reunion shows, which were equal parts commemoration and chaos, were really more like gatherings for fans to reminisce, a place to feel ODB's spirit. A place to convene and say who he was and that what he stood for will live on, that there will never be another like him, and no amount of lighters held high to the sky can make up for the loss. And sadly, it seems that Wu-Tang reunions are easier; half a dozen have been planned each summer since he died. It's like they shed the one member who was noticeably absent and notoriously difficult. Sadly, ODB is a lot more reliable dead than alive. It's easier to conjure what he stood for than to make him stand in one place.

ODB isn't Tupac; there isn't a foundation set up in his name teaching kids the glories of the performing arts and providing Freedom Trails to walk along in his honor. ODB doesn't have a former Black Panther mother paying the way of remembrance—Tupac's intellectual legacy barely survived him: Even with her foundation for the arts, it's his cultivated gangsta persona—now painted in Times Square, pastel portraits with a Crips bandanna tied at his forehead and a tough-love look that could never mask his sweet face. ODB isn't Biggie; he doesn't have enough backlogged material to release an album a year for a dozen years. ODB's not even Eazy-E, who died with an estimated $35 million estate. ODB has only his legacy of sporadic genius and the people who honor it.

ODB has to continue being the ODB he was in life, even in death.

I'd like to see classic marble statues in front of the Brooklyn Museum, or rococo portraits of ODB swathed in leopard furs and pheasants and holding half-filled crystal goblets. I'd like to see drug rehabilitation centers and mental illness facilities erected in his name. I'd like to see his kids grow up and dominate with the same intensity as their dad. I'd like to see the people who loved ODB honor him by living life simply, living life from the gut but maybe with slightly more caution. I'd like to see ODB remembered for the glorious character he was and the man that few knew.

ACKNOWLEDGMENTS

INDEX

ACKNOWLEDGMENTS

This book is for ODB, with awe and affection and sadness.

More than thanks, more than gratitude, I'm in debt to my agent, Jud Laghi, for seeing this before I did, my mom for patiently reading every word I've written, Hana for making it seem like the world is wearing a prom dress, my grandparents for leading lives of simplicity and love and kindness, my dad for sharing jazz and words and coffee, and my stepmom, Marilyn, and stepfather, Jeff, who helped raise me by committee and whom I can't imagine life without.

Thanks to Chuck Eddy for printing the original story in *The Village Voice*, Joe Levy for assigning it, and everyone who was willing to share their stories about ODB—RZA, GZA, Cappadonna, Meth, Buddha Monk, Dante Ross, Jarred Weisfeld, Cherry Jones, Icelene Jones, Robert Shapiro, Dr. Poissant,

ACKNOWLEDGMENTS

Steve-O, Blowfly, Tom Bowker, Chang Weisberg, Sophia Chang, Steve Rifkind, Phife, Pras, Wyclef, ?uestlove, Soren Baker, Chad Duering, Brian Cohen, Angela Yee, Gabe Tesoreiro, Jesse Pearson, Suroosh Alvi, Sam Spiegel, Busdriver, Popa Wu, 60 Second, Shorty Shitstain, and all the strangers at shows who talked to me.

And much gratitude and love to Bill Vourvoulias, James Lochart, Perry van der Meer, Jebediah Reed, Matthew Thompson, Sarah Jacoby, Maer Roshan, Dana Nelson, Carrie Odell, Sally Tannenbaum, Pam Mann and Terry Meginniss, Emma Mann-Meginniss, Amy Osburn, Miriam Kramer, Ethan Minton, Niko Higgins, Dana Shapiro, Adam Sack, Brett Forrest, Mason Pettit, Adam Duerson, Caryn Prime, Sharif Corinaldi, Alan Light, Effie Phillips, Dr. Schwartz, Dr. DeAntonio, Erin Stack, Zoe Ani, Karey Green, Ethan Brown, Mim Udovich, Greg Seibert, Jeremy Engel, Max Hart, Meesha Haddad, Mike Ryan, Monserrat Fontes, Nancy Meakem, Nicole Citron, Rachel Benoff, Hardy Fischer, Robert Christgau, Thien and Vic, Josh Dean, Stephanie Vo, Sarah Poulter, Craig Melzer, Michael Kornberg, Cesca Adey, Elena Schneider, Cindy Zaplachinski, Autumn Bernstein, Tyler Brodie, Griff, and Cody.

Thanks to everyone at Gleason's, particularly Stuart Bakal, who trained me to work in three-minute intervals; Bob Duffy, who graciously shared his office; Bruce Silverglade, Charlie and Carlos, Blimp, and anyone who sparred with me. Also thanks to the Eggplants.

Finally, thanks to FSG: Denise Oswald for her deft use of a purple pencil, Jessica Ferri (MRL), Aaron Artessa, and Don McConnell.

INDEX

INDEX